Praise for *Women* (

This book is an unmissable asset for anyone interested in the ordination of women. It documents, with incredible detail, the stories of forty-seven Catholic women who were ordained despite the opposition of the official church. It describes their call, their struggle to surmount barriers, their inner motivation, and the spirituality that guided and still guides them in their ministry. Fascinating and significant data, underpinned by the authors' highly professional scholarship and compassionate understanding of real people.

—John Wijngaards, DDiv, professor emeritus, Missionary Institute London; chair, Wijngaards Institute for Catholic Research

In a carefully crafted ethnographic study of the Roman Catholic Women Priests' movement, Callahan and Rodriguez offer a hopeful and joyful message to anyone who feels marginalized by institutional religion.

—Gary Macy, professor emeritus of theology, Santa Clara University

Callahan and Rodriguez offer a stunning pneumatological and ethnographic reversal of expectation on the "ordination of women" question within the Roman Catholic Church by rigorously examining the ongoing ministries and "spirits" (1 John 4) of women ordained in apostolic succession (if *contra legum*, canon 1024). Scripturally, theologically, and phenomenologically, the authors provide ample testimony to Spirit's fruit and ecclesial renewal in (and because of) the faithful perseverance of over forty womenpriests living their priestly vocations. That this is done with such clear love of a church that refuses such women, even with theological-ecclesial integrity *and* prophetic challenge, makes this a compelling read and a remarkable testimony to God's ongoing work in the world, sometimes *despite* the church.

—Lisa M. Hess, ordained clergywoman (PCUSA); professor of practical theology and contextual ministries, United Theological Seminary (Ohio), and author of *A Companionable Way: Path of Devotion in Conscious Love*

What can it mean to willingly invest oneself in a religious institution that tells you that you cannot, that you should not, lead? How do you follow the Holy Spirit into leadership amidst oppressive structures? These are some of the most difficult questions Roman Catholic womenpriests must struggle with, and this compelling and beautifully written book explores the diverse and multiple answers these women articulate. The wider Christian community has so much to learn from their journeys, and to ignore them is to miss out on the surprising joy the Spirit breathes into the world in the twenty-first century.

Why ever would a woman want to be a Roman Catholic priest? This book offers the surprising, compelling, and powerful stories of women who have chosen to do just that, even as the official church excommunicates them for doing so. The wider Christian community has so much to learn from their journeys, and to ignore them is to miss out on the surprising joy the Spirit breathes into the world in the twenty-first century. Quixotic, compelling, full of both joy and sorrow, the stories of Roman Catholic womenpriests that Callahan and Rodriguez have gathered into this book offer captivating glimpses into a church in transition in the twenty-first century. The book also offers a concise yet substantial historical overview of the question of women and the priesthood in the Catholic church, with careful attention to both church documents and contemporary theological wisdom.

I have a front-row seat to the struggles of women seeking to lead in the Catholic church, not simply because of my own journey, but because I've followed my mother-in-love Dagmar as she became a Roman Catholic womanpriest as part of the Danube 7. This book is a compelling, carefully researched, and thoughtfully contextualized engagement with the movement of Roman Catholic womenpriests. Callahan and Rodriguez have given us a profound gift that has much to teach all of us who care about Christian community, leading with the Holy Spirit, and embodying church in the twenty-first century.

—Mary E. Hess, PhD, professor of educational leadership,
Luther Seminary

What better time for this carefully researched and profoundly inspiring work than now, with the hope-filled dawning of a new church that calls for and listens to the voices of its women, lay and religious, as equals in a synodal, not hierarchical, church. The authors reveal the love, concern, and spirituality of these women in their lives as priests, albeit illegally ordained. They have dedicated their lives to a church that still runs away from them. The women in this text were called by and responded to their call from—they argue—the same God who called all who came to serve God's people before them.

—Diana L. Hayes, JD, PhD, STD, professor emerita,
Georgetown University

women called to
catholic priesthood

women called to catholic priesthood

from ecclesial challenge to *spiritual renewal*

Sharon Henderson Callahan
and Jeanette Rodriguez

Foreword by

Christine Schenk CSJ

Fortress Press

Minneapolis

WOMEN CALLED TO CATHOLIC PRIESTHOOD
From Ecclesial Challenge to Spiritual Renewal

Library of Congress Cataloging-in-Publication Data

Names: Callahan, Sharon Henderson, author. | Rodriguez, Jeanette, author.
Title: Women called to Catholic priesthood : from ecclesial challenge to
    spiritual renewal / Sharon Callahan, Jeanette Rodriguez.
Description: Minneapolis : Fortress Press, [2024] | Includes
    bibliographical references.
Identifiers: LCCN 2023031190 (print) | LCCN 2023031191 (ebook) | ISBN
    9781506498393 (print) | ISBN 9781506498409 (ebook)
Subjects: LCSH: Ordination of women--Catholic Church. | Women in the
    Catholic Church. | Women priests.
Classification: LCC BV676 .C335 2024 (print) | LCC BV676 (ebook) | DDC
    262.14082--dc23/eng/20231026
LC record available at https://lccn.loc.gov/2023031190
LC ebook record available at https://lccn.loc.gov/2023031191

Cover design: Laurie Ingram
Cover image: Flower Beings by MarinkaG/iStock.com

Print ISBN: 978-1-5064-9839-3
eBook ISBN: 978-1-5064-9840-9

This book is dedicated to women who trust what the Sacred has called them to be. We recognize the ancestresses who have modelled many ways to fulfill their divine humanity. We acknowledge the many allies, women and men, who encourage young girls and women to pursue their heart, imagination, and gifts for the greater good of the cosmos. We dedicate this text especially to the many women who have demonstrated courage, persistence, humility, and love in transforming lives.

CONTENTS

FOREWORD

For over thirty years it has been my honor to accompany women who experience a call to priestly ministry. Many discerned they would honor that invitation by continuing to serve as lay ecclesial ministers, chaplains, spiritual directors, and parish administrators within the institutional church. Others discerned they would honor their call by entering into what I believe to be a prophetic liminal space opened by the Roman Catholic Women Priests (RCWP) movement.[1] These women were ordained *contra legem* (against canon 1024[2]) and willingly accepted the penalty of excommunication rather than disobey what they understood God to be asking of them. It should be noted that excommunicated persons, while barred from validly receiving the sacraments, are still members of the Roman Catholic Church. Ordained Catholic women believe their prophetic refusal to obey an unjust law will, by God's grace, redounds to the good of the whole church. I admire and respect all of these women—those ordained in fact and those ordained in the silence of their hearts. Each woman occupies an important and necessary place in the vineyard of church reform. As I see it, each one's ministry is already bearing rich fruit—both now and for the future.

In addition to the testimony of women following what they believe to be the Holy Spirit's call to priesthood, there is other evidence that the Spirit may be calling us to a new way of being church. In the 1990s two highly regarded US statisticians, Richard Schoenherr and Lawrence Young, projected that by 2005 there would be a 40 percent decline in the number of US priests, and that the number of Catholics would increase by 60 percent.[3] At the time I was working as a cofounder and executive director of the church renewal organization FutureChurch. Our founding mission was to open ordination to all those called to it by God and the People of God so as to preserve the Eucharist as the center of Catholic worship. In the beginning this meant educating about and advocating for opening ordination to women and married men.[4]

Looking back, I well remember the optimism of those early years. Surely, we thought, by 2005 the bishops will come to their senses and put the sacramental and pastoral needs of the people of God first. We expected church leaders would open ordination and reform the clerical system. That did not happen. Centuries of entrenched all-male leadership—one that that not only distrusted women but apparently also distrusted men who loved women enough to marry one—would not easily change. Yet it was—and is—increasingly apparent that the Catholic church desperately needs to expand those permitted to provide priestly ministry to her people.

Schoenherr and Young's projections proved devastatingly accurate. Bear with me for a moment as I share data trends that attest to the timeliness of this book and provide outside evidence that suggests how the Spirit may be leading the church today. Between 1965 and 2022 the number of diocesan and religious order priests serving the US church decreased by 42.2 percent, going from 59,426 in 1965 to 34,344 in 2022. During this same time period—according to the Official Catholic Directory—the number of parish-connected Catholics increased by 50 percent, growing from 44.3 million in 1965 to 66.5 million in 2022. The diocesan priesthood is also aging. Just 66 percent of diocesan priests were actively engaged in ministry in 2022 compared to 75 percent in 2000. In 2000 there was one active diocesan priest per 2,795 Catholics. In 2022 that ratio increased to one active diocesan priest per 4,179 Catholics. The number of priestly ordinations increased slightly with 451 in 2022 compared to 442 in 2000.

Yet new ordinations are woefully insufficient to offset priests who are retiring. Mary Gautier, a senior research associate at the Center for Applied Research in the Apostolate at Georgetown University, found that the US church needs "two to three times" the annual number of diocesan ordinations to keep up with parish demand: "It's only about a third to a half as many as we would need to compensate for the larger number of priests that are dying and retiring."[5] Worldwide statistics are scarcely better. The number of the world's Catholics more than doubled between 1970 (653.6 million) and 2020 (1.36 billion), for a 108 percent increase. Yet by 2020 the number of priests worldwide had declined by 2.2 percent. In 1970 there were 419,728 priests compared to 410,510 in 2020. One of five of the world's parishes do not have a resident priest.[6]

The unrelenting shortage of priests continues to put great pressure on US bishops who believe they must have a priest in each parish church to adequately minister to the Catholic people. For far too many bishops, an easy solution has been to shrink the number of parishes to fit the number of priests available. The trend is to herd Catholics into ever larger churches. To do this, bishops are merging financially viable and ministerially effective parish communities and then hoping to sell their churches. Between 2000 and 2022 US bishops closed 2,807 parishes for a 14.6 percent decline overall.[7] Too often the preponderance of closures affects small, socially conscious parish communities that served low-income neighborhoods. In the Archdiocese of Boston, an informal statistical study found that 60 percent of the seventy-seven parishes suppressed in 2004 were located in towns with low or modest income.[8] In the Diocese of Cleveland, all fifty-two closures in 2009 involved inner city parishes or inner ring suburb parishes, the majority of which were solvent if burdened with aging buildings.[9] Cleveland regularly vies with Detroit as the poorest large city in the nation.[10] The closed Cleveland parishes had provided important ministries in poorer areas in which the church served as a trusted anchor in troubled neighborhoods.[11]

As grace builds on nature, I humbly submit that these dramatic trends suggest the Spirit is asking us to open ordination rather than to close parishes. We already have a pool of well qualified candidates. Lay ecclesial ministers serving in the US church now substantially outnumber the number of priests with 44,556 lay ministers serving in 2022 compared to 34,344 priests.[12] Historically, 80 percent of lay ecclesial ministers are women.[13] A 2021 sociological study of forty women ministering in the Catholic Church found that they "feel a call to the ordained diaconate or would image and discern such a call if the diaconate were open to them." Furthermore, they "adapt to live out that call by operating as 'de facto deacons,' engaging in strategic deference, strategic dissent and emotional management."[14] The preceding data bears its own tragic witness to institutional blindness. Church leaders appear to be choosing eucharistic and ministerial scarcity rather than accept the Spirit's abundant priestly calls to women and, I would argue, to married men—especially those who have left the active ministry to marry.

Throughout my years of friendship and accompaniment of women struggling with an invitation to priestly ministry, I have more than once prayed that our bishops would just listen to their experience of God's call to them. Rather than rejoice that faithful Catholic women wish to devote even more of their life's energies to God, bishops too often respond with dismay and disapproval before summarily dismissing women's priestly calls. Yet, their stories—as exhaustively chronicled in this study— are replete with evidence that the Holy Spirit may indeed be doing something new.

It is the Holy Spirit's job to renew and reform the earth—and the church (Ps 104:30). This is something Pope Francis himself has proclaimed: "It is the Holy Spirit who forms and reforms the Church and does so through the Word of God and through the saints, who put the Word into practice in their lives."[15] In consultation with church leaders around the world, Pope Francis has called for a multi-year synod on synodality. Item two of the 2021–2024 synod preparatory document clarifies the role of the Spirit:

> . . .*what steps does the Spirit invite us to take in order to grow as a synodal Church? Addressing this question together requires listening to the Holy Spirit, who like the wind "blows where it wills; you can hear the sound it makes, but you do not know where it comes from or where it goes" (John 3:8), remaining open to the surprises that the Spirit will certainly prepare for us along the way.*[16]

The preparatory document then names the urgent need for all Catholics to participate in confronting and converting our culture of clericalism, the very culture that refuses to acknowledge the possibility that the Holy Spirit may be calling women to ordained ministry:

> *The whole Church is called to confront the weight of a culture impregnated with clericalism, inherited from its history, and forms of exercising authority in which various types of abuse (of power, economic, conscience, sexual) are inserted. A conversion of ecclesial action is unthinkable without the active participation of all the members of the People of God.*[17]

The whole point of the synod on synodality is for bishops and people to listen to one another and together discern how the Spirit may be leading the church today. In his 2015 address for the fiftieth anniversary of the institution of the synod of bishops, Francis spoke passionately about the need for such listening:

> *a synodal Church is a Church of listening . . . It is a reciprocal*
> *listening in which everyone has something to learn . . . It is*
> *listening to God, to the point of listening with him to the cry of the*
> *people; and it is listening to the people, to the point of breathing in*
> *them the will to which God calls us.*[18]

Thanks to Callahan and Rodriguez, we now have valuable documentation of Catholic women's experiences of listening and being led by the Spirit onto an uncharted, but joy-filled priestly path. I pray our bishops will listen too, and that their stories will be taken seriously by everyone in our church. Even more, I pray they catalyze a long overdue discussion—indeed a church-wide discernment—as to what our ever-renewing Spirit may be asking of us today.

Christine Schenk, CSJ
Feast of Pentecost, 2023

ACKNOWLEDGMENTS

The elders of this land have taught us that the words before all else are always words of gratitude. A book that rises from the heart and soul of individuals cannot be written without their trust and generosity. So many have helped us put this manuscript together. We begin, of course, with the Roman Catholic womenpriests themselves, who unabashedly and with deep trust, shared their struggles, pains, hopes, aspirations, and deep faith. We thank you. We are also grateful and thank the members of the various congregations that we visited both nationally and internationally, who offered us hospitality and were eager to share their experience of having a womanpriest, which they tell us has renewed their faith and commitment to the church. Their journey narratives were often heart filled, inspiring, and challenging. Special thanks to Bishop Christine Mayr-Lumetzberger of Austria, one of the "Danube 7," for receiving us in her home, introducing us to members of her community, and showing us the Danube where the story of the RCWP began. We are incredibly grateful for the time and trust she extended to us.

This research allowed us to collect the stories of forty-seven women on four continents. Hence, we are grateful to all those who supported and believed in our work by financially investing in it. We thank the late Fr. Pat Howell, SJ, who believed in the vision, hope, and creativity of the Second Vatican Council. In 2019, his leadership of the Institute for Catholic Thought and Culture at Seattle University ensured we received our initial award to conduct research on this topic. Next, in 2020, the Louisville Institute, awarded us a full Project Grant for Researchers. We thank them for their encouragement and financial support, their flexibility as our plans changed while doing the research, and their support in gathering other researchers who helped us clarify our methodology and focus.

We especially thank Seattle University's Institute for Catholic Thought and Culture for generously sharing their resources and staff to assist us: Jessica Palmer, Estefania Kendall, and Sophia Cofinas. Others at the university offered support as well: Dean Powers of the College of arts and sciences, Sarah Bricknell of the Office of Sponsored Projects, and librarian Mary Sepulveda were consistent in their support. Research is always made easier with the help of our librarians and archivists. A special thanks to William Fliss of Marquette University who helped us access the archival records of the RCWP movement.

As women researchers we recognize the contribution others have offered through the centuries. The multiple women saints who eventually became recognized as doctors of the Church paved the way for women scholars to offer insight and research on a variety of topics related to ministry, theology, and spirituality. We specifically honor the work of more contemporary scholars such as Carolyn Osiek, Phyllis Zagana, Jill Peterfeso, Miriam Therese Winters, Elizabeth Johnson, Mary Hunt, Sandra Schneiders, Christine Schenck, Rosemary Radford Ruether, and others too numerous to name. Those named have directly influenced us in our own theological and ministerial journeys.

Writing is even more pleasant when you have "a room of your own" to work; thanks to the Iona Community in Scotland and the Catholic Retreat House for providing us hospitality and a place to think, reflect, and write. Finally, we are grateful and praise the Spirit, yes, the Spirit because we believe from the inception of this project doors opened up, bridges were built, and we have felt that the Spirit has been involved all along in helping us articulate this commitment and desire to both love and serve the church.

With gratitude,
Sharon Henderson Callahan
Jeanette Rodriguez

ABBREVIATIONS

AA	*Apostolicam Actuositatem* (Vatican II Decree on the Apostolate of Lay People)
CARA	Center for Applied Research in the Apostolate (Georgetown University)
CIC	Code of Canon Law
DV	*Dei Verbum* (Vatican II Dogmatic Constitution on Divine Revelation)
DH	*Dignitatis Humanae*
EG	*Evangelii Gaudium* (Apostolic Exhortation, Joy of the Gospel, Pope Francis)
GS	*Gaudium et Spes* (Vatican II)
LG	*Lumen Gentium* (Vatican II)
OS	*Ordinatio Sacerdotalis* (Pope John Paul II)
PO	*Presbyterorum Ordinis* (Vatican II Decree on the Ministry and Life of Priests)
SC	*Sacrosanctum Concilium* (Vatican II Constitution on the Sacred Liturgy)

❦ 1 ❧

INTRODUCTION

"The Spirit of God Sweeping over the Water"[1]

"Demands that the legitimate rights of women be respected, based on the firm conviction that men and women are equal in dignity, present the Church with profound and challenging questions which cannot be lightly evaded."[2]

IN THE SPRING of 2015, I, Jeanette,[3] participated in a pilgrimage/seminar to Greece focused on women's leadership in the early church.[4] One person dominates the story of the founding of the church in Philippi, according to the Acts of the Apostles: Lydia. Lydia is the first person in Philippi of whom it is said that "the Lord opened her heart" (Acts 16: 14) to receive the word as given by Paul and Silas. She opened her house as well to provide hospitality and hosted the very first gathering of those who wished to hear them preach (Acts 16:15). Dr. Carolyn Osiek helped the participants understand that from Luke's narrative, we have evidence that Lydia's house was the place where the first church group in Philippi was formed and continued to meet (Acts 16:40). There are several stories like this of many different women who heard the word, embraced the word, opened their homes, led gatherings, and preached. In addition to being prominent leaders of the early church these women were witnesses to Christ and partners in mission. Dr. Osiek contended that the record of these women reveals the intimate involvement of women in the first years of the formation of the church. They were workers alongside their male counterparts and partners in the ministry of collaborating in communicating the gospel in as many ways as possible.[5]

During that trip, I met a Roman Catholic womanpriest. At first, I was taken a little aback; cautious, maybe even dismissive. But as I watched her interact with others and witnessed her unabashedly expressed faith and joy in that vocation, I decided to approach her and listen. During those periods of sharing I listened, asked her about her journey, her struggles, aspirations, and how she came to this ultimate choice. She made a choice that would lead her to respond to a deep call against the practices of the institutional Roman Catholic Church. I walked and talked with her throughout our time in Greece. An idea about studying and listening more closely to other women who heard and answered this call to ordination began to form in my mind.

When I returned, I decided to conduct some research on this movement of women becoming ordained Roman Catholic priests who claimed apostolic succession. I consider myself a "border theologian" doing what might be called "theological ethnography" which studies Christian faith experience among different cultural groups. And in conjunction with the wisdom I find in the libraries and diverse disciplines, I go to the living "texts," that is, the wisdom of the people in the "*cotidiano.*" My work has sought to lift up the wisdom of historically minoritized voices embodied in our mothers, sisters, daughters, and grandmothers, and so on (while also honoring our grandfathers, fathers, brothers, sons, husbands, and partners). For me, the challenge was to bring these voices, insights, and "ways of knowing" to the table of both academic and theological credibility. My colleague, Sharon, specialized her studies in ministry and leadership. As a professor and academic dean in a School of Theology and Ministry, she prepared men and women for ordained leadership as well as lay leadership in most mainline churches including the Roman Catholic church. We had collaborated on many projects, so I asked her if she would like to join me in conducting a qualitative, ethnographic research project. She agreed.

I, Sharon, have conducted multiple ethnographic studies related to competency for ministerial leadership in both Roman Catholic and mainline Protestant ecclesial communities. As an academic dean within an Association of Theological Schools (ATS) accredited school, I participated in international meetings dedicated to understanding the role of ordained ministers and the theological and ministerial education needed to prepare them. As a representative to the Association of Graduate Programs in Ministry,

I collaborated with other Roman Catholic educators in preparing lay and ordained Catholic ministers, deacons, and priests for over twenty-five years. In that organization, we consulted annually with representatives from the United States Catholic Conference of Bishops (USCCB) and their subcommittees related to lay ecclesial ministry. Like Jeanette, I have also conducted qualitative, ethnographic research in other countries, especially in Kenya, China, Taiwan, the Philippines, and Vietnam, and together we worked in Mexico. In addition, as director of the Doctor of Ministry program, I taught ministers how to design and implement qualitative studies related to their areas of ministry. Over seven years, I chaired and oversaw the research methodologies of almost thirty doctoral projects. Like Jeanette, I am interested in themes and stories and the insights they give us about phenomenon we study, especially as it pertains to ministries in the Christian Church. Thus, when she asked, I immediately agreed to collaborate with her on this project.

Jeanette had already framed the question when she approached me. She asked the very title we have adopted: Are women ecclesial challenges in the church, as most patriarchal teaching suggests? Or do women offer something to the body of Christ that may renew it and sustain it as it interacts with the world? Clearly, as women, we have contributed to the church even if we have at times been problematic. Thus, it is natural for us to consider women loyal workers who sustain and renew the church. We think their spirituality, or "the way in which they live in accordance with basic values,"[6] offers an opportunity to listen deeply toward understanding how God works in our lives. Our approach mirrors the synodality approach of Pope Francis and the bishops around the world who are engaging in deep listening sessions to understand what the Holy Spirit is doing in today's cosmos. Hence, this book seeks to listen deeply and share the spirituality behind this "vocation" of womenpriests that goes "*contra legum*," against Canon 1024.[7]

In 2002 the first group of Roman Catholic women was ordained by several bishops on the Danube River in Austria. Known as the "Danube 7," these newly ordained womenpriests were later excommunicated by Pope John Paul II. Later, several anonymous male bishops re-ordained two of these women as bishops: Christina of Austria and Gisela of Germany. This ordination ensured that other women could be ordained within the Catholic Church. Roman Catholic Women Priests has rejected the penalty of excommunication, claimed their response to a higher authority, and asserted that the power of the sacrament of baptism is so strong they cannot be unilaterally excommunicated. This group stems from the Danube 7 and is differentiated from other groups of womenpriests such as Old Catholic or Ecumenical Catholic womenpriests.

In this book we will explore this "call" to priesthood and the spirituality that nurtures and sustains the women's journey. Bishop Patricia speaks of this call as an inner attraction that stays with one over time and tends to flare up into one's consciousness now and then. She notes there may be a struggle within each, as one considers whether she has the necessary gifts and talents confirmed by friends and community. She names the moment of the early 2000s as the time for challenging laws of exclusion even as laws of apartheid were challenged in her home country of South Africa. She links attentive listening to obedience: to self, signs of the times, individually and together, to the Spirit.[8]

Her reflection mirrors the definition of spirituality proposed by Rev. Roy Lazar, who states that "spirituality is relational in the sense that is also concerned about how one relates to oneself, to others, to nature and to God."[9] These responses can lead to the spiritual life or "the sum total of responses which one makes to what is perceived as the inner call of God and when the individual has decided to make this call the centre of activity and choice, he or she may be called a spiritual person."[10]

We, as authors, are interested in in-depth and rich description of the spirituality that supports womenpriests as they lead congregations. Thus, we took a qualitative approach that examines the leadership and spirit of those leading in their natural setting. As Roman Catholic women ourselves, we became instruments "of data collection, who gather words or pictures, analyze them inductively, focus on the meaning of participants, and describe a process that is expressive and persuasive in language."[11] As researchers we intended to "build a complex holistic picture" that "analyzes words, reports detailed views of informants, and conducts the study in a natural setting."[12]

As phenomenological researchers we practiced deep listening to our subjects, the womenpriests themselves. Our discipline of listening, reviewing what we heard, verifying with their own congregants and writings constituted a research methodology that sought to deeply understand the women's experience as they spoke and wrote about it. Thus, we chose to concentrate on lifting their voices throughout rather than judge or converse with what they revealed. Other researchers such as Jill Peterfeso in her excellent work *Womanpriest, Tradition and Transgression in the Contemporary Roman Catholic Church* examine the deep historical and cultural context of this movement. Her work is insightful and succinctly describes the movement, while we hoped to focus on the women's stories of their own spiritual journeys.[13]

To this end, we contacted the organization of womenpriests and bishops in the United States. The leadership of the organization agreed to allow us to conduct on-site visits (field notes and observations), interviews of the priests and bishops (consent forms obtained with permission to withdraw from the study at any time), surveys or focus groups of congregants (all identities protected by protocols for confidentiality), and examination of artifacts in congregational settings. Through the extensive gathering of multiple data points, the researchers sought to provide a thick description of the phenomenon of womenpriests in the Catholic tradition.

We collaborated to provide an initial triangulation of sources and interpreters. In addition, the multiple sources of data offer increased opportunity for validity of the research. We also acknowledged the caution of research experts Norma K. Denzin and Yvonna S. Lincoln when they write that "the use of multiple methods, or triangulation, reflects an attempt to secure an in-depth understanding of the phenomenon in question. Objective reality can never be captured. We know a thing only through its representations."[14] The researchers sought to know the essence of womenpriests' experiences as thoroughly as is possible while acknowledging the limits of qualitative and quantitative methodologies.

Our work sought to understand the phenomenon of RCWP spirituality. We designed a semi-structured interview process and physically interviewed thirty-three RCWP members. We reviewed the individual stories contained in a previously published account of womenpriests and chose an additional nine women to include in the work (names are listed in the appendices).[15] While we read extensively about the Roman Catholic Church's theology of priesthood and its consistent rejection of women as suitable for ordination, we resisted reading about the movement itself until we had interviewed most of the women and had coded their responses for themes. We wanted the study to be ethnographic, that is, rooted in the experience of the women themselves without imposing or accidentally applying preconceived notions to their experience. We transcribed each interview, coded it individually and then collectively. We entered the transcripts and re-coded using NVIVO, a software system designed for the purpose of assisting researchers in organizing multiple layers of research data. We observed two ordinations and three live Masses and during the Covid-19 pandemic observed several online Masses. We met with five communities and traveled to RCWP groups in the United States, Austria, and Scotland. We intentionally sought material and insight from the major locations of womenpriests throughout the United States, Latin America, Europe, South Africa, and Canada. We spent almost a week reviewing, cataloguing, and coding material housed in the archives at Marquette University.[16]

This research focused on the spirituality of the womenpriests as women daring to defy a law within the tradition they love. Most of them participated in their parishes and communities for many years. They risked previously held and deeply meaningful beliefs about themselves, their world view, and their view of the sacred. They gathered others willing to risk similar values. Indeed, both clergy and lay participants dared to shift their deepest held beliefs because they have come to know something new. They are willing to risk condemnation, excommunication, and shunning from those with whom they previously worshipped, played, and celebrated. Something profound shifted in the priests and the people in their congregations, and now sustains them in their new ventures. The researchers sought to understand the womenpriests' ways of attending to, naming, understanding, and living in harmony with the Sacred they know.

Thus, the qualitative study includes a phenomenological aspect. The researchers studied womenpriests and bishops in their natural setting. Our hope was to take what John Creswell describes as the "complex, time-consuming process of data analysis,"[17] to identify themes and categories that illuminate the call, response, and sustaining spirituality for these women in the church. As women ourselves, living our own call to faithfulness, we recognize the potential impact of this research and its "deep involvement in issues of gender, culture, and marginalized groups."[18] Thus, we agree with

Creswell that this is an "emotion laden, close to the people and ultimately practical study."[19]

Our work, then, presents information gathered about forty-two Roman Catholic womenpriests from a pool of approximately three hundred and fifty priests situated in the United States, Canada, Columbia, Europe, and South Africa. It is a global movement. The women range in age from thirty-three to the late eighties. They serve communities as small as fifteen people and as large as 1,500 men, women, and children. Most are "tentmakers,"[20] since there is no organization to offer them healthcare, retirement, or job security. Some rely on professions they pursued while also volunteering or working for the church. Others have counted on spouses to assist in their ongoing economic security. Of our group, most moved into the priesthood by way of vowed religious life or lay ecclesial ministry. Throughout this book, we focus on the women's stories as they told them. As author Carol Christ has written, "women stories have not been told. And without stories there is no articulation of experience. Without stories a woman is lost when she comes to make the important decisions of her life. She does not learn to value her struggles, to celebrate her strengths, to comprehend her pain. Without stories she cannot understand herself. Without stories she is alienated from those deep experiences of self and the world that has been called spiritual or religious."[21]

We hope lifting their voices at this time of synodality in the church will offer the church an opportunity to listen deeply to the stories these women reveal.[22] As the documents from the various churches on the several continents have revealed, the church as a whole is concerned about the place of women in the ecclesial community. While individual synodal submissions from various gatherings of bishops may include the desire for more place for women, this text offers people an opportunity to hear, to deeply listen to the spiritual calls, journeys, practices, and contributions women make as priests.

Chapter 2 explores the context in which these womenpriests respond. The Second Vatican Council (1962–1965) convened to explore the signs of the times in relation to the Roman Catholic Church. Hoping to "open the windows" to the movement of the Spirit, Saint Pope John XXIII called all the bishops together to consider how the Church might respond to newly emerging global realities. As the document on the Church in the Modern

World (*Gaudium et Spes*) declared, "the world which the council has in mind is the world of women and men, the entire human family seen in its total environment. It is the world as the theatre of human history, bearing the marks of its travail, its triumphs and its failures."[23] Most of the women we interviewed either experienced the changes in their lives as a result of the Second Vatican Council or they are now inheritors of the fifty years of appropriation of its documents. They describe themselves and their communities as "Vatican II people." This chapter, then, unpacks what that might mean.[24]

Chapter 3 begins the exploration of the womenpriests' stories concerning their call to God, to God's service, and to the priesthood itself. Scripture texts describe multiple call stories. From Adam and Eve as first humans through Abraham and Sarah as primary carriers of God's covenant with God's people, stories include women and men who experience the sacred in a variety of ways. Christian spirituality centers a person's call on an experience with Jesus which leads to some type of response. Paul names the response as a "walk in the Spirit" (Rom 6:11). The first document of Vatican II, the Constitution on the Sacred Liturgy (*Sacrosanctum Concilium*) states in a firm manner that "the spiritual life, however, is not limited solely to participation in the liturgy." Christians are "indeed called to pray with others, but they must also enter into their rooms to pray to the Father [sic] in secret [see Matt 6:6]; furthermore, according to the teaching of the apostle, they must pray without ceasing [see 1 Thess 5:17]."[25] Later, the Dogmatic Constitution on the Church (*Lumen Gentium*) affirmed that all men and women share in God's divine life and are chosen and "also predestined to become conformed to the image of his [sic] Son (Rom 8:29)."[26] As women who were and are influenced by the Second Vatican Council, our interviewees spoke eloquently about their own call by God. We reveal these calls in their own words as much as possible.

Chapter 4 explores the responses to their calls over their lifetime. Spiritual journeys are recorded throughout the Scriptures in the stories of Abraham and Sarah, Jacob and his wives, Joseph and his brothers, Moses and his many thousands of people. In Christian scriptures, Luke casts Jesus's life as a journey, and the story of the disciples (Mary and Cleopas) walking to Emmaus is often seen as a metaphor for the Christian disciple's life. As Lazar noted, the "life of holiness and sanctity is a gift from God, however one has to cultivate and nurture it by responding to it in a generous way."[27] This chapter, then, follows their journeys of faith as they revealed them to us.

Chapter 5 explores spiritual practices the women integrate to sustain their journeys. We found they drew from the main threads of spirituality in the Roman Catholic tradition: monastic, pastoral, Franciscan, Ignatian, liberation, and eco-spirituality. Lazar noted that the council invited all Catholics to participate in a deeper spiritual life. He observed that this included works of charity, "mercy and justice along with spiritual activities of prayer and meditation."[28] The womenpriests' practices also include spiritual ways of being normally considered outside Roman Catholic traditions, usually from Eastern traditions. The chapter tells their stories using their words and combined they offer a highly diverse way of nurturing their spiritual lives.

Chapter 6 examines how womenpriests' spiritualities impact their priestly leadership. Using the four marks of ministry exercised by the early church according to the Acts of the Apostles, this chapter reveals how the women interact with the people of God in their communities. The four marks include *Kerygma, Koinonia, Diakonia*, and *Leiturgia*. These early church activities approximate some of the models of church identified by Avert Dulles, SJ. Combined they shed light on choices the women make as priests, their sense of priestly identity, and their hope for the universal church. This chapter concludes with a discussion of the womenpriests' integration of the marks of Acts and the models of church through their leadership of a discipling church. Within that model, they offer three major contributions: widening their tent, expanding understanding of Eucharist, and embracing prophetic leadership that prioritizes collaboration rather than hierarchy.

Finally, in the epilogue we return to the question we posed as we began our work. We ask you the reader, to consider the stories, the insights, the teachings, the context. Then we ponder their contribution to spirituality as a walk of faith, their ordination as response to call, their embrace of the cost of excommunication and their hope for the church. As the synodal process continues even as we write, every nation that has submitted a report so far suggests that there is a problem in excluding women from every level of participation in the life of the church. We offer a few insights from our work and ask you again: Are womenpriests a challenge to the church? Renewal of the Church? Both? Neither?

2

CONTEXT

*"The joys and hopes, the grief and anguish of the people of our time,
especially of those who are poor or afflicted, are the joys and hopes,
the grief and anguish of the followers of Christ as well. Nothing that
is genuinely human fails to find an echo in their hearts."*

—GS, 1

"WE'RE VATICAN II people!" So exclaimed a group of congregants gathered during lunch in Southern California. They noted how many in their congregation suffered rejection by priests and more rigid churchgoers. Some were divorced and remarried and denied communion. Some had left the priesthood or religious life and married. Some discovered and claimed their nonbinary sexual identity. In the words of the people gathered, they were all Vatican II people of God who no longer found the Catholic Church a place for them to meet the sacred and to thrive as disciples. Their embrace of Vatican II framed our understanding of the women we interviewed and studied.

The Second Vatican Council (Vatican II) looms as the most important theological event of the twentieth century. Set in Rome from 1962 to 1965 and convened by a supposedly interim pope, this event assembled the largest ever group of bishops, theologians, and advisors to reflect on and renew a world religion and its future in a changing society. Following two world wars that disrupted the order established by Western European monarchs, Vatican II sparked research and hope in scholars, lay leaders, and vowed religious Roman Catholic women. Contemporary with the civil rights and women's movements of North America in the 1960s, the emancipation movements of colonial governments, and the liberation movements of Latin America, this council fueled new energy toward examining the meaning of Christian religious belief in the midst of a deeply transforming world.

The council inspired a major religious movement that extended responsibility for discipleship to all the baptized. It increased Catholic understanding of what Martin Luther King Jr. termed the "beloved community." The documents released by the council invited experimentation and hope for opening the doors of the Roman Catholic Church toward the contemporary era in which it existed. Rejecting the closed, anti-modernist disposition of previous hierarchical authorities, Saint Pope John XXIII, in collaboration with almost 2,500 bishops, approximately twenty-five women, and several ecumenical consultants, "sought to renew ourselves . . . under the guidance of the Holy Spirit."[1] Many significant changes emerged from the experimental nature of the immediate post-council church.

Of these changes, six conciliar shifts directly impact the content and tone of the women studied in this work. First, television coverage allowed people to witness the incredible diversity of cultures and ethnic origins represented in conversation over four years of council deliberations. Second, the council situated the major role of discipleship on the laity. The council documents spoke increasingly of the people of God, community of believers, and the universal discipleship of the baptized. Third, the council fathers recognized an absence of voice among over half the participants in the local churches. One participant, Cardinal Suenens, requested the presence of women at all future sessions. One US woman, Sister Mary Luke Tobin of the Sisters of Loretto, joined approximately twenty-five other women who proceeded to influence the content of major documents. They made major contributions on documents related to religious life and their participation set the stage for hope of future inclusion. Fourth, the council invited major Protestant ordained ministers, Jews, and Orthodox bishops to participate as witnesses to the conversation. Like the women and *periti* (theological advisors), these representatives influenced council documents through their conversations with participants before, during, and after formal council sessions each fall.

Fifth, the council addressed issues of spiritual formation and community worship through its Constitution on the Sacred Liturgy (*Sacrosanctum Concilium*). This document produced discussion that transformed the liturgical life of the post-council church by moving the celebrant closer to the community, requiring the community to be present as constitutive of worship, changing the language of worship to match the culture celebrating

God's presence among them, and endorsing the development of holiness as constitutive of the life of followers of Christ through the Spirit. We shall see how these initiatives impacted people formed by the documents of the council and their emphasis on the community, the language used during worship, and the ritual itself.

Sixth, in 1965 the Council released the Declaration on Religious Freedom (*Dignitatis Humanae*). This document stated clearly that the dignity of the human person encourages one to exercise fully their own judgment and assume responsibility for their actions. It further links this freedom to the human spirit and free practice in society. Thus, "this Vatican council pays careful attention to these spiritual aspirations" and considering "truth and justice" it "searches the sacred tradition and teaching of the church."[2] As a result of this effort, the document argued, one "has the right and duty to seek the truth in religious matters so that, through the use of appropriate means, they may form prudent judgements of conscience which are sincere and true."[3] Further, the document explains that "all are bound to follow their conscience faithfully in every sphere of activity so that they may come to God, who is their last end."[4] Together these six movements shaped an evolving context that formed and eventually compelled some women to seek ordination challenging Church law: Canon 1024.[5]

Global and Cultural Adaptation

These six major shifts in understanding fostered hope and experimentation throughout the world. Bishops in most countries formed synods that met occasionally to coordinate how Catholic Christian discipleship might be best lived in that cultural context. This process of consultation and synodality birthed the liberation movement in Latin America with the major conferences of Rio de Janeiro (1955), Medellin (1968), Puebla (1979), Santo Domingo (1992), and Aparecida (2007). Most recently the Amazonian conference of 2021 continued the process of synodality initiated through the Second Vatican Council. Similarly, the African bishops gathered in two major synods (1994 and 2009) to determine how multiple African countries might interpret changes in liturgy and church governance, specifically in light of African traditional religion. They, too, are currently participating in the synodality process convened by Pope Francis in 2021. Asian countries held their own synod (1998) offering theological reinterpretation of Christian norms as they affect traditional Asian cultures.

Throughout the world, then, bishops consulted with priests and laity in a new way. The Second Vatican Council established a methodology that included circulating written documents, convening groups for responses to issues, and writing letters and instructions to enhance faith in particular cultural contexts. This process continues today as evidenced by Pope Francis appointing a group of bishops to serve as his consultants, calling for a global consultation on the family (2013) that included multiple sources for gathering information, and convening local councils in Brazil, Germany, Canada, and the United States. In October 2021, for example, he called on the universal church to listen deeply to the people of God so that together the Church could move forward in responding to the current context.

Victoria spent time in Nicaragua and it changed her perspective. Patricia stood up against apartheid in South Africa where she served many years as a Dominican Sister. After her theological studies in Rome, she began to support women's ordination. As an ordained bishop she sought to dismantle the cultural and patriarchal barriers blocking women in ways similar to those of resisting apartheid. Marina Theresa, a lay ecclesial minister from Columbia, served people of African descent in Ecuador. At the invitation of both Episcopalian and Roman Catholic bishops she pursued additional education so she could better serve the most marginalized. Two Judys crossed global borders when they worked in Latin America toward spreading the gospel. They assisted both Olga, who was later ordained a bishop, and Marina Theresa who later immigrated to Florida where she works with Black and Latinx Catholics. Juanita takes people to the Holy Land almost annually, while Shanon shepherds pilgrimages to Bingen, Germany. Esperanza works with marginalized Latinx who cross the border in California and Chava works with immigrants from Nicaragua, Mexico, and Guatemala. Women-priests are found on every continent except Antarctica and they share an openness to global insights and cultural understandings.

The global church with its multiple cultural and language contexts continues to call forth men and women to lead people to God through Christ in the power of the Spirit. For example, the Church of El Salvador, as led by Saint Monsignor Romero, retrieved the church of the poor and the church of the martyrs. As migration to the North from the South continues to impact western European dominated countries and the Church in those countries, the movement and work of the global Church continues to challenge and convert the people of God.

People of God

Within the Vatican II documents one finds evidence of two major notions of church. The first emphasizes the institutional nature of the church protected by a predictable hierarchy and rooted in Matthew 16:18: "I tell you that you are Peter and upon this rock I will build my Church." The existential angst following the two world wars of the twentieth century, however, suggested that locating all authority, holiness, discipleship, and agency in an ordained priesthood failed the world in a time of great need for moral courage. As Kenon Osborne observed, leaders searched for ways to reinvigorate the Christian believer as a baptized disciple of Christ empowered by the Spirit of God.[6] Theologians such as Yves Congar, Edward Schillebeeckz, Bernard Häring, and Karl Rahner proposed centering the mission of the church in the laity, the baptized. As a result, the documents of Vatican II, particularly *Lumen Gentium*, reflect the second and emerging notion of church as the community, the people of God gathered together in Christ.

The multiple synods that have followed since Vatican II promoted this notion of community and shared responsibility. This principle placed responsibility for actions at the foundational level in which a decision could be made. It attempted to flatten the power of the hierarchy of the church in order to redistribute responsibility to all the laity as their birthright and call through baptism. In the United States two USCCB-commissioned studies of the priesthood articulated how these documents formed seminarians for the post–Vatican II parishes they would lead. Each found that the increasing presence of women on parish staffs, and the allocation of tasks previously reserved to the priests, required priests to learn new skills of collaboration and shared decision-making.[7]

Bishops created pastoral and presbyteral councils to assist them in setting goals for dioceses. Similarly, parishes initiated pastoral councils to promote shared responsibility and accountability for the life of the parish. Eventually, most aspects of ministry including Catholic charities, education, youth ministry, schools, evangelization, and missionary outreach developed boards of consultants that essentially flattened hierarchical control. By 1996, many studies found that most Catholic ministers considered ministry a team enterprise and the church the people of God or the community rather than the institutional hierarchy.[8]

From the 1990s through the current synodal consultation, however, a movement against the more egalitarian way of being church re-emphasized the power of the hierarchy and the institutional church. This exploded with the exposition of pedophilia scandals and the eventual revelation of cover-ups by the hierarchy. This continues even as Germany and France release their respective studies (2021, 2022) on pedophilia scandals in their countries.

As womenpriests spoke about their leadership styles, they eschewed top-down management styles in favor of consultative and collaborative models. Teresa, Pat and Donnieau all spoke of their work to enliven the gifts of the people within the community so they could share the gifts and nurture community life. Most congregations that gather with women-priests include twenty-five to one hundred people. These smaller groups care for one another, reach out to support each person, and choose to expand their care to various people in their communities. Jeanette states she wants to be present to her people. She continues "the ministry of presence, the ability to be present, to be there, to really be that Christ presence with them . . . that's what connected me." Suzanne spoke about forming "a community that would spiritually sustain people." Both women count on the people in the community to make decisions for the community. Bridget Mary writes "the goal of the group RC Womenpriests is to bring about the full equality of women in the Roman Catholic Church. At the same time, we are striving for a new model of Priestly Ministry."[9]

Women Ministers

Throughout this era of synodal collaboration, priestly ordinations failed to match the increase in lay populations. From 1970 through 2021, ordained priests in the United States alone fell from a total of 59,192 to 34,923. At the same time the age of active priests increased such that over half the number of priests are now over the age of 65. In addition, the US Catholic population grew from 47.9 million people to 66.8 million.[10] During this same period, the world priest population remained somewhat stable with a drop of only about 5,500 priests. The Catholic population, however, increased from an estimated 653.5 million to almost 1.3 billion. Parishes without a resident or assigned priest increased as did those serviced by a deacon or a person appointed by the bishop according to Canon 517.2.[11] Thus, the notion of "priest shortage" became a theme throughout the world.

This notion of "shortage" fueled creative imagining of other sources and ways to fill the perceived void. Most of the response to opportunity emerged from lay people newly recognized in the Vatican II documents, and women comprised between 70 to 85 percent of those stepping into new roles of responsibility. Indeed, most of the Roman Catholic womenpriests we studied followed their call through volunteer, paid lay ecclesial work, vowed religious life, or social justice outreach efforts such as the Catholic Worker movement.

As the Center for Applied Research in the Apostolate (CARA) documents, the invitation of Vatican II resulted in people responding in the thousands to new opportunities for discipleship and ministry. Multiple studies related to competencies for ministry emerged. In addition to the Bishops' studies of ordained ministry, multiple groups examined the phenomenon of lay people assuming responsibilities for ministries in education, formation, prayer and healing, visiting the sick, and prison ministries. These studies documented the shift from an all-ordained ministry to a more team related ministry practice over a forty-year period.[12] Organizations emerged to oversee the quality of programs preparing lay ministers. Indeed, by 2005, the USCCB published a document, *Co-Workers in the Vineyard*, that named the importance of lay ministers to the total ministry of the Church.[13] By that time, dioceses in the United States authorized multiple methods for educating and forming lay leaders. Throughout this period from 1966 through today, women have constituted between 70 to 85 percent of lay ecclesial leaders. In programs designed to educate and form leaders, over 70 percent of the student body have been women.

By 2005, CARA statistics showed that the number of lay ecclesial ministers had increased enough to serve every parish in the United States. New experiments with leadership included job titles such as "Pastoral Life

Coordinator," "Pastoral Life Administrator," and "Sacramental Minister." Lines of power through ordination began to be blurred somewhat as parishioners experienced women and married men in roles of significant pastoral leadership, including celebrating worship without a priest.

Throughout this time of growth and re-organization, the women we interviewed served in many of these parishes as paid and volunteer lay ecclesial ministers. They often related their own conviction and hope that they would be ordained as a result of Vatican II's call to *resourcement,* the continued return to biblical texts with increasing attention to translations and historical contexts. These numbers and the closing of parishes reveal that the promise of renewal that many felt after Vatican II did not result in full inclusion of women. This disappointment proved a major influence in women choosing to move toward ordination.

Suzanne, a priest and bishop, spoke about her connections to a priest at Santa Clara while she attended college there. She and others were encouraged to actively participate in special masses that relied on their participation as readers, acolytes, and preachers. She and her friends thought this would lead to ordination. Dianne reflected that she thought in 1985 she would be ordained in her lifetime. As part of post–Vatican II theological education, she anticipated that new biblical understanding offered the Church the way to change its practice of exclusion. Christine, a priest and bishop, spoke about her time as a Benedictine in Austria. She noted that her order was "pastoral," meaning they did preparation for masses, teaching, outreach, sacramental preparation, and other duties related to sustaining the pastoral presence of the Church. She thought women in her order would be among the first ordained to the priesthood, since they were so prepared. She spoke about this as a "time of hope about married clergy and that someday women would be ordained." She later observed that Pope John Paul II closed the door to this expectation. Clearly, women who agreed to be ordained anticipated the possibility much earlier and with the full blessing of the hierarchy.

Ecumenical and Interreligious

During this same fifty-year period, more Protestant ecclesial communities ordained women to pastoral leadership. In the mid-1950s, the Swedish

Lutheran church voted to allow ordination of women to be ministers. Anglican churches specifically in Hong Kong and later throughout the Anglican communion followed. Interestingly, ordained male ministers from both Lutheran and Episcopalian/Anglican traditions were admitted into the Roman Catholic priesthood even though they were married. Since they were male, and the ecclesial communities also ordained women, the transfer to Roman Catholic ordination caused the Vatican to worry about ecumenical relationships. The ongoing ecumenical dialogue, opened through the Decree on Ecumenism (*Unitatis Redintegratio*), offered opportunity for Roman Catholic theologians to interact with those of other Christian ecclesial communities. The concerns related to ordination centered on apostolic succession of men. Thus, communities such as the Evangelical Lutheran Church in America, Anglicans, or Episcopalians were considered already ordained due to Roman Catholic acceptance of their shared apostolic succession. On the other hand, women who shared apostolic succession in those traditions could not be accepted by Roman Catholics due to their gender. This became a key element in the Roman Catholic Women Priests movement.

As seminaries and universities expanded offerings for master of divinity programs, women and men from all Christian traditions sought their education and preparation for ministerial leadership in accredited schools closest to their geographical proximity. In a very real sense, this cross-fertilized Christian ministerial leadership. As women joined master of divinity programs, they often compared notes about who would be ordained and where they may be placed. Significant studies, starting in the 1970s and continuing through 2020, document the discrepancy between the permission to ordain, the actual practice of ordination, and the placement and advancement of ordained women in most mainline Protestant ecclesial communities as well as many Pentecostal and traditionally Black churches.[14] These studies demonstrated that ordained women are paid less, earn less in their retirement, have less access to healthcare and are not considered for "promotion" to larger church communities that can offer a living wage. So, like many of the RCWP, these ecumenical partners in ordained ministry suffered financial hardship and often relied on tent-making professions to sustain themselves and their families. The sisterhood that has arisen from this shared experience contributed to the support RCWP received from Protestant and even Jewish and Unitarian Universalist pastors as the RCWP sought places to preside over worship, gather communities of faith, and ordain new priests and bishops.

Other studies of congregational life documented the size of most Protestant and Evangelical communities. Chaves, a sociologist of religion, has conducted a series of extensive sociological studies that recorded the average size of most Protestant congregations as seventy-five people. While some congregations exceed two thousand people (mostly large evangelical mega churches), the majority range between twenty-five to seventy-five people.[15] Further research revealed that ordained women in Protestant traditions are often assigned to the smallest and most rural congregations and left there throughout their ministerial careers. The close association of womenpriests with their ecumenical counterparts encourages them as they convene smaller congregations that match the norm for other ecclesial communities. Thus, as noted, many of the womenpriests serve small groups ranging from twelve to one hundred people, with very few approaching a larger number such as the 1,500 registered at Spiritus Christi and pastored by Myra and Celie.

Morag revealed her fascination with, and appreciation of, a woman minister in the United Church in Scotland. She confessed she was a teen at the time, and it sparked a keen desire to pursue ordination herself. After retiring, she returned to university and earned a master of divinity. While in the program, faculty and students in the Anglican Church and the Church of Scotland asked her to consider ordination in their traditions. She knew she was "Catholic in her 'DNA'" and is the only listed RCWP member in the UK. Similarly, while in divinity school, a United Methodist pastor invited Dagmar to lead a United Methodist community after graduation. Others revealed similar invitations and opportunities.

Another womanpriest decided to leave her vowed religious community so that when her bishop called her into his office, she could protect that community. During their conversation, the bishop asked her to change allegiance from her Roman Catholic affiliation and urged her to pursue ordination as an Episcopalian. To him it was better that she was ordained an Episcopalian priest than that he was compelled to excommunicate her.

Many went to Protestant sponsored seminaries. Chava worked for the university that sponsored her seminary and was able to explore theological traditions in a safe environment. While maintaining her deep Catholic belief and practice, she ventured into work with the growing agricultural migrant community. Victoria attributed her work with the marginalized in New York and San Francisco to her education at New York Theological Seminary. Joanna and Celie traced their journeys through their ordination in other ecclesial communities to their work now as Roman Catholic womenpriests.

The ecumenical and interreligious connections include shared space, invitations to share worship services, and shared efforts toward social justice. As the womanpriest invites people to the service and to communion, she proclaims the liturgy is for everyone, and all are welcome. As a result, the congregations reflect religious diversity. When pressed about their choices, each identified their deep attachment to Roman Catholic tradition as embodied in their DNA.

The Influence of the Constitution on Sacred Liturgy

To begin our research, we observed an ordination liturgy. Held in a Lutheran church in Oregon, the liturgy included some men, some families, and a designated section for those who would be reprimanded if their pictures were included in the documentation of the celebration. Several Roman Catholic womenpriests concelebrated with one male Lutheran minister present. Joy infected all gathered. From the beginning, the presiding priest, one of the women we interviewed, welcomed all. She repeated the phrase "all are welcome" several times throughout this event, including at the reception of the Eucharist. At the reception following, we researchers discovered Jews, non-believers, and other Christians gladly participated in the ordination as well as weekly liturgies. This initial encounter led us to ask an additional question of all interviewees. The question concerned their understanding of the Eucharist, and the answers led us to consider the impact this movement contributes to the practice of, and theologies related to liturgy, especially the celebration of the Eucharist.

Essentially, the Constitution on Liturgy (*Sacroscanctum Concilium*) intended to support the baptized in their pursuit of holiness. The teaching, then, of Vatican II, encouraged all the baptized to enter into the life of Christ and to become disciples. That is, the documents urged Catholics and all

Christians to approach God as if on a journey of faith and life. Thus, many began to write and reflect and create opportunities that assisted people in nurturing their faith.

The sacramental life of the church itself approaches spiritual awakening as a journey. There is an initiation to life with God and it is called baptism. This sacrament assures people they are from God, oriented to God and loved unconditionally by God. The sacrament also initiates people into a community that is dedicated to living Christlike lives with and for one another. The journey continues with another initiation as children grow in the ability to understand the need for food on the journey. That food consists of Scripture, bread, and wine through the Eucharist. As one proceeds on the journey, people make mistakes and reconciliation celebrates the reunion and renewed fortification of grace that Christ offers through that sacrament. As people age, another stage in their maturing faith is celebrated in confirmation which again dedicates and formalizes the choice to become a more fully realized Christian, a follower of Christ. It is often said that the two career choices represent the adult sacraments: marriage for most and ordination for a few celibate males. Finally, sacraments are celebrated to move one through the final passage into new life.

Vatican II documents and teaching renewed and emphasized the importance of the Christian journey as movement toward holiness. Roman Catholics believe and celebrate Christ present sacramentally throughout one's life. As Dagmar exclaimed "I want all the sacraments! I want to be present to all the grace and love Christ has to offer." Others have wondered why those neither married nor ordained don't have a sacrament to sustain them. In the early church, for example, virgins, widows, and martyrs were highly respected and valued. Indeed, vowed religious women follow in the footsteps of widows and virgins. No sacrament officially supports these ways of moving toward holiness. According to the universal Christian church, the number of sacraments, their practice and application changed over the centuries. During the Reformation period, the Roman Catholic Church named seven.

As pastoral theologian Edward Hahnenburg synthesized, the document on liturgy emphasized four goals, each of which the RCWP embrace. The church sought (1) "to energize Catholics, (2) to update church institutions,

(3) to encourage the unity of all Christians, and (4) to reach out to the whole world."[16] The document encouraged full participation; thus, the liturgy was translated into local languages from the universal Latin. Combined with the ongoing attention devoted to translating Scripture into more contemporary language, the liturgy attempted to reach people in their cultural contexts. The liturgies we witnessed as researchers continued this practice of adapting language to be inclusive of all peoples and to encourage unity in an effort to reach out to the world around them.[17]

Section three of the constitution affirmed the practices of popular religion as worthwhile efforts on the journey to God. This began with the notion that other signs "impart grace" and "are sacred signs that bear resemblance to the sacraments: they signify effects, particularly of a spiritual kind; which are obtained through the Church's intercession."[18] Thus, for ordinary believers, "the liturgy of the sacraments and sacramentals sanctifies almost every event in their lives; they are given access to the stream of divine grace which flows from the paschal mystery of the passion, death, and resurrection of Christ . . . There is hardly any proper use of material things which cannot thus be directed toward the sanctification of humans and the praise of God."[19] As people experienced this radical openness to individual spiritual practice and invitation to holiness, opportunities exploded. They included Scripture studies, retreats, spiritual direction, novenas, spiritual renewal efforts, and so much more.

Experimentation with extending spiritual life to the laity encouraged cultural contexts to insert more influence on the sacramental imagination of the Church. Thus, the *dios de los muertos* practices of the Latin American communities impact the North American celebration of All Saints and All Souls days. House altars from various countries now find themselves in many households as people remind themselves of the communion of saints that includes those formally canonized and those ancestors of faith not formally canonized but equally important in a person's journey. For example, the devotion to Our Lady of Guadalupe, somewhat restricted originally to Mexico, now includes her veneration as Our Lady of the Americas with churches throughout North and South America celebrating her in formal liturgies as well as devotions adopted through encounters with Latinx populations.

Jane, a priest, bishop, and scripture scholar, translated the entire lectionary for weekly mass celebration so that people could pray without patriarchal language hindering their spiritual imaginations. With Kathleen's keen guidance, people shared the prayer of consecration and offered each other a variety of breads that accommodated diverse food sensitivities as they broke bread at Eucharist. Kathy created altar banners that highlight major saints in feasts through her quilting art. Victoria set scripture stories to music and created one person plays so the scriptures came alive and assisted peoples' imagination and spiritual growth. Esperanza, Olga, Marina Theresa, Judy, and Chava ensured there were translations of Scripture at community celebrations so that culturally diverse communities could share their spiritual journeys. Dianne, Myra, and Jane ensured music lifted peoples' hearts and minds to God. All congregants were called to read, lector, serve as eucharistic ministers, sacristans, and musicians.

Primacy of Individual Conscience

One of the final and most important documents completing Vatican II freed Roman Catholics to use their reason and theological understanding to choose how to form and live according to their conscience. The *Declaration on Religious Freedom* (*Dignitatis Humanae*) opens with a powerful statement: "A sense of the dignity of the human person has been impressing itself more and more deeply on the consciousness of contemporary man [*sic*]. And the demand is increasingly made that men [*sic*] should act on their own judgment, enjoying and making use of a responsible freedom, not driven by coercion but motivated by a sense of duty."[20] This amazing document continues "On their part, all men [*sic*] are bound to seek the truth, especially in what concerns God and His [*sic*] Church, and to embrace the truth they come to know and to hold fast to it."[21]

Recognizing that religious freedom for all humans is based on the dignity of being human, the document maintains that all are to be given the right to seek the truth, "especially religious truth. They are also bound to adhere to the truth, once it is known, and to order their whole lives in accord with the demands of truth."[22] These radical statements freed many Roman Catholics to pursue their own study of the teachings of Christ through examination of Scriptures and the traditions of the Church. Indeed, most master of divinity programs require thorough examination of the inherited tradition informed by a critical eye as to how understanding developed over the course of human history. As a result, feminist and liberationist critiques developed new ways of approaching the study of inherited traditions. The inclusion of multiple cultural traditions led communities to embrace new lived experience of the Christian tradition.

These trends of study and cultural experience combined over the last fifty years to provide new interpretations and understandings of the roots of the Christian heritage. The document acknowledged that Christian faith must be a free act of faith. It also suggested that the Church itself grows in understanding of truth in relation to itself and others.[23] While the document stands against religious oppression by governments and other religious groups, it opens the door for individuals to appropriate their faith without the oppression of any religious organization. Indeed, one section of the document assures families of their own basic rights, in accordance with their religious beliefs. It encourages families and family members to exercise freedom of choice and to reject unjust burdens as a matter of contributing to the common good.[24]

As outlined in these few paragraphs, the document on religious freedom helped lead to the phenomenon this text considers: the valid but illicit ordination of women as Roman Catholic priests. Esperanza exclaimed that she was taught the primacy of conscience by her Sisters of the Immaculate Heart of Mary teachers. Attending schools they taught from first grade through high school, she reported that she is now a full member of the community. They teach how important it is to ask questions. She declared, "It's in the questions!"

Ida Raming and Iris Müeller both wrote extensively before and after Vatican II about the need to question the practice of ordaining only men. Raming produced a major PhD document that disputed the tradition of relegating ordination to men. She sought to help the church find in its history and practice the opportunity to move forward in more equality during this new time in the church. Similarly, Scripture theologians appointed by Pope Paul VI were divided in their opinion that there was no scriptural impediment to ordaining married men and women to the priesthood.[25] Relying on tradition initiated during and after the twelfth century, Pope Paul VI issued a Declaration (1976) accompanied by a commentary that intended to settle the question with a negative answer while simultaneously inviting further research and conversation.[26] Having investigated theological and scriptural sources through their studies and exercising their freedom of conscience, RCWP challenges the teaching of Canon 1024 that "a baptized male alone receives sacred ordination validly."[27]

Creative Problem Solving for Providing Ordained Ministry to a Newly Alive Church

Within ten years of the end of the Council, biblical and historical research encouraged by Popes Pius XII, John XXIII, and Paul VI uncovered new information that challenged traditions in the church related to ministry. Many articles surfaced arguing for a radical return to Christian roots in liturgy, home/house churches, smaller communities, expansive understandings of leadership and ministry, and new forms of organizational structures that might flatten the strict hierarchy of the institutional church. Theologians, scripture scholars, and laity embraced the opportunity to study and contribute to substantive scholarship related to all the themes of "aggiornamento" (open windows to contemporary cultures) unleashed by the Second Vatican Council.

The studies combined with ongoing liberation movements around the world increased pressure on the Vatican to embrace change. As we have seen, laity answered calls to work in the evolving ministries in the church. Vowed Religious women entered new ministries and left their roles in Catholic schools, encouraging a new wave of lay men and women to assume this important role in the church. Similar experiences occurred in health care and social justice oriented ministries. As we have shown in previous sections, women entered into paid ministries in record numbers. The change seemed to be happening fast, and several theological faculties addressed issues related to ordination hoping to contribute to the *resourcement* and *aggiornamento* flourishing in the church. Biblical scholar Robert Karris registered his disagreement with the pontifical interpretation of the biblical commission's declaration when he wrote:

more in accord with the data we have surveyed is the view of twelve of the seventeen members of the same commission [Pontifical Biblical Commission] *who do not agree with their five colleagues that in the scriptures there are sufficient indications to exclude the possibility of the accession of women to the presbyterate. On the contrary, these twelve think that the "church hierarchy, entrusted with the sacramental economy, would be able to entrust the ministries of Eucharist and reconciliation to women in light of circumstances, without going against Christ's original intentions."*[28]

Yet, it seemed that the tenor of embracing change shifted as resistance to the seemingly fast movement emerged. Paul VI complied with the more conservative and traditional group in the Biblical Commission and wrote a document (*Inter Insigniores*) that answered "no" to the question of expanding ordination to women and married men, without quite closing the discussion. Thus, scholars increased their efforts to change the course of the Church. Finally, now St. Pope John Paul II intended to close all discussion with a firm "no" to expansion on the two theological grounds related to tradition and the priest acting sacramentally "*in persona Christi.*"[29] Later, Cardinal Ratzinger, who would become Pope Benedict XVI, declared that the teaching on women's ordination "has been set forth infallibly by the ordinary and universal magisterium" and he cited a second apostolic letter (1998) by Pope John Paul II, *Ad Tuendam Fidem.* Disagreeing with Ratzinger, theologian and ecclesiologist Richard McBrien relied on canon law itself to counter the argument writing that canon "749.3 stipulates that if there is any doubt about the infallible nature of a teaching, it is not infallible."[30]

By 2000 reports of major scandals of pedophilia and sexual abuse of women by Roman Catholic priests caused thousands of Roman Catholics to question their loyalty to the institution. Given the apparent retrenchment from Vatican II ideals as expressed in documents of 1962–1965, women and men questioned hierarchical decision-making. By 2002, women and many priests, and some bishops, responded in a new way to the "priest crisis." On the Danube River between Germany and Austria, three bishops ordained seven women to the priesthood. They were immediately excommunicated, as were those who participated in the ordination in any way. All of them reject the excommunication. The precedent started a movement that has now produced over three hundred and fifty Roman Catholic Women Priests (RCWP) working throughout the world.

Summary

Throughout this chapter, we sought to illumine the voices of the women in response to their exclamation "We are Vatican II people!" The chapter sketched the landscapes in which the women were formed and now minister. The women and their congregants used words, phrases, and images reflecting the vision and documents of Vatican II. While we offered hints through some of their statements, the following sections describe their spiritual journeys more completely.

3

IS IT I, O HOLY ONE?

"Speak God, for your Servant is Listening."
—1 Sam 3:9

"Listen carefully . . . with the ear of your heart."
—Rule of St. Benedict

DONNIEAU DID NOT know as a child in parochial schools that there were no womenpriests. She just thought there were no womenpriests at her parish. In second grade, immediately after Mass, she ran with excitement to her pastor, practically dancing for joy because she knew that she wanted to become a priest when she grew up. When she exclaimed her good news to him, he responded "Oh but you can't! You can't be a priest. You are a girl. You can be a nun!" Crushed, the second grader who initially ran to tell him of this epiphany that she had with all the joy that came with it, felt deflated; no, devastated. As she ran away in tears, she literally bumped into one of the beloved sisters at the school, Sister Ignatius. "I just walked into her; I just remember running into her. She put her arms around me, looked down at me and said: 'You will be what you were meant to be.' And that changed me." When she grew older Donnieau sought out a spiritual director and worked with her for almost two years. She recalls, "the first year I just lied to her! I lied to her—my spiritual director! What I mean by lying to her is that I kept a secret in me about feeling called to priesthood because of the fear that had been instilled in me about falling out of sync with the Roman hierarchical church. But in the process of spiritual direction and discernment I finally came to my spiritual director in tears and I said: 'I feel called to be a priest; I still can't be a priest because women can't be priests.' And I'm sitting there sobbing and I'll never forget, my spiritual director leaned back in her chair, looked at me with great compassion and said: 'Do you have any idea what's happening in the church?' I was confused and then she said: 'Let me tell you about this movement of Roman Catholic womenpriests.'"

For many RCWP, God seems to open one door after another as God calls them to something forbidden in the church. Myra says it succinctly: "One door after another God has opened for me. And I kept remembering my promise, you open the door and I'll walk through it. When the door opens, I am obligated by covenant to go through it." Each womanpriest shares a story of call followed by wonder at how this call could be answered within the current Roman Catholic structures. These call stories mirror stories preserved in Scripture and in lives of the saints. They inspire others to wonder at their experience of the sacred.

Attending to Experience

Paula served as a lector in her parish and read the call of Samuel (1 Sam 3:1–19) at Mass. When she finished reading, she returned to her seat by her husband and silently prayed, "Speak God your servant is listening." As she related the story, she described how she was experiencing the moment: "I get goosebumps when I tell this story. I heard in my heart God say: 'I want you to be a priest.' I was shocked; that was the first time I ever thought about it." As she continues, she describes her awareness that such women priests existed. Indeed, she admitted that she and other women in a group prayed for women who were called to priesthood. She never believed she would be called. "As I was there in the pew, I looked up and saw our priest on the altar and I said 'No God, I don't want to do this male thing. I don't want to be part of that.'" As she declined God's offer, she heard "Things could be different." She continues, "With that, I said to myself, 'This is God, this is God speaking to me.' And I began shaking terribly and crying. And Ed [her husband] said, 'Paula keep listening, it's from God and God will continue to call you.' I said 'OK'."

Encounter with the Holy begins with a restlessness, a longing, perhaps a recognition that goes beyond intellectual assent and includes something that is felt through the senses. In some ways, as Marina Theresa said, the Spanish word *inquietud* captures this phenomenon better than English. *Inquietud* refers to a restlessness that one feels, as if something was missing, but not really knowing what it is until one sees it, hears it, or feels it. Moses's curiosity to see more, then his reverence in removing shoes as he approached the burning bush illustrates this impulse in Scripture. This notion best describes the experience of the women as they speak of their call from God.

Marcus Borg, a biblical theologian, contended the following about the personal quality of God's presence:

> *I think God 'speaks' to us. I don't mean oral or aural revelation*
> *or divine dictation. But I think God 'speaks' to us—sometimes*
> *dramatically in visions, less dramatically in some of our dreams, in*
> *internal "proddings" or "leadings, "through people, and through the*
> *devotional practices and scriptures of our tradition. We sometimes*
> *have a sense—I sometimes have a sense—of being addressed.*[1]

Donnieau was inspired through her participation in the Mass, Paula heard Scripture speak to her personally, and Myra described a bargain, an internal prodding.

Georgina Zubiria, RSCJ, a theologian from the province of Mexico-Nicaragua, highlights the importance of the senses and affect to understand that which moves the human heart.[2] She writes that speaking about God is difficult. She notes that we always run the risk of reducing the experience of the divine into finite words and ideas that ultimately place God in a box.[3] Yet, she argues our very senses and feelings mediate this experience of God and contends that "our experience of God is born, grows, and is nourished through our humanity, through words and gestures, symbols and rights, human experience and conviction."[4]

As we considered the womenpriests' experiences of the divine, we specifically explored the impact those experiences exerted on their senses. Thus, as Paula revealed, she shook and cried as she sat in Mass—a public place. Her husband, next to her, leaned into her and whispered in her ear. She had a private experience of God in a communal celebration. Paula's husband recognized that her emotional response—shaking with tears—was connected to her experience of God. This example illustrates a basic insight of Ignatian Spirituality, which connects feelings and our emotional awareness to our ability to understand God's activity in our lives. As Wilkie and

Noreen Cannon Au explain, "human experiences such as joy and desolation, as Ignatius contends, are the very way in which God communicates God's very Spirit to us."[5]

Paula's story revealed that her husband recognized the power of the divine to impact a person. Clearly, he felt her shake, and he had participated in ministry with her for years. Thus, together they could, as Zubiria acknowledges, recognize the "intuitive and perceptive capacity, our intelligence and feeling" that "permits us to recognize the transcendent in the imminent".[6] Thus, this story allows us to experience with the couple, how feelings are "wired and manifest and make transparent, God's love and presence and commitment to humanity in an embodied, incarnational way."[7]

Other stories of Roman Catholic womenpriests testify to their experiences with the sacred. Each exemplifies *inquietud*, an attentiveness to, and yearning for, God. Each easily recalls their first experience of call. They demonstrate an ability to hear and recognize this call is not something that just hatched at one point in their life. Like ancestresses in faith such as Mary, Elizabeth, and Sarah, the faith of these womenpriests is grounded in the long tradition of faithful people who listen and obey God's call.

Call Stories

Celie tells us that at an early age: "I remember sitting in the pews at church and looking up at the consecration and feeling I suppose what you would call a shimmer, a feeling of 'Oh! that's who you are!'" She notes that due to irregularities in her family, she wasn't baptized or allowed or drawn to be Catholic during that Mass. At the same time, she reflects, "I think . . . for me it just felt so much like God's call to my spirit. I hope as I share this story, this journey with you that this dimension as part of the story will move us beyond any argument or debate because I think it is valuable to hear from women describing how there has been a pull on their spirits. Let people know that God does call women not through arguments but by believing in that pull of the Spirit." Her experience of awe and immediate recognition of a holy "shimmer" during the elevation of Eucharist initiated her journey, even before she was baptized.

Many of these women speak of the same longing, pulling, or recognition. Jane, for example, shares that when she went to a specifically Catholic liturgy, that she walked in and her first response was "Aahhh, this is where I belong." She had felt the presence of God at the age of three! While swinging on a swing outside she celebrated God's love by singing "church songs" she learned in Sunday school. Yet her feeling of belonging occurred later in a Catholic liturgy. Kathy described her call as a young child, sort of like a telephone call. She heard the voice of God and sought to live with that Holy One throughout her life. Each speaks of physical and emotional experiences.

Maria recounts several moving stories about her evolving relationship with God. As a young girl she was orphaned during World War II and placed in an orphanage. She suffered from malnutrition when she was found and was slightly handicapped as a result. She was mistaken for a Russian child, and only later did people discover she was German. "I was one of those children people would point at. It was always my fault and I never defended myself." She found solace at the edge of the orphanage property while she watched the sun set and rise each day. For a while she was forbidden to do so, but one day a new headmistress noticed her.

> *She took me by the hand, which no woman had ever done. And she told me she was going to make a bargain with me. If I would do what she would ask me to do . . . she would grant me something that I very much wanted to do. She wanted me to go to the village school, and I wanted to be permitted at sunset to go to the edge of the island and shout my "Hello!" Shout my pains and stories of the other children into that sun, sinking sun, because I believed that with the sinking of the sun into the ocean, it would rise again newly. Because I believed there was someone who held beginnings in the hand. And that feeling which first came to me when I was standing in rubble in Germany. It was sort of a very, I don't know, it was like a touch, it was like a breath . . . It became very familiar. I didn't know what to call it so I settled on YOU. We have "du" and "sie." This presence to me was very familiar and it still is.*

After the war, she lost a boy she loved as she helped young children in danger travel from East to West Germany. She describes herself as very angry at God during that time. So angry, she hated to even hear the organ play music in churches as she passed by. After she emigrated to the United States, she happened to walk by a chapel: "It was a lovely little chapel at St. Vincent's hospital. And the light was streaming in and a priest was preparing the altar." As she watched the priest move slowly and obviously painfully, she felt her heart stir with compassion. "Even from the doorway I could feel his pain. I was drawn to that and I went in and I asked what he was doing. He said he was laying the table of God. And I asked, "For whom?' And he looked at me and said 'Oh child, for everyone!' And you see I know hunger in absolutely every form . . . I know what it meant to be invited to a table for everyone. And so I asked this priest what I needed to do to come to that table." He taught her for two weeks, baptized her, and confirmed her. Through him she discovered God with a thirst she could only satisfy through her own conversion, theological exploration, and lifetime of service. She continues to call God by the diminutive German word for "You."

Like so many others (Victoria, Jean, Pat), Esperanza conducted Mass as a child with her siblings and cousins in the backyard. She reflected that she loved the Mass and found no trouble at five or six "staying still" because she "could drink it all up." As a girl she was part of the choir while the boys were taught Latin so they could be servers. She also learned the parts of the Mass and sang for an ordination in the Cathedral. "I was in the high choir loft when I saw the priest laying down. I just went 'Oh my goodness I want to do that!'" From that time forward, Esperanza received signs that she was to be a priest.

As Pat reflected on her call and journey, she noted that there were no "fireworks." Rather, she spoke about the "quiet voice within, the Haggia Sophia speaking to me quietly." She, too, loved the Mass and felt the call when she was eight or nine years old. She knew that to answer the call was impossible because she was the wrong gender. Despite this feeling, she made an altar at home and practiced being a priest. She made up what she did because the priest's back was to her during the liturgy. "I made my own rules and that's what I did." In Austria, Christine remembered that even at a young age she never doubted that she was called to be a priest. She was moved by liturgies, enjoyed the community, and always knew that being a priest was her call. She reflected that she considered that call "mine." She named her gift as "I had the gene of God like the gene of music."

Myra recalls a time when she brought to prayer the question of whether she should preach as she was invited to in her parish. She didn't hear anything, so she took it as a no. She went downstairs and started vacuuming her house. She recalls that she felt something tug at her shirt and so she stopped the vacuum. She looked around and no one was there. She started vacuuming again and again she felt a tug. "And then I knew it was God calling me because there was nobody there. The tension that I was feeling pulling on my shirt was real, but nobody was there." She returned to her room upstairs and got on her knees and prayed. "And I heard this audible voice 'Yes, I called you to preach and to teach my word.' I thought 'What?!' I started to argue with God. 'God! I'm Black! I'm a woman! I'm Catholic! How can you call me to do that? This doesn't make any sense.' I didn't hear a response. I thought: 'Really! You're not going to say anything else?' So, I thought: 'Fine! I'll do it. But then you need to enter a covenant with me. The first one would be that you must teach me how to do this. You must give me the resources to teach me how to do this. The second thing, God, is that you have to open the doors for me. If you open the doors for me, I will walk through them. I will not kick them in; I will not convince people that you called me to preach or teach. I will not manipulate my way into ministry. I won't do any of that. If you don't open the door, I'm not going! If you open it. I'll meet you on the other side.'"

Olivia writes about her sign toward ordination. She describes her journey as an "interior awakening to my call and the simultaneous recognition of the call by other persons close to me, including my family and ordained priests. She was reluctant to own that call but remembers a time she spent with her mother-in-law in 1978. She was ministering behind the Iron Curtain at the time, and visited her eighty-year-old mother-in-law, Sima. She was in what is now Bosnia and Herzegovina and she was asked by Sima to "anoint and pray with a dying villager as no parish priest could be found to administer the sacrament for the sick and the dying." She continues, noting that her mother-in-law didn't know how to read or write, "but Sima called me to consider priesthood." Olivia acknowledged, "that deeply spiritual woman . . . knew how to read my heart to cultivate seeds sown there by the Spirit. Whenever, I pause to review the steps leading and calling me to ordination, I always remember the role Sima played."[8]

Dana Reynolds writes about her call using stories of listening and hearing and picturing God. She reflects on Joan of Arc and her response to her heresy judges in 1431. According to Dana, the judges confront the notion that God speaks, and argue that this is only Joan's imagination. She quotes Joan as replying: "How else would God speak to me but through my imagination?"[9] Dana continues to recount that Joan heard many voices: "Saint Margaret, Saint Michael, and Saint Catherine. These voices guided her to leave home and family, and dress in men's clothing, to lead an army and help crown a king. She often saw the saints that spoke to her and it is said that white butterflies followed her whenever she rode into battle. The fact that she would not deny her mystical guidance ultimately led to her death at a fiery stake. She was nineteen."[10] Like Joan of Arc, Dana encountered God in a deeply experiential way that included voices and images. She recalls that "whenever I was sketching ideas, writing an icon, or creating a visual journal, I felt connected creatively to a place I eventually named the sacred imagination. This metaphoric field of pure potential within each of us is the place where the Holy Spirit fuels creativity, sparks dreams and visions, and seeds our calling."[11]

Catholic Imagination, Sacramentality, and Call Narratives

As we reviewed these and other stories, we recalled Andrew Greeley's writing about Catholic imagination. He contended that Catholics work within a liturgical imagination "linking graceful stories of God and church . . . the core of the Catholic religious heritage."[12] Roman Catholic womenpriests tell their stories filled with Catholic stories and liturgical experiences. They are replete with Scripture and saint tales.

Greeley reminds us that "Catholics live in enchantment world, a world of statues and holy water, stained glass and votive candles, saints and religious medals, rosary beads and holy pictures."[13] He continues that as a result, Catholics tend to recognize the "Holy lurking in creation. As Catholics, we find our houses in a world haunted by a sense that the objects, events, and persons of daily life are revelations of grace."[14] Catholic imagination can appropriately be called sacramental in that it opens a person to recognize the presence of God in all things.

Understanding the presence of a creative God in all things constitutes spiritual life, the innate human capacity to transcend our limitations through ideas, values, symbols, and rituals. The recognition of God in life elevates us to discover, rediscover, retrieve, or uncover a hidden meaning or truth connecting us to the divine. A review of the spirituality of these women indicates a delicate balance between intuitive and logical, receptive and active modes of consciousness. These media are activated and come alive within the context of sacramentality.

Sacraments may be understood as an opportunity for a living encounter between God and the human person to be experienced through ritual action. Catholics believe that through sacramental signs one can encounter a communal ritual experience. The Constitution on the Sacred Liturgy named the liturgy as that "through which the work of our redemption takes place, especially in the divine sacrifice of the Eucharist."[15] Indeed, the constitution continues that participation in the liturgy "builds up those who are in the church, making of them a holy temple of the Lord, a dwelling-place for God in the Spirit" (see Eph 2:21–22).[16]

The women's stories reflect Catholic imagination with sacramental roots. Celie experienced a shimmer in the elevation of the Host at a eucharistic celebration. Morag visited sisters who had cared for her mother. Not yet Catholic, she found herself finishing her Sunday visits attending Benediction and sitting in front of the exposed Host in the monstrance. Gabriella recounts her experience at five. The "Spirit showed herself to me in the darkened, incense-filled church as we chanted during Benediction. Spirit showed herself to me in the mystery and symbolism of the Mass during Eucharist. Spirit showed herself to me when I was alone and afraid."[17] Joanna recounted a similar type of experience. She noted that she was about seven or eight and sitting in a Catholic church with the priest's back to her. She vaguely remembered the smell of incense. She looked at the statues in the front and she thought: "Mary, Joseph, and Jesus. Those are my real parents. I can get anything I want if I pray hard enough." She thought further: "And I don't know if that was a call, but that was my first recollection . . . I thought I wanted to be a nun, really the only option that time, until you got a boyfriend. But I was very holy and devout and went to church every Sunday and did everything until I married somebody Jewish [laughter]. I kept saying 'God, you have to tell me who to marry and look who you brought me!' which just expanded my horizons. So that was that was my earliest recollection." Each of these stories relies on signs, smells, visual art, sacraments, and sacramental practices.

As Myra recalled her story, she reminisced about how her whole family enjoyed music. Together, they sang, played instruments, and danced. They often relied on music from Michael Jackson and Annie Mae. She recalled that one day, a neighbor approached the family and asked them if they would please play music for her church community. Myra was doing Christian based work, but never joined a particular community and the family didn't know the hymns. "The neighbor assured us that they would teach the family everything they needed to learn. So, they did." And she reflected: "We joined as an invitation to sing. It was about helping my neighbor; we went to Mass and heard the homilies. I fell in love with Jesus. And then I knew I wanted to be there; my family was there. Lots of kids with lots of Blacks and lots of whites. It was home."

Jane grew up Presbyterian in Southern California and she described her parents as conservative religiously but liberal socially. In her neighborhood with thirteen girls her age, ten belonged to the Catholic parish. If Jane spent the night with one of the Catholic girls, she was allowed to go to Mass with her the next morning. She reflects:

> *In my little girl way, it was much more concrete than my reflection on it.* [Some tears in voice.] *First of all it was a sense of reverence. I loved the silence. There were parts of the service that were silent. It was . . . you know I liked kneeling, I liked sitting, I liked having a little book to try to follow. I couldn't do it very well, but I would try to follow along, the way my friends were trying to show me. One thing I loved about it, was it felt, and I think historically this was accurate, it felt more egalitarian to me.*

She continued reminiscing,

> *And I saw these all these little kids at mass, and they were all clean and ironed and combed but they just had on school clothes. (Which*

they wore uniforms then.) But it made me feel like it's a different concept of God. That you don't have to dress up for God. You have to be respectful. So those were things. I loved blessing yourself going into the church. I still love to do that.

She reflected further about what that early experience with her friends gave her as an adult and as a womanpriest:

the first time I walk through the sanctuary, I always bless myself. I think I have a child's love for circumambulation at communion. Everybody gets up. Everybody goes to the altar. There's no word for it. Everybody receives food. Not me [then]. But I loved those things about it. So, the music I didn't like because we had great music at our church. But I loved the chanting when there was chanting.

Later she discovered the liturgical year and noticed the changing colors on the altar. She said:

Color is really important to me. We received a lot of criticism for still using vestments. But I think vestments matter because of color for one thing and for another because it's kind of a uniform. And it really is not supposed to be about Jane, it's supposed to be about the role. So color is really important to my spirituality.

When Jane spoke of Eucharist, she again noted aspects of Catholic imagination that inform her spirituality:

And I love the concept of, you know, one bottle of wine. And Gary Macy writes about this. Every single bottle of wine is unique. That wine comes from one season and it will never exist again. And the bread is one loaf baked by a person with love in our community. And our new bread baker is a man. And then everybody here shares that same cup and that same bread [tears] and we take it into our physical bodies and we all metabolize it. [She is teary in her voice when she says the last line.] And for a little time, we

are chemically, biologically [small laugh] *connected in a way that*
we wouldn't otherwise be. And I love the circumambulation. And
when the music has good theology, obviously I love the music.

Jane's reflection is replete with Catholic imagination—the kind of attention
to senses and mystic experience that attracted her to this faith stance and
currently sustains her.

Jane and Myra frame their calls in music and movement and color. For
two millennia Catholics have used multiple arts to communicate the word of
God. In the early church carved stones marking graves, mosaic altar pieces,
symbols of fish, and many paintings and sculptures depicted the stories of
Jesus and the disciples and saints and martyrs. Even remnants of bodies,
garments, and items people used became ways to remember and to access
the holy. In the 600s Celtic Christians carved stories of salvation into stone
"high crosses" to evangelize the people and draw them into relation with
God, Jesus, and the community of believers. Monks copied the scriptures
and writings of saints and biographers and illustrated the manuscripts to
highlight aspects of Christian life. As technologies allowed, churches grew
to gothic heights with open spaces for windows. Stained glass windows
filled cathedrals throughout the Christian world and told the stories most
important to local communities. During the Middle Ages, people celebrated
saints and other feast days with festivals, masses, drama in the form of plays
and puppet shows, and often accompanied these with attention to the saints'
relics.

Bridget Mary wrote her story filled with images from her Irish American Catholic faith—her DNA! She described her earliest memories of
the Sacred: "In Ireland we gathered around the turf fire each evening to
recite the rosary. I had a sense early on that heaven and earth were closely
connected, and the saints and angels, the Blessed Mother and Jesus were
always nearby. I fell in love with God at a young age and felt a deep sense of
God calling me to devote my life to the Gospel."[18] Dana acknowledges her
own story of relationship with God as embedded in art. She enters a state of
knowing herself as a divine creation and feeling herself in the literal presence
of God, connected to mystery. She writes "in this mystical place, the gateway
between heaven and earth, revelations are gifted, sometimes through the
voices of angels, sometimes through symbolic visions."[19]

Call stories, then, reveal the way one hears and responds to God's initiative in one's life. As we see in the stories told by these women, their call is first and foremost, a response—a response to an experience that generates awe. In this case a response to the love of God and to what God has done for them. "Our love of God, our spiritual life, therefore, is not of our own doing. It is the Holy Spirit at work within us, that Spirit who calls, gathers, enlightens, and sanctifies each of us together with the whole Christian church."[20] Diane describes this experience of call: "If we are opening our hearts and minds, and opening our whole being to the Spirit, the Spirit of Love that flows through everything . . . we can trust." Joanne affirms that for her, it is always a discernment of love.

The Roman Catholic womenpriests, prepared through Scripture and informed by their liturgical lives, use their Catholic imaginations to describe elements of their experience. Just as the Scripture writers and editors conveyed call stories using words and symbols people knew, these theologically prepared women spoke of their experience using elements of their Catholic imagination. Thus, like Abraham and Sarah who met angels/ messengers in the desert and fed them, they look for signs as interior recognitions of God's activity.

Throughout the Hebrew Scriptures, we read and recall many "call stories." Rebekah, called to marry Isaac, then circumvents the law of inheritance so that the younger son, Jacob, can receive the blessing of God's covenant. Both Leah and Rachel help Jacob respond to God's call. It is Rachel who assists Jacob in amassing a herd large enough to provide for his people upon his return to Israel. It is Rachel who gives birth to Joseph— the savior of Egypt and Israel during massive famine. Then, the midwives, Moses's mother and sister, Miriam, have the wits and courage to outfox the Pharaoh. It is Pharaoh's own daughter who works with God's plan to save the Hebrews from oppression. It is Jethro's daughter who marries Moses and helps him rescue God's people then sets him free to lead them to the land promised to them. In their own ways, each of these call stories reveals both a deep relationship with God, as our womenpriests described, and a willingness to follow in spite of laws and practices to the contrary. Similarly, Deborah, Judith, Esther, Huldah, Naomi, and Ruth offer models of women hearing God call them, responding in faith and saving their communities from destruction. As womenpriests responded to their calls, they followed a path that John's gospel reveals as "come and you will see" (John 1:39).

In all these stories there are aspects that we explored with the women ordained as Roman Catholic priests. Each of their stories began with first noticing God's presence. Their *inquietud,* restlessness, curiosity to know more led them to seek God through their Catholic imaginations. Similarly, these stories culminate in decisions to act that seem counter-intuitive or *contra legem* (against the law.) As Rebekah, Miriam, Shiprah and Puah, and Rachel and Leah bent the practice of favoring the eldest son and obeying the powers of institutions, these women answered calls that forced them to form and examine their own understandings of life in concert with the sacred. "Over the pope as the binding claim of ecclesiastical authority, there still stands one's conscience, which must be obeyed before all else, if necessary even against the requirement of ecclesiastical authority."[21] Or, as Myra framed her response, one who waits for God to open that door of what may seem impossible. "One door after another God has opened for me. I kept remembering my promise: 'You open the door and I have to walk through it!' When the door opened, I was obligated by covenant to go through it."

Summary

Our subjects' stories demonstrate the myriad ways the Divine speaks priestly callings into being. Like every person who answers Yes to God's call, each then travels a journey of faithful response. The next chapter reveals some of the journeys these women travelled. Like Mary who humbly allowed God to "do as you will." She then discovers that the one who was to be "the Son of the Most High, and the Lord God will give him the throne of David" (Luke 1: 32) was actually to be born in a stable of poor parents, crucified and buried to rise again as the hope of new life. We will find in the next chapter how Roman Catholic womenpriests answered, suffered, and persevered on their journeys.

4

JOURNEY

"What are you looking for? . . . Where are you staying? . . . Come, and you will see."

—John 1:38–39

"I respond one step at a time. The path reveals itself as I step forward."

—Diane, womanpriest interviewee

JANE TOLD THE story of knowing God as she pumped on her swing in her back yard at about three years of age. She described it as a knowing, not a call. But the knowing drew her to want to draw closer to God. So, her journey with God began.

As we saw, many women experienced God present to them when they were attending Mass. The combination of song, movement, scripture, clothing, stained glass windows, statues of holy ones, and the priest's elevation of the Host all combined to inspire young girls to try to create similar events at home. Like many Catholic boys, these girls—some of whom were not Catholic at the time—shared a fascination with the liturgical rituals of the church. These rituals moved them to seek more intimacy with God. Donnieau described her conviction that she would be a priest and her story of running with joy to the priest to tell him. Like Jean, she didn't know that girls couldn't be priests. Confused by this desire with no legitimate outlet, the women trusted as Mary did in response to Gabriel's words that "nothing will be impossible with God" (Luke 1:37). Like Mary they journeyed in trust that God's will would be done (Luke 1:38).

These women are not unlike so many women's stories the church celebrates in its veneration of saints. Sarah, for instance, moved from Ur to Canaan with Abraham (Gen 12:5). She fixed the meal that Abraham served to the messenger/angel/Trinity visitors who foretold she would birth a son

(Gen 18:9). According to the story, she was in her nineties when the son arrived after missteps with Haggar, a misadventure in Egypt, a willingness to move from place to place, and finally a single child who would be the fulfillment of promise of children as numerous as stars.

The women we interviewed found ways to stay faithful to God, just as Sarah did. They spent a lifetime waiting on God's time for fulfilling the promise of vocation to the priesthood they heard. Encouraged by the Document on the Laity, these faithful women tried "to actually grow closer to Christ by doing their work according to his will."[1] They exerted their energies "in extending God's kingdom, in making the Christian spirit a vital energizing force in the temporal sphere."[2] Most followed their lay vocation by becoming "members of any of the associations or institutions approved by the church."[3] They sought to make "their own the forms of spirituality proper to these bodies."[4] This chapter looks at their journeys with an eye to how these contemporary journeys of faith were encouraged by the Second Vatican Council.

As Diane explained, spiritual journeys evolve one step at a time. While each journey is unique, some patterns emerged. Ten of our interviewees entered vowed religious life. At least twenty married and have children and grandchildren. Others married later in life, and a few remained singularly focused on their ministries. Most eventually worked as lay ecclesial ministers in their respective parishes. At least ten hold doctoral degrees and served as faculty in universities and schools. Some found their paths leading through arenas of social justice with the Catholic workers movement, antiracism or immigration outreach. Others entered public health systems and ministered as nurses, public health consultants, or chaplains.

The first group of seven located themselves in Austria and Germany. Even the first US womanpriest, Dagmar, was an Austrian by birth. Eventually, Patricia from South Africa, and others from Canada and the United States sought ordination. Outreach to Latin America invited Olga and Marina Theresa among others. Some are publicly represented on the RCWP website while others enjoy "catacomb" status to protect their families and associates. Morag is the only womanpriest from Great Britain. As chapter five will demonstrate, most waited until they retired from other professions to seek ordination, and they are mostly worker priests who contribute to their own livelihood. Only a few younger priests are attempting to support themselves in their ministries. The impact of the cost of education coupled with no expected compensation for ministerial service restricts ordination to those financially secure enough to support themselves. This at times limits wider cultural and ethnic representation. We included representatives from each of the countries and twelve percent of the respondents are of African or Latina descent.[5]

Each womanpriest reported their search for the best way to serve God within the confines of church law. Like St. Augustine, each admitted that their hearts were restless as they searched for the best way to answer the God that called them. Each grappled with closed doors, ostracization from friends, parishioners and family, and the threatened expulsion from the religion they practiced and loved. Like Jeremiah, each at times cried out in pain wondering how God could call them to ordained priesthood, when everything in their religion's rules rejected that call. Just as St. Thérèse of Lisieux mourned that she could not realize her dream to be ordained, their stories reveal the pain they experienced as they travelled in faithful and resilient persistence through the labyrinth they walked toward ordination.

This chapter considers the journeys these women navigated from answering their baptismal call to holiness through pursuing their additional call to ordination. Journey stories have become their own literary genre. Joseph Campbell identified the hero journeys in his seminal work *The Hero with a Thousand Faces*. Based on myths primarily concerned with men, he charted twelve stages on the path to what Jung might name individuation.[6] Women's journeys differ from those men have taken over the millennia.

Feminist scholars Alice Eagly and Linda Carli found that women's routes to realizing their call in almost every profession or ministry follow, not the path of men, but potentially three phases. They named "three types of barriers [that] obstructed women's advancement" in pursuing their vocations.[7] They described these as: "the concrete wall, the glass ceiling, and the labyrinth."[8] The next sections consider the womenpriests journeys as they dealt with these three obstacles.

The Concrete Wall

Using this analogy to describe the womenpriests' stories allows us to present their journeys in a context. As Eagli and Carli described, the first roadblock seems impenetrable, thus it is described as a concrete wall. Two major issues impacted the womenpriests in ways that seemed impenetrable. The first concerns their formal relation to the church they espouse: excommunication. The second concerns the theological and pastoral understanding of women as defined by the mostly male hierarchical institution over the last two thousand years. The womenpriests contributed work toward dismantling these aspects of the wall preventing ordination.

Excommunication

Excommunication due to Canon 1024 built the concrete wall that Donnieau literally ran into when she joyfully skipped to her priest at age seven. Every woman who feels called by God to be ordained a Roman Catholic priest runs into this wall. Roman Catholic women encountered, studied, and embraced the practice that other Christian ecclesial communities and even some Jewish communities exercised in ordaining women.

A wall consists of "explicit rules and clear-cut norms."[9] Women in every profession other than homemaking, "were denied entry to prestigious careers because of the assumption that their proper work was in the home."[10] This dichotomy of roles exists in the contemporary church.

The Roman Catholic Church compiles its rules for belonging and governance in what is called Canon Law. These canons govern the activity of the Church. In 1983, after fifteen years of experimenting with new forms of liturgy, governance, and organizational change, the Church published a revised Code of Canon Law. That Code included many opportunities for lay people to assume various roles related to ministry in the church. Men and women were encouraged to give their time and talent, pursue ongoing education and religious formation, and participate in the governance of the local church. At the same time, men were barred from ordination if they were married and women because of their gender. The pain of violating the rules could be excommunication, depending on the seriousness of the violation. Excommunication meant one was no longer welcome to receive the sacraments, be buried in a Catholic cemetery, or work for the Church. Essentially, the canon concrete wall was supported by millennia of patriarchal theologies related to the roles of women in creation and the world. Raming and Müeller began the work of chipping away at the concrete.

Women's Roles in the Church

Many women scholars sought to remove the concrete wall of exclusion due to gender. They include the combined works of theologians and Scripture scholars such as Elizabeth Schüssler-Fiorenza, Mary Hunt, Rosemary Radford Reuther, Carolyn Osiek, Maria Pilar Aquino, and Ilia Delio. They also number women scholars who became ordained as RCWP: Ida Raming, Iris Müeller, Jane Via, Bridget Mary Meehan, Mary Theresa Streck, Shanon Sterringer, and Patricia Fresen. Together they argued for revisiting the teaching on ordination as well as other theologies related to women. Indeed, by 1977, Anne E. Patrick documented many hundred articles published in support of considering the ordination of women in the Roman Catholic Church.[11] She concluded her article by summarizing:

> *What is especially at issue here seems to be a difference in understanding the nature of the activity of the Holy spirit in the Church. This difference might be summed up in the question: Is the Spirit given mainly to protect the past of which we are "sure" or to guide us into an uncertain future, confident that God will make up for what is lacking in our best human efforts?*[12]

As a womanpriest, Jen claimed that "if the Catholic Church changed its theology of women, the entire world would change." Indeed, her ancestresses in ordination and theology, Raming and Müeller, spent their lives researching and writing about new understandings of women and rooting those understandings in the *aggiornamento* (open the church to the work of the Spirit) and *resourcement* (renew the sources of Scripture and Tradition) concepts that undergird the theologies of Vatican II. *Aggiornamento* consisted of the invitation to look forward and move the church into deeper conversation with and even transformation in current cultural contexts. *Resourcement* exhorted scholars to return to the roots of the faith, scripture, and tradition. While different in their energies—one forward looking and one reinterpreting the past—these two movements of the Second Vatican Council invited scholars to apply new understandings to culturally and theologically rich traditions and root the Catholic community in its origins with Christ, the Spirit, and the apostolic traditions. The Roman Catholic womenpriests attended to these Vatican II mandates through their pursuit of education and reinterpretation of the roles of women in the world and the church.

Prior to Vatican II, Müeller and Raming wrote a petition to the Vatican Council that called for women's ordination.[13] They both completed doctorates in theology by 1970. Following the Council, Pope Paul VI asked the Pontifical Biblical Commission to study the role of women in the Bible. The appointment of the commission led to an expectation that there might be new consideration of the exclusion of women in ordained ministries— specifically priests and deacons.

Biblical scholar John Donohue wrote about the 1976 findings reported by that commission. He observed that the seventeen participants in the commission voted unanimously that the New Testament does not settle "once and for all and in a clear way that women cannot be ordained priests."[14] The commission also found in a vote of twelve to five that "scriptural grounds alone are not enough to exclude the possibility of ordaining women";[15] and by a similar vote that "Christ's plan would not be transgressed by permitting the ordination of women."[16] Given these findings by a Rome appointed commission, many women and men were hopeful that the concrete wall of the canon would be removed. Unfortunately for them, Pope Paul VI issued a Declaration (1977) on the subject which argued the Church didn't have the authority to authorize women's ordination.[17] His declaration affirmed the concrete wall that barred women from ordination as priests while also suggesting that more dialogue might chip away at the concrete.

Following up on the hope that dialogue was possible, in 1977 Leonard and Arlene Swidler edited a book of essays supporting women's ordination in response to Pope Paul VI's declaration. Leonard Swidler, a professor of religion at Temple University, listed Raming's 1970 comprehensive doctoral dissertation as a significant contribution to reconsidering the decision banning women priests. By 1976 Raming's book, *The Exclusion of Women from Priesthood: Divine Law or Sex Discrimination?* had been published in German and in English. She convincingly concluded "that the traditional arguments supporting the law are invalid."[18]

At the time she wrote, others continued to study and write. By 1994, however, Pope John Paul II issued an apostolic letter (*Ordinatio Sacerdotalis*) intended to close the conversation permanently. This apostolic letter further generated a response (1995) by the Congregation for Doctrine concerning the binding nature of that apostolic letter. Both attempted to conclude discussion. Indeed, many theologians interpreted the two documents as forbidding, under pain of retribution, any conversation about ordaining women as priests at any level. In the Vatican, the matter was closed, and the concrete wall stood strong and impenetrable.

On the other hand, women theologians and womenpriests continued to study and illuminate scriptures and tradition. Jane Via, one of the women-priests who is also a scripture scholar, wrote about women in the early church who followed Jesus and seemed to participate in apostolic teaching and discipleship. She observed, that in the canonical gospels, and genuine letters of Paul:

> *(1) the absence of any evidence for ordination as Roman Catholics have practiced it in the last millennium and as contemporary Roman Catholics know it; (2) the radical inclusivity of Jesus' ministry to women as a class; (3) documentation for the leadership of women in virtually every existing ministry of the first century church.*[19]

She continues to write to reframe the church's understanding of women and their place in society and the church.

Later, theologian Ilia Delio summarized:

> *the church has a deep structural problem that is entirely bound to ancient metaphysical and philosophical principles, not to mention imperial politics, that at this point requires either a radical decision towards a new ecclesial structure or the acceptance of the possibility of a major schism . . . structure concerns relationships, and the types of relationships that comprise church structure are based on outdated philosophical notions of nature, gender and personhood.*[20]

Similarly, several women we studied wrote a statement reflecting their commitment to break open the barrier to fully living their call. Coauthors

Bridget Mary Meehan, Olivia Doko, and Victoria Rue announced that "Roman Catholic womenpriests are a new and ancient model of priesthood, within the Roman Catholic Church."[21] They cited the barriers to ordination and declared their intention to "work positively within the Church."[22] Like Delio, they acknowledged the patriarchal structure of the Church. Like Via, they reject previous scripture interpretations that relegate women to inferior status.

Interestingly, they reflect some of the language in Pope Francis' declaration, *Joy of the Gospel*. Reclaiming their spiritual heritage, they attempt to create a "discipleship of equals."[23] Just as Pope Francis states that the laity constitute the majority of the Church and the ordained are in service of the laity, the womenpriests write "the present gap between clergy and laity needs to be eliminated. As ordained women, we must find a way to call forth the gifts of each member of the community. We all are church, not just some."[24]

Womenpriests continue to write and minister; they stand on the shoulders of the many women who preceded them in vowed religious orders and holy lay lives. They continue to study the texts and to consider alternative interpretations, and they are joined by an increasing number of scholars in this work. Their work continues to hammer at the concrete wall even as it still stands.

The Stained Glass Ceiling

More people are familiar with the image of a glass ceiling as it applies to all women in all professions. Barbara Brown Zikmund studied Protestant women breaking through that barrier toward ordination. She adopted the notion of a "stained glass ceiling" to describe the journeys women in mostly mainline Protestant traditions pursued from the 1950s to the 1990s. Over the past century, some women in Christian and Jewish communities found ways to move into the leadership of their communities of faith through ordination and the rabbinate. Their work demonstrated what Eagly and Carli noted as penetrating or breaking the glass ceiling. Zikmund and others documented how women had been ordained, but also repressed in terms of appointments, compensation, opportunity for advancement, retirement, and benefits.[25]

Roman Catholic womenpriests watched the progress of their ecumenical and interreligious sisters. They saw progress in other traditions as hope for their own eventual inclusion in their own tradition. They joined groups such as the women's ordination movement, Call to Action, and Future-Church. Each group had worked for many years seeking to persuade the hierarchy to ordain women and married men.

The pedophilia crisis in the archdiocese of Boston gained international attention and set in motion a new impetus for breaking the glass ceiling. Even at this writing, the Roman Catholic Church in every country remains weakened due to this pervasive moral crisis. What most of the hierarchy continues to misjudge is the deep wound the hierarchy caused in its almost universal protection of offenders rather than the children the offenders harmed for life. The futile attempts to cover up the systemic protection of the system of the church (clericalism) over the people of the church spurred some to new action.[26]

Christine had been working with women in Austria and Germany. She had written a curriculum and was helping form women for ordination to the priesthood. Eventually, three male bishops stepped forward to preside over an ordination. Almost thirty were ready to move forward. "Three groups started: one in Linz, one in Innsbruck, and one in Vienna . . . Most of them theologians, teachers, religious sisters, or nurses, embarked on a long and intensive preparation program."[27] Gisela claimed her place as one of the seven to move forward on the Danube in 2002. "I was one of these women, and I felt myself ready to work against the inequality of the Vatican. In my youth I loved my church . . . more and more I saw the fight of the church hierarchy as a fight to show everybody that the space around the altar was off limits to women."[28] Iris and Ida were ready; they had been ready since the 1960s! So, seven of the thirty were ordained: "Dr. Ida Raming, Dr. Iris Müeller, Dr. Gisela Forster, Christine Mayr-Lumentzberger, Viktoria Sperrer, and Pia Brunner."[29] One was originally anonymous, but Christine wanted representatives from several places. She invited Dagmar Celeste, an Austrian who emigrated and lived in the United States to participate in the sacramental celebration. Dagmar eventually revealed she was the seventh, the anonymous person hidden for a time because of her position as having been previously married to the former governor of Ohio. Suddenly, the stained-glass ceiling was burst by seven women who were ordained in apostolic succession by willing male bishops. The Danube offered a place in which no ecclesial jurisdiction was compromised. To ensure the movement could move forward, a male bishop subsequently ordained Gisela and Christine as women bishops. They would eventually ordain women in countries throughout the world.

The Labyrinth

Having broken through the glass ceiling, womenpriests continued to believe in their call and to work with their situations in faith. Many women authors document a more circuitous path for women who reach positions of authority in their chosen field. Researchers Eagly and Carli discovered a *Wall Street Journal* article that documented how many women had actually navigated a way to break what people referred to as the glass ceiling.[30] Thus, by 1997 some were celebrating the success of women who had made it to the top, claiming barriers were a thing of the past.[31] Yet, as late as 1998, Zikmund documented a continued "stained glass ceiling" as it applied to women ordained in mostly mainline Protestant communities. Full equality had not been achieved for women in any career, much less in ordained ministries. A new image took shape to describe the journeys women took as they pursued what seemed first a concrete wall, then a glass ceiling, and now a circuitous path.

Eagly and Carli noted that a new observation captured the various ways women navigated their journeys. They cited an entry by Karin Klenke who in 1997 wrote about how paths that twisted and turned with obstacles and setbacks resembled a labyrinth. Thus, they write, "the labyrinth contains numerous barriers, some subtle and others quite obvious."[32] Others have written about the labyrinth as a spiritual process.

Lauren Artress, an Episcopalian priest, writes about the labyrinth as guiding one to deeper meaning. She reflects: "through the simple act of walking the singled, but circuitous path—alone or in large numbers—the mind can quiet and the heart can open. It changes lives by helping people find their center, their grounded nature. . . . the path becomes a larger metaphor of the Path of Life that—whether we are conscious of it or not—we are all walking together."[33]

We found this metaphor helpful in describing the twists and turns of each womanpriest's journey toward ordination. As we moved into the process of listening to their stories, we heard their pain and their joy: the obstacle that causes a turn and an opening they can move forward through. We asked the womenpriests about the obstacles they encountered and the ways they sustained themselves in their journeys. We organized their responses so they include both the encounter of the obstacle and the stepping into openings as they moved through the labyrinthian journey resulting in their ordination. In the following sections we cluster their responses into the following barriers: pursuing approved ministries; education; personal obstructions and allies including family, lay colleagues and ordained male clergy; physical and spiritual suffering; and doing their internal transformational work. Clearly, each category offers both obstacle, opening, and stepping into joy. That is the way of a true labyrinth.

Approved Ministerial Paths

Lay ecclesial ministry emerged as an option for lay women immediately after the Second Vatican Council. Parish Councils gathered lay leaders to consult with the priest about the direction of the parish, the financial costs and resources, as well as the pastoral concerns. School boards emerged to consult with priest and principal about the same things in relation to Catholic Schools. Similarly, religious education boards assisted the new position of Director of Religious Education in determining how to form young people in their faith.

Initially vowed religious sisters switched from previous ministries to these more direct interactions with parish people. They encouraged promising lay people to volunteer, access educational opportunities, and eventually replace them as they moved to other parishes or ministries. From 1966, the year after the council closed and no record of lay ecclesial ministers was kept, through 2020 this ministry grew from zero to over 39,000 men and women serving the over 17,000 parishes in the United States.[34] Such growth is not found in other Western countries such as Canada, Scotland, England, or Ireland. Fewer are found in other European countries, but South American lay ministers flourished as a result of the synodal processes the bishops initiated post–Vatican II. The *Communidade des bases* movement transformed lay experience and ministry in South America as well.

Many womenpriests served over thirty-five years in parishes as directors of religious education, liturgical ministers, catechists, adult education providers, chaplains, spiritual directors, and some as heads of parishes who oversaw the life of a parish with the assistance of a sacramental minister who said Mass, heard confessions, and baptized, wed, and buried congregants. They accompanied the people of God, convinced of Vatican II teachings that all are called by Baptism to be disciples—that is, learners of Jesus's way. They assumed roles of leadership while accepting poor pay, few benefits, and little if any promise of retirement income. Like St. Paul, they became tent-maker disciples, counting on income sources outside their ministries. Thus, many worked until their retirement age, so they could receive a steady income from social security as they moved forward in ordained priestly service.

Teresa, Shanon, Jen, and Diane offer a glimpse into the classic path within lay ecclesial ministry in the United States. Each of them heard the call to priesthood, and each pursued the closest route they could find given their status as single or married women. They each volunteered in their respective parishes. As paid positions opened, they each accepted jobs within the parish. Knowing their own lack of preparation, each pursued graduate education in theology and ministry. Like others in this category of service, some worked at the diocesan level to ensure catechetical preparation for all in their region. Others worked directly with people in the parish. Some with religious education for elementary age children, others with adults, yet others with teens. Their work touched people at every level of ministry except celebration of the sacraments as presider.

Similarly, Juanita, Helen, Mary Theresa, Christine, Patricia, Suzanne, Jeanette, and Paula followed the path of vowed religious women. They pursued education in a variety of ministries but found themselves mostly in parish-based or spirituality-based outreach.

Other womenpriests, such as Morag, Donnieau, Esperanza, Kathy, Myra, Vikki, and Chava, sought opportunities to serve in health-related ministries. They pursued education that allowed them to nurse, offer public health services, conduct research, and alleviate mental and emotional suffering.

Education

Some pursued education for the sake of teaching. Victoria, Jane, Mary Therese, Donnieau, Bridget Mary, Judy, Juanita, Vikki, Pat, Patricia, Morag, Iris, and Ida—all earned degrees that prepared them to teach in a variety of disciplines from theology and scripture to public health, mental health, and social work. In other words, almost all the womenpriests pursued both education and career opportunities as they navigated paths to answer God's call. None of these combinations, however, allowed them to pursue the one thing they each felt called by God to be: an ordained priest in the Roman Catholic Church.

Education became key in their ability to find an opening amid so many obstacles. Maria reflected on her journey. As noted in her call story, she developed a practice of recognizing a "You" while she was a child in an orphanage during World War II. Luckily, she had a matron who understood her need to be away to collect herself at the end of every day, a practice she continues to the present. She suffered the aftermath of rebuilding Germany post war and lost an important love in her life. Even as she assisted other children through the dangers of emigrating across the Berlin Wall, she suffered threat of death and loneliness. She found herself angry with God, who seemed absent from her struggle. Having encountered a wounded priest who invited her to the table, she reflected on her wounded life: wounds from war and a hunger for life beyond with God. She pondered further: "I decided I wanted to study theology. For me it was literally a matter of life and death." Through her connection with this unnamed priest, she found herself studying at Marquette University under the tutelage of such theologians as Karl Rahner and Bernard Cooke. She noted that from that time on, she learned "to associate love and the power of love with Jesus in many different ways. But it was always the Spirit who gave me the courage to move into that one step further, one step at a time."

Like Maria, Jane converted to Catholicism and found herself hungry for the food of Scripture and theology. She, too, enrolled in Marquette University and she completed her doctorate in sacred scripture. She moved to San Diego and started a career as a faculty member on the Catholic faculty in Theology and Religious Studies at the University of San Diego. She taught priests and lay people together and also served the diocese as a lay faculty for ongoing education of laity in the diocese. When she was ready for tenure, the normal professional progression of university faculty, the bishop stopped her progress. She had signed the petition related to reversing the church teaching on contraception. Her name was listed in the *New York Times* issue with hundreds of others. That signature and publication proved to be another concrete barrier in her path as educator, lay woman, and priest. Denied tenure, Jane pursued another doctorate, and earned her J.D. She became the prosecuting attorney for the city of San Diego. Throughout her legal career, her desire to serve as priest never left her.

Patricia earned a doctorate in sacred theology in Rome as a Dominican sister from South Africa. When she returned home, she found herself teaching at the university. She, too, educated and formed men for priestly ordination, all the while struggling with her own vocation to priesthood.

Christine was convinced that ordination of women would happen in her lifetime. Since she worked with men preparing for ordination, she decided to create a program of theological study combined with spiritual and ministerial formation for women who would become priests. After she and six others were ordained on the Danube, she continued to serve other women seeking ordination. Patricia was ordained a year later (2003). Since both Christine and Patricia had worked with educating male ordained candidates, they combined their talents with Ida and Iris to offer women in Western Europe the opportunity to be ready for ordination. After her ordination in the United States, Jane worked with others to create a curriculum of study that would combine personal reflection, spiritual direction, and theological understanding. Recognizing a lacuna in theological preparation designed for some who had limited resources and few geographical opportunities to access priestly formation, Bridget Mary and Mary Theresa created a curriculum of study that offered online, less expensive, degree granting education through Global Ministries University. As the movement grew, womenpriests found openings to counter the obstacles by creating new opportunities.

People: Obstructors and Allies

Women often speak of collaboration as their contribution to leadership. Organizational consultant Margaret Wheatley suggested that even quantum sciences reveal that the natural order is infused with a predisposition toward attraction and community. Wheatley's work in the 1990s offered leaders a vision of constant communication, fostering organizations that attracted others to their "force field," and relying on people in communities. She noted that connections are the fundamental elements of all creation. Thus, leadership, she argued, must be relational, connective, communicative, and influenced by meaning and love.[35] Theologians might call this Trinitarian.

Many stories of people called by God include those who accompanied them. Abraham left Ur with Sarah and Lot and family. Jacob returned from exile due to the clever thinking of his love, Rachel. Moses refused to conduct the mission God called him to without the assistance of his brother Aaron. Indeed, Moses needed a lot of help: his mother, the Pharoah's daughter, the midwives Puah and Shiprah, his sister Miriam; his wife and his father-in-law Jethro. Eventually over seventy-two helped govern the group that left Egypt. Jesus chose people to accompany him after praying (Luke) and Luke also identifies seventy-two disciples and women who followed and learned and carried on the work Jesus begins. Even Paul takes John Mark, Barnabas, or Luke with him on his journeys. His letters thank many men, women, couples, and ministerial partners who oversee the communities he entrusts to them.

In light of these lessons from Scripture figures and contemporary leadership scholarship, we asked the women to talk about those who accompanied them on their journeys. Just as the biblical folks we mentioned, womenpriests encountered those who posed obstacles and those who assisted them in finding openings in their journeys.

Kathy is from a parish of about 2,500 families. She told everyone in her parish that she had been ordained. "So just telling people you knew, they were fine with it." Olga counts on the support of her sister and "the laity who are each time more conscious that they are the ones who support us and allow us to give service to them." Diane participated in a Jesuit Christian Life Community and the group has remained together for the last twenty-five to thirty years. She acknowledges "that group has listened to every piece of this for all these years." Diane mentioned that her spiritual director and supervisor of thirty-six years has also supported her journey. Indeed, all the women accessed spiritual directors throughout their journeys. Some also benefited from counselors and teachers and academic advisors. They knew they needed to discern God's work in their lives and that "like any other complex art, discernment cannot be learned offhand. To grasp the theme of God's presence and action amid the discordant notes of our lives requires a proficiency acquired through ongoing practice."[36]

Shanon encountered major challenges during her educational pursuit. Allowed to pursue a Master's degree in the seminary that prepared men for ordination, she was denied the opportunity to earn the same degree as the men. She worked intensely with her spiritual director for many years. In addition, she worked with a seminary advisor who called her to make a choice. It was the conversation with that Episcopalian advisor that moved Shanon to choose to become a Roman Catholic womanpriest. Although Maureen could not pursue ordination with her male colleagues, she presided over liturgy in the home of a professor at a Catholic university. Several male ordained priests and some vowed religious women attended with other lay people. Morag expressed her admiration for an Argentinian theologian who taught in Scotland. She exclaimed "she belonged to everybody! She was dynamite!" Like others, Morag's master of divinity did not translate into qualifications for ordination in the Roman Catholic Church. One day after the ordination on the Danube, one of Christine's neighbors visited with a cake, reminding Christine that, as she recalls, the neighbor said "in case your ordination took place, I promised to bring you a cake." Indeed, in the midst of major potential backlash, many people contributed to Christine's efforts to be ordained first as priest then as bishop. She remembered how different people in the community contributed: sewing, finishing work on the chapel, offering food for the workers and those who celebrated in the chapel.

Dagmar, Marina Theresa, Olga, Joanna, Juanita, Kathleen, and so many of the women count on each other for support. Olga and Marina Theresa specifically relied on Judy and Judy for allied support as they navigated the ecclesial and political realities of Colombia. Marina Theresa admits to being rescued from physical persecution in Colombia as she was brought into the United States by the two Judy priests. Now she works in a healing profession and copastors with the remaining Judy, especially emphasizing ministry to people of African and Latinx descent. Many of those ordained in the United States counted on Patricia to oversee their formation processes and their ordinations. Having created the first formation programs, Christine has travelled the world to encourage and ordain womenpriests.

Christine assisted men in becoming priests while she was a lay catechist. During that time, she met and befriended several men who were ordained. She reflects on one who is "now a parish priest and we have a very good relationship and friendship." Several womanpriests mentioned male priests who accompanied and taught them how to celebrate the sacraments and care for the people of God. Pat called out the impact Roy Bourgeois, a Maryknoll priest, had on her process. "I was at the Ontario Institute of Education. My eyes were this wide. I loved him! He was an inspiration. Then he gets thrown out of Maryknoll because he attended an ordination. Please!"[37]

One such priest consulted weekly with Jane before she was ordained. He assisted her in becoming more comfortable leading liturgy. Similarly, Victoria answered a direct call from a priest to begin a service of ministry directly outside St. Patrick's in New York City. Together they concelebrated mass and distributed food and counseling, especially to the LGBTQIA+ community as well as those experiencing homelessness. Subsequently, she moved to California and started a ministry close to the site of the Oakland Cathedral that was destroyed in an earthquake. She recalled that twelve people cleaned the park, disinfecting what they could, and removing needles so that together they could feed, minister to the homeless, and offer liturgy. Eventually, she said "the Franciscans came to help and to feed people." She remembered that together they often fed over two hundred people while holding an outdoor liturgy for up to fifty people.

Like others, Shanon found Jesuits supportive. She recalled that in Austria, when she was about to be ordained, a Jesuit declared to her "I'm a feminist" and he organized the liturgy of her ordination. Helen encountered a man helping her to fix a toilet in her parish plant. He confided to her that he was actually an ordained deacon who had renounced practicing as deacon because: "I have seen that women have been left out of this. And I have decided that I'm not going to be a deacon again until women are accepted to the priesthood." Interestingly, this conversation happened in the Archdiocese of Seattle after Archbishop Raymond Hunthausen retired. The archbishop had discontinued the diaconate program to allow for exploration of women's ordination to diaconate ministries. These were not approved while

he was archbishop, and subsequent bishops reinstated the male only ordination process for the diaconate.

Jean remembered "I received lots of emails from priests congratulating
me or wishing me well." They expressed regret that it had to be through
a path of excommunication. She said, laughing, "One guy welcomed me
to the brotherhood, to the brotherhood!" Others in the diocese have been
"respectful . . . and there was a fair amount of undercover support." Even a
person with authority in the diocese, after he accepted her resignation from
work, gave her a peace sign quietly as together they left a funeral.

Kathy noted that two priests in her old parish offered moral support.
One promised her "I would never refuse you communion" while another
wrote her a letter "wishing her the very best." Similarly, Marina Theresa
observed that "I am feeling like I am Jonah. Because like Jonah, like the
prophet, when I was in Ecuador, a bishop told me come on. Be a priest. The
bishop told me I should be ordained a priest."

Maureen consulted a male priest as her spiritual director. She was
discerning how to proceed, and finally, he said to her "Maureen, sometimes
you just need to say, 'To hell with them.'" He passed away but wrote down
what he wanted people to say about him during his funeral. She was unable
to go, but the bishop was there, and he read that the priest lamented "He
didn't live long enough to see a woman ordained a Roman Catholic priest."
She noted that he was talking about her! According to witnesses who were
there, she was informed "The bishop sat there very stiff lipped as the whole
church stood up and applauded!"

Judy noted that a Salesian often encouraged her as they were ordained.
She said he wrote and said "I accept you as a priest." He then imagined
himself resting as he relied on the two womenpriests (both Judys) "to work
alongside him with the poor." He just wanted "to do liturgy.

Family

Family members bring additional challenge as well as support on the
labyrinth. Womenpriests, like most women balancing career, family, self,
and others, juggle to the best of their ability. Bishop Suzanne and Chava
mentioned the cost to family. As bishop, Suzanne worked 24/7 for over ten
years to help the organization grow. Her administrative skills helped create a

working website and form committees for care, education, and liturgy. She speaks to cardinals and bishops at large Catholic gatherings hoping to create a culture of acceptance and professional colleagueship. She acknowledged this cost her time with her family. Several women worried about supporting their children as single moms. Others grieved the fact that members of their families don't understand or accept their choices to be ordained. More than one noted that she wouldn't be buried with other family members in the Catholic cemetery. Some tried to remember financial and practical cautions from parents concerned for their well-being. Ordination has caused discomfort and concern among family members who prioritize church law over those challenging this one canon.

On the other hand, family members also support womenpriests. "My husband Bill is the first and main supporter," says Diane. "Without his willingness to to bring in a real salary so we could raise our kids and pay our mortgage I would not be able to do this." She highlighted the importance of a partner who earns enough to support the work of womenpriests and lay ecclesial ministers:

> *I would not have been able to do Spiritual Direction, where you just really don't get any money back, because . . . I was paying for childcare and . . . the sisters paid me $12 an hour . . . we didn't have a lot of money. But we did have a solid job before the kids were born."*

Diane noted that her partner was not "much of a churchgoer." Even so, his ongoing support allowed her to become the minister she was called to be.

Like Diane, Christine named her husband as her biggest supporter. He, too, supported her financially as well as emotionally and spiritually. Together they met a former priest and bishop who shared a house with them. When her husband died, this friend continued to support Christine in her efforts locally and internationally. Together they built a chapel in their shared property. Jean also named her husband as a principal supporter. He had been a Marist priest who had been laicized. They were happily married with children when she was ordained. She recalled that when she was preparing her ordination ceremony, one of her aunts told a story about Jean as a little girl exclaiming "If I had a penis, I could be a priest." Jean laughed at remembering this story, because she was astonished that she had said such a thing, since she didn't recall even knowing the names of body parts at that early age. She also acknowledged her parents, who even though they were confused and in their late 80s, affirmed her by their presence at her ordination.

Mary Therese also named her husband as the most inspirational and solid ally during her time of discernment. As a vowed religious she joined her future husband, who was a priest working in social justice ministry. They worked together for several years, then left their prior vocations to marry and continue their ministry to the children suffering in a cycle of poverty. Together they created a ministry she now continues as an ordained woman-priest. Her work over thirty years in her diocese garnered respect that helped her overcome the many barriers to her ordination. She admitted "when I was in my process of going through and doing all of this, we never did anything that challenged the diocese . . . so many of my friends are pastors and priests . . . I had no challenges . . ." She went on to say that even in the local newspapers covering her ordination, priests who were quoted said "I can't imagine anybody refusing her communion."

Paula also acknowledged the support of her husband, a laicized priest who kept deferring to her as ordained. She explained, that even when parishioners asked them to concelebrate, her husband declined saying "you know what, we've seen enough men priests. We need to see womenpriests! And my job is to support my wife and other women." Her entire family and her eleven siblings came to celebrate her ordination.

Several women mentioned their daughters as major supporters. Kathy noted that one of her daughters is in a Marian small faith community and together they are very supportive of Kathy's ordination. Similarly, Paula praised her three daughters and celebrated their support and lives of faith.

Celie counts her mother as her major ally and supporter. In a similar vein, but with a twist, Esperanza described her mother as having her own problems and not particularly involved in Esperanza's development. Indeed, her grandmother served as the most influential person who supported and accompanied Esperanza in her early years. Yet, as Esperanza reflected, she acknowledged that just before she was to be ordained, she visited her mother who was watching TV at the time. When Esperanza finally confessed that she was about to be ordained her mother said "That's good Esperanza!" Esperanza reminded her mother that she would be excommunicated and her mother replied "All right, that's ok." Esperanza reiterated the excommunication threat and her mother finally commanded "Turn the TV off and come over here. You are worried about the stupidest things sometimes!" They had a discussion about who could baptize and how that meant she could do priestly things. When her mother had forcefully convinced Esperanza that she should proceed, she said "OK, turn the TV back on!" Esperanza reflected, "That tough old lady was the one that eased my soul by telling me how stupid I was to worry about excommunication."

Ordained Male Clergy

Ordained church leaders confront multiple issues when they work with women who seek ordination. Their vows of obedience to the bishops demand they uphold church teaching and canon law. Their pastoral experiences sometimes convince them the teaching needs revision. Both attitudes are present in the womenpriests' experience. The uncertain responses one can anticipate both enforce the limits of the ceiling and offer hope that it can be shattered.

Kathleen spoke about her journey as child asking every priest if she could be ordained. She remembered that each said no, and her dad would pull her away. She stayed involved with music; a woman recruited her mom to sing and Kathleen joined her. Kathleen also joined the Catholic Worker movement on the east coast, and when she and her family moved to Olympia, Washington, she became a catechist working with children in the parish. At one point, she discovered she was celiac and could not receive the Host the parish offered. She approached the priest, and asked if they could provide a non-wheat based wafer for all those who could not receive the Host as offered. The priest replied, "We'll give you a prayer." And she answered, "I want Eucharist." She teared up as she remembered that the priest and eucharistic ministers present walked away from her. She continues her story. "Here I am preparing children for the Easter sacraments of baptism, confirmation, Eucharist and reconciliation, and I can't go! They all noticed that Kathleen doesn't go to communion. It was affecting their journey and mine. I said 'I can't do this anymore.'"

Like Kathleen, Helen found herself publicly shamed by her previous pastor when she tried to go to communion in the parish she had led for over fifteen years. She recalls "I never put myself in a position again with him [the pastor], although I did go to Mass occasionally and others would give me communion or a part of their Host. I didn't want to make a public scene, but I didn't like being humiliated either. I just let it go." She notes that another pastor told people they couldn't go to Mass with her.

Christine was "a chaplain in a hospital, and was there every Sunday to distribute communion and visit the sick . . . did little liturgies, many, many, many in the hospital. Then we had the students from the seminary and some of them had terrible problems to handle even the little box with the host in it. And I said 'Oh my God, how will they become priests when they are not able to handle distribution of communion? This is the easiest thing to give people." She also mentioned the church reform movement and the scandals. She thought "I will only do what is mine." And she moved forward to write a preparation program for ordaining women.

Jane remembers the final straw that moved her to leave her parish. The priest gave a homily related to the Eucharist and what makes it valid. She recalled him saying something like "you know in America we don't treat the Eucharist properly." He then claimed that "not understanding the Eucharist is the Eucharist because a priest consecrates it is like saying it is as bad as pedophilia." Jane was shocked and went to her friends after Mass to check out if they heard what she heard. None of them was offended or upset. She said, "That's it. I'm done."

As documented in previous chapters, Vikki's bishop thought it would be better to change religious affiliation than get ordained as a RCWP. The bishop of St. Louis stopped communicating with the Jewish rabbis since one of them agreed to host an ordination in her synagogue. He publicized every aspect of Elsie and another's ordination and excommunicated both, as well as the woman, Bishop Patricia, who presided at the ordination. Juanita, who has driven miles to pick up vowed religious and a male priest who join her community, admits "we have to keep that kind of quiet so the diocese doesn't know about this." While they are allies, their presence creates obstacles.

Shanon spoke movingly about her pain in leaving the institutional Catholic community she had served for over twenty years:

*I was shattered. I realized at that moment, that as much as I
was trying to stay inside the institution and work for the change
as much as I could, it felt like the Holy Spirit just kept putting
obstacle after obstacle that kept pushing me somewhere else. So, in
a very tearful meeting with the church council of the parish where I
served, the council agreed with me. They pretty much knew I had a
vocation and that I tried really hard to follow the rules. This bishop
never follows the rules. They are not following the rules but they
want us to follow the rules! It was a painful six months, and during
that time I left my job willingly before the diocese fired me.*

And just as so many others (Teresa, Donnieau, Kathleen, Chava, Paula, Suzanne) have said about ensuring financial stability, her friends immediately said to Shanon "you are unemployed and unemployable now!"

Judy shared that her partner Judy, also a priest, was dying in the hospital and she had a devout Catholic doctor who knew her story and asked her if she would like to speak to a priest. She agreed that he would call the priest from the parish she still attended. That priest had befriended the two Judys. Judy continued "So he came and the first thing he did was ask her to repent of her priesthood . . . She looked at him and asked 'Father, do you repent of your priesthood?' He answered in the negative. She responded 'Neither will I.' Then he gave her the rites. I had already given the rites, and some of the other womenpriests gave her the rites." Still mourning the loss of her partner, Judy can't return to the parish with the male priest who led with the request to renounce the ordination. "I feel cut off. I do go to a faraway parish with visitors, a parish where they don't know me. I love the liturgy."

Lay Colleagues

Patricia wrote "Because of my ordination, I had to leave the Dominican Order. This was a great sadness for me and my life has changed considerably since then. But, as so many ordained women have discovered: some doors close and others, often the ones you never dreamed existed, open for you." Vikki also had to resign her association with a special vowed religious community in the Midwest. When she decided to pursue ordination, she and her superiors agreed together to protect the order. Several others have followed this path. The loss of support—even though all agree it's the way to go—hurts in the separation. Even as they resigned their association with orders to protect those remaining in the orders, some found the individual members shunned them for their decisions to be ordained.

Diane recalls how she raised her kids in the same parish in which she worked. She was part of the leadership of a charismatic community within the parish. She pursued school, became trained in spiritual direction, and worked with folks who grew in faith and knowledge with her. When she finally became ordained, she had to leave the parish, and most of the people in the parish dropped her as a friend, spiritual director, or confidante. She copastors a vibrant community, but together they mourn the loss of the larger community they shared for so many years.

Even before her ordination, Donnieau noticed how she took her participation as a Catholic more seriously than her peers. She reflected "I think the friends I had along the way that were Catholic, they would see me as a bit odd, a bit strange, because I was focused on trying to understand how we see God through many different lenses. So even on a connection level, just going to church, having Catholic friends, there was still that sense of pushback. That sense of 'Can't you just sit here and just sing this song and go get communion and just be the good quiet person that you always appear to be.'" Since her ordination, she has continued to ponder her relation to God and to the community and to herself. She notices her immediate responses to some things are leftovers from early childhood training. She continues "I recognize some things impact me at a deep level as I have gone on this journey. It has allowed me, if anything as a benefit, to have a greater deal of compassion for those who really can't see what journey really means, because I still have my own struggles."

Physical and Spiritual Suffering

Christine, one of the Danube 7 and the first bishop, remembered the trauma and conflict surrounding that ordination in 2002. She remembered that her friends were afraid for her to break canon law, and they became hostile toward her, as did members of her home parish. "They became very hostile when I invited them to my ordination." They had all been part of an ongoing church reform movement. And the day before the ordination the speaker of that movement confronted her "in a public interview on the TV." Christine talked about how difficult it was for her, and the power of the anger and conflict against her personally and the ordination itself. It caused her to wonder, "Should we not do the ordination? Is this the right way? Should we continue or should we stop the whole thing?" The press was against the process saying, "these terrible witches want to become priests . . . and they can only find a bishop that is not proper enough." She confirmed the work they had done and the validity of their call and moved forward. As a leader, she confided, one must move forward in confidence, even when chaos and conflict surround the work. She accepted her role as shepherd and believed that "God will be with us and we are protected."

Shanon worked with her diocese and in a parish for many years. She sought every kind of education and formation open to her as a lay woman. She developed a love of Hildegarde of Bingen and, with a group of people, began a retreat center close to their parish. They studied Hildegarde's life, letters, songs, and art and made pilgrimages together. Through her studies, she encountered a time of choice. Should she become an Anglican priest?—a path open to her. Or should she stay committed to the path she was on as a lay minister? This is a question most of the womenpriests asked themselves.

Several things influenced Shanon's decision. A priest in the diocese committed egregious crimes and remained relatively unpunished, while women were limited in their ability to contribute fully to the life of the Church. She resigned from work with the diocese but stayed as lay minister. Then, a bishop she knew well, stationed in India, was convicted of embezzling funds from his ministries. He was chastised but remained an ordained priest ministering in India. The scandal impacted Shanon in a major way. Like Teresa of Avila, John of the Cross, and Mother Theresa, she entered a dark night in her soul. She felt lost, helpless, angry at the injustices, and questioned the character of other priests and bishops in the Church she loved.

Throughout her anguish, she worked with a spiritual director, and prayed unceasingly, and finally, one director asked her to either leave and become an Episcopal priest or be the change she sought in her church. Again, she suffered as she pondered her choices. Finally, she said "I kind of just realized one day after I got out of my dark night. We talk about it and we talk about it and we know women served as leaders and priests in the early church. I thought we are just going to have to do it. We are just going to have to be that change. And we have to do it with as much charity and compassion as possible." She left her benefits, her retirement, her companions in faith and her parish. Yet, she knows "I'm not angry. . . it's been very peaceful. I feel that I am just being the change as positively as I can."

After years teaching in the Catholic school, Paula retired and entered the process to become ordained a womanpriest. Supported by her husband and three daughters, she participated in the formation process. Prior to her ordination, she experienced a health problem not unlike the woman with the hemorrhage who met Jesus on the road. After losing and receiving several pints of blood and a stay in the hospital, she was released. Yet, she knew something was not yet right. She went to another doctor who found a tumor that was not in a place doctors felt comfortable removing. She received shots in her stomach for six months to assist in both reducing the tumor and protecting a clot that had formed on it. Eventually, Paula insisted that the doctors operate saying to a Catholic nurse: "You'll understand what I am going to say. God has called me to be a Roman Catholic womanpriest. And God needs women, our church needs women, and I just feel that God is not going to call me to this important thing and take me home. And so we're going to have the surgery, and I'm going to get better, and I'm going to be ordained a Roman Catholic womanpriest, and I am going to do what God has called me to do." They did the surgery and she survived and was ordained.

One of her daughters reflected with her that she got her cancer because she eats her anger. Paula noted how astute her daughter was and agreed that "her anger builds up . . . until it becomes a tumor." She agreed, "That is what happened to me. I was angry at the way people were treated. As women in the church, and as all lay people, we were not treated equally. Women are certainly second class." She noted she learned to express her anger, to shout it out, to get in touch with herself.

Several womenpriests have dealt with cancer. Bridget Mary, Judy, and others spoke of their physical struggles with cancer. Judy noted that her partner Judy "had already beaten one leukemia called APL" after a three-year battle. "She was beautiful and everyone was praying and so happy to have her back." Eventually her fourth cancer caused her death.

Esperanza spoke openly about her perception of God calling her to something the church forbids upon pain of excommunication. She named God as cruel and acknowledged how much it hurt when she told this story: "I was considering becoming a eucharistic minister. I didn't want to do it because it hurt too much. It hurt too much to be there and to know that this is as far as I was going to go. . . . So I said that's it, I'm withdrawing from all of this. I'm not leaving the church but I'm not volunteering anymore because it's too painful." She had an intimate relation with God and like Jeremiah, felt free to confront God with her perceived injustice. Thus, just as Jeremiah bemoaned the day he was born and even his mother's rejection of him, this womanpriest shouted, "You're a cruel God." She notes that she continued to pray over the years and was at daily Mass one day, when no one went to help the priest distribute communion. The priest looked at her and gestured for her to come up, and of course, she assisted the priest. All the while she laughed to herself, because this God whom she railed at called her forward anyway, and she knows her "God has a sense of humor."

Olga tried to help the mother of a friend who was suffering and needed anointing. The priest of the parish was busy teaching classes at the university, and the neighboring priest claimed it wasn't his responsibility to assist. Olga pursued her own ordination to alleviate the suffering of others around her.

Celie recalls being very aware that as a girl she could not be a priest. Her family system also "includes divorce and LGBT people in an important way." Even as a young girl she wanted to be priest even though she wasn't baptized, and her family didn't conform to Church expectations. Celie followed a different path through ordination as a Unitarian Universalist pastor. She experienced difficulty relating to her youth; she started her master of divinity as a Unitarian Universalist candidate at the age of twenty-two. During her studies she experienced discomfort as the youngest person in her group and as a fully Christian theist in a more universalist culture. Upon her graduation from seminary and ordination as a Unitarian Universalist minister, Celie answered a call to a Unitarian congregation. As a Christian Unitarian, her belief in God "was at the far end of the personal relationship with God for Unitarians." While serving that community, she met with ecumenical colleagues, including those at a neighboring Catholic Church. There she saw a woman on the altar. The experience of witnessing a woman celebrating Eucharist in a Catholic church rekindled her early experience in church. She exclaimed "I knew I couldn't unsee" this testimony to women as priests. She thought "Ok, God has been preparing this." Ten years after seminary, she became Roman Catholic and resigned from her position as pastor of the Unitarian congregation. She reflected, "I sometimes felt not terribly nurtured. I had tremendous difficulty letting go of my parish that I served at the time. I had quite a struggle for a couple of years before I finally decided to let go." When she did let go to enter the process of ordination as a RCWP, "it proved much more difficult than I thought." She was unemployed, moved in with her mother, a person she counts as her greatest ally, and suffered through Covid's early years trying to make ends meet through part-time employment. She admits "I didn't have a lot of success for a while." She noted that several RCWP cautioned her against ordination, because of "the financial ramifications, the lack of a place to serve." As a young person, only in her midthirties, the elder womenpriests warned her of the costs in income, retirement, healthcare, and financial stability. She persevered and as a more recent convert, she continues to work to understand the past hurts of people who are struggling with their faith. In addition, as the youngest womanpriest, she faces the ongoing challenge of leading people mostly twice her age.

Doing the Work

The most common path for all women attempting to enter ground previously closed has been simply to do the work. As countless authors have noted, women have entered into most professions by showing up, working hard, and staying the course. The labyrinth, then, offers a metaphor for the process of moving three steps forward and two steps back. As we have seen, each obstacle turns the participant to find another way, an opening. Womenpriests did the work of ministry, sought and earned equivalent degrees and spiritual formation for priestly ministry, and dealt with rejection, illness, and economic instability. Throughout their journeys they met people who barred their way and celebrated allies who nurtured them as they discovered new openings. The labyrinth is a tool of spiritual transformation. Eventually, the person finds the way to the center. As author Tom Dickey asserts, "labyrinths represent a universal pattern in human consciousness."[38] Each woman spoke of their journey as a search for God's will for them. This meant, as Diane said, "one step at a time."

Kathy spoke in very practical terms. She felt prepared to accept the rejection through the process of formation in the RCWP. She acknowledged that the obstacles and rejection hurt, and also that "knowing that it was going to happen, gave me less concern." She continued, "I was doing what I needed to do. That's where I have to go. I have to go there!"

Diane admitted to "doing her work and doing it for a long time. I had a lot of work to do . . . but you know I'm still doing it. I stayed on the road I was on . . . and that was the answer, even when things got hard with local parish stuff. So, when I thought 'I can't stand it any longer,' I continued to minister. I was cantoring, and I was lecturing, pretty much I was on the altar every weekend. I'd take little sabbaticals once in a while and I'd always get sent back by God." She took extra time during her formation to "work through the resistance" she had. She noted that she was tired of hearing what the Pope said and what the catechism said, what the rule said, and what others thought everyone had to do. "It was squelching at best. Smothering." As one who had worked for the church through her lifetime, "I was accustomed to being an abbess for a long time. I had been directing formation programs for years . . . I've always been a kind of bossy boss, so even though I do it in community, in a team, I didn't know how to be a novice . . . I had a lot of work to do."

Shanon spoke at length about her painful decision to leave ministry in the institutional Church so she could answer her call to ordained ministry. She sought help, as did all the women we studied, and she finally "came to a place where I understood that the authority and validation doesn't have to come from only one place and the institution."

Others reflect on their relationships with priests and the hierarchy. Olga sated "I do not feel excommunicated. Not too long ago, I went to my hometown to take my baptismal certificates. I admit my heart wanted to jump out of my chest while the secretary prepared my request. I have not left the Church. I have not renounced my baptism. I am not a stranger before the congregation and the clergy. No one has attacked me or the other female priests while we have been working within the church." Maureen spoke to a priest about her ordination. He said, "The pope says women can't be ordained, so women can't be ordained." She reflected, "The status is *persona non grata*. I feel like we have a common call . . . I really believe that there's no deviation in the calling between a man and a woman."

When Juanita finally accepted ordination, she was "kicked out of her parish." She thought to try a different parish and was accepted by the priest, but the people complained to the archdiocese. Juanita went to the pastor and affirmed that he "was a great pastor" and confirmed that she "didn't want him to lose the parish." She asked, "Just give me a blessing." And he gave her "a beautiful blessing." Subsequently, she continued at the parish, even though lay women continued to complain and judge. When the priest was transferred, the new priest not only gave her the blessing she requested, but "he gave me communion. He opened my hand and gave me communion." Afterwards the same women found him in the sacristy, and she heard them screaming at him and then "they came out and screamed at me: 'How dare you! You're an excommunicated woman! How dare you receive communion!' They finally left the parish, and I contacted the next priest by email and he responded, 'Whatever he allowed you to do, go ahead and do.' That's been good for the last six years. Eventually, I saw our bishop and sat down with him to tell him everything I was doing and I told him I worked with the homeless out in the streets with Casa de Clara, and he said to continue to do what I'm doing. He's been amazing."

Patricia compares the work with the institutional church to the "long march to freedom" that characterized the South African journey to dismantle apartheid. She worked against "unjust discrimination against women in the church"[39] toward "a discipleship of equals."[40] She called for prophetic action, which she defined in terms of obedience, that is, listening. She further spoke about the need to listen deeply to herself, her formed "conscience, values, sense of what is right and wrong, listening to my heart."[41] In spite of her rhetoric to call for action, she admitted "like so many other women, I always suppressed it [her call], since it was unthinkable. But it kept coming back, often at the most unexpected moments."[42] She writes, "Many people who knew me confirmed their sense of my call to priesthood, including seminarians, priests, friends, and even a bishop. No one, however, thought that ordination for women was possible in the Roman Catholic Church."[43]

Christine continues to connect with bishops and priests. She resists going to the parish in her home area to protect the life of the church there. As "a good Catholic girl who joined the Benedictines" and then left and got married, Christine eventually went "into conflict with my friends, especially the local bishop at the time. We were very good friends and he had to act officially against me with letters and so on. We had a very complicated relationship of many years. Now we are in good friendship again." She noted that they had both grown older and they are now "respectful and on one stage of conversation." As a Bishop and leader in the movement, she admits that the burden of leadership causes her to ponder deeply how to proceed so the best outcome can be achieved.

Teresa faced a challenge of living authentically. Like Diane, Teresa recalled years of working on herself in relation to God and others. She remembered a charismatic group in the parish where she served as youth minister. One day "they came into the office and they said 'Teresa, we need to pray over you, we just got the message from the Holy Spirit and we need to pray over you.'" She allowed them to do so. As she told the story, she remembered that this happened repeatedly while she was at the church. As a non-Charismatic, she admitted that she sort of "rolled my eyes" but she allowed the prayer. During one of her appointments as a liturgical minister, her male priest colleague gave her a stole and the priest colleague she worked with next also gave her a stole. And people came up to me and said, "You are our priest. You are our priest. We all recognize it."

Over the years, she had worked as a lay pastoral coordinator/ administrator in two dioceses and three parishes. Having spent years in archdiocesan sponsored education and formation opportunities, she earned her master of divinity degree. She served several parishes as liturgical coordinator and pastoral administrator/coordinator in two dioceses. Her call to priesthood never left her and she continued to struggle to stay hopeful and faithful within the parameters she found herself. She didn't take initial steps to move toward ordination until two things happened. First, Pope Benedict XVI wrote that women consecrating Eucharist was as harmful to the faith as priests committing pedophilia.[44] Teresa describes her horror at the statement and admits it was the final straw for her. About the same time, she was about to be replaced by a male ordained priest. Her bishop congratulated her for her years of work in a parish no one had wanted. She had fostered a vibrant community and helped rebuild church property, bringing it up to the current building code. The parish was paying its way. Her success as a pastoral coordinator soon attracted interest among male priests in the diocese who asked to be appointed to the parish she had led as a lay woman for the past ten years.

Even then, she confessed she "took almost five years to complete my preparation [for ordination] even though I already had my master of divinity completed years before. I couldn't enter the priesthood feeling as if I'd been victimized by the Church. I needed to freely open myself and I needed to not take hatred with me. I needed not to do something if it was a violent act against the traditional church. So, it took me a while to get to the point where I no longer felt like I wanted to break things and hurt people."

Shanon pursued a master in ministry as she served her parish and the diocese. She entered the process at the seminary and joined classes with men preparing to be ordained. At some point, she knew she couldn't continue, because the seminary didn't award a master of divinity degree to women, only to men. She found ways around this through applying to nearby Ursuline College. The sisters were willing to accept her seminary credits, but they didn't offer a master of divinity. Shanon had to leave the educational process and deal with her feelings of anger and inadequacy even as she sought to serve to the best of her ability. Eventually, she sorted things, earning a master's degree after which she earned a doctorate. Her doctoral studies helped her do the type of *resourcement* that found her exploring texts and recovering early teachings of the church.

Maureen described her work in graduate school as "heartbreaking, because my classmates who had earned the same degree as I had, went on to ordination . . . I went to their ordinations . . . then I went home to fill out an application to get a job—and I did end up finding a job as a theology teacher at a girls' Catholic high school." She eventually left that position and found a job teaching in a public school system. She continues to work in this way for benefits, retirement, and a livable wage. She speaks of her suffering in the context of women "suffering because they're being so stifled. And I think you know the spirit of God is not going to be contained forever you know."

Donnieau pursued education as a way to validate her call and her place in the world. She spoke about sitting "in the space of just this biggest confusion . . . because I felt called to do this work. I studied other faith journeys. I've studied other Christian perspectives. None of them made sense to the very core of who I am." She pursued "counseling, psychology, mental health," because "there is a lot of healing in that." At the same time, she confessed "but still this longing was so strong, this yearning, this stirring was so strong in me, saying in so many words: 'You're not done!'" She was listening to the Spirit, still feeling a sense of inadequacy after having earned doctoral degrees in areas related to psychological and spiritual healing. Still, she found she was looking for a more complete way to answer her call. She even "started to go back to maybe it's that spiritual stirring of maybe I need to go back and try to join orders as a nun." Eventually, though, she found her peace in becoming a womanpriest.

Stepping into Openings and the Center: Joy

Pope Francis begins his declaration in *Evangelii Guadium* with: "the joy of the gospel fills the lives and hearts of all who encounter Jesus . . . With Christ joy is constantly born anew."[45] St. Paul speaks of joy as a sign of God's presence in believers. Certain biblical passages note that this encounter with God creates a noticeable shift in a person's being. Thus, at what the church calls the transfiguration, Jesus shines like the sun with Elijah and Moses (Matt 17: 1–3; Mark 9:2–10; Luke 9:28–36). Barbara Reid, scripture scholar, notes that of all the transfiguration stories, Luke mentions that Jesus is praying. And rather than transfigured, his "face changed in appearance."[46] She compares this shift to that observed by the people when Moses was seen after he encountered God. His face was radiant when he was with God on Mount Sinai, and he covered his radiant face after spending time with God in the Tent before the ark of the covenant (Exod 34:29–35). Similarly, Hannah's face was lifted up after God heard her prayer (1 Sam 1:18). The purpose of the spiritual labyrinth is transformation, a lifting up or joy upon completion.

During our reflective time after each interview, we often commented how much joy the womanpriest we had just encountered demonstrated.

We interviewed Teresa first. As faculty and researchers, we both knew Teresa early in her education and ministry. Our experience of her during the interview was followed by our surprise. For many years, we knew Teresa's anger and frustration at the church she served so well as a lay ecclesial minister. During that first interview with her, she demonstrated only peace and joy. She spoke about her path to that joy and her work to release her anger. She didn't want to be a catalyst for people to rally around with picket signs. So, she invited them "to go a different route." Even today, people will come to her when the male priest at the canonical parish is too busy. She's been called to do burials, weddings, and baptisms, and called to patient bedsides for the sacrament of the sick. Catholics who say they don't have a relationship with the assigned priest call her. Yet, she attempts to continue relationships with male priests and bishops as a sign of the unity of the Church.

Maria remembers the community at Marquette as changing her entire life. This informs her work today. The first priest she encountered after her ordination gave her a blessing. Subsequent priests were informed of her status by the bishops. Now, however, if the priest can't go to an emergency, they call her and she goes. She goes to the lay person to receive communion when she attends mass at what would be her parish, so as not to embarrass the priest. She says the parish still considers her a member.

After worrying about her age, returning to school after many years, completing enough theology, and managing her workload, Juanita applied to RCWP and was accepted for formation for ordination. When she heard that "Yes!" she recounts "Everything opened up. When I let go and let God take over, everything just fell into place."

Joanna travelled a unique path. Her journey took her outside the Catholic tradition through marriage and childbearing. She was mentored by a couple who formed their own church, and she was eventually ordained in that tradition. After a painful divorce, she enrolled in courses sponsored by Marianne Williamson. Through her interior work and counselling, Joanna returned to the Catholic church, where she discovered that love was the motive for all her action. Eventually her Catholic community called her to be ordained and she approached with an open heart. Now, she serves a small community, and she describes her willingness to "stand with them as they work for social justice." Her smile broadens when she speaks of the work she does with her community.

Jean reflected on her journey of pain at the death of two children at childbirth, her divorce, and her remarriage in the Church. She learned to understand grief and love in a different way. She admitted that "when things like this happen in your life, you have to find a way to go on and to make something good out of it. So they could have goodness in their own life . . ." She now copastors a vibrant community with her husband.

Gisela writes of her experience with both pain at the persecution by the Church and joy at the freedom to finally answer God's call. She met with a bishop after she received her excommunication papers from the pope. "We met and I told him of the vision of us women: to bring priestly ordination to all women of the world who want to be ordained. He said he would support us."[47] She recalls her ordination as a bishop, another event fraught with worry and persecution followed by driving away that night ready to "bring our hearts, our feelings, and our desires to the people of the world who have a big longing for equality and justice for women. Welcome! Welcome to all women priests and women bishops!"[48]

Summary

A spiritual journey begins with a call. Once a person meets the divine, one decides how to respond. Some do as Peter and Andrew did in John's gospel. They "come and see" Jesus. Others find ways to follow their *inquietud* through daily life. In all cases we studied, these womenpriests were curious and humble. Like Moses and Miriam, they resolutely attended to God's activity in their lives and the lives of their communities. As in the case of biblical characters, each followed a path that offered inspiration, significant challenge, suffering, and accompaniment on the way. As Vatican II highlighted, all baptized are part of a pilgrim people of God. The spiritual quest seeks life with God.

Just as women in many contexts found ways to surmount barriers in fulfilling their vocations, these women attempted every possible path they could find. Unable to break through the concrete wall, they broke through the stained-glass ceiling by walking the labyrinth of their lives. Eventually, each decided their only choice was to disobey the law. Like Jesus and his disciples in several gospel accounts, they broke a law of their religious tradition. Jesus and his disciples ate grain on the Sabbath (Luke 6:6), healed peoples' lives on the Sabbath (Matt 12:10; Luke 13:14; Mark 3:1–6; Luke 13:10–17; Matt 12:11) and preached on the Sabbath (Luke 4:16). We see Jesus take time out to pray, and after prayer, Jesus makes important decisions (Mark 1:35; Luke 5:16; Matt 26:39). Our next set of questions asked these womenpriests how they nurtured and sustained their journeys of faith. The next chapter considers their responses.

❧ 5 ❧

SPIRITUAL PRACTICES AND DISCERNMENT

"Pray always without growing weary."[1]
"Persevere in Prayer, being watchful in it with thanksgiving."

—Colossians 4:2

AS THE LAST chapter demonstrated, the paths to womenpriest ordination in the Roman Catholic Church vary. Filled with uncertainty, opposition, clear signs of call, and a nagging and unrelenting "still small voice within," each woman found ways to sustain connection with God and others on the journey. The French philosopher and scientist Pierre Teilhard de Chardin once said, "Joy is the infallible sign of the presence of God."[2] He further outlined ten things one gives up to experience joy. First among those is fear, the kind of living in fear that burns up energy, goes nowhere and prevents a person from becoming the one they are created to be. Next, he suggested one gives up negative self-talk, a sign of being one's worst enemy. Third, he advised that one must live in the present, and fourth, give up others' dreams or limitations for a person so they can live into their own God-given self. Fifth, he urged people to give up resistance to change because literally everything changes. Indeed, biologists note that change is part of life—either change to die or change to live, it is always change. Sixth, one should look inward to develop oneself free of comparison with others. Along the way, one stops trying to impress someone else (seven) or blaming others or the self for how life is (eight). At the ninth step one stops complaining or making excuses, essentially relying on God to help us become who God created and gifted us to be. Finally, Chardin encourages us to never doubt God's plan for us, and that God wants us to use our talents and ability to make our world a better place. These are Chardin's steps to joy.

We noticed these women's joy as we interviewed them. After our interviews we commented on this to each other and wrote about it in our reflection journals. The previous chapter demonstrated how so many of them walked these steps. Their journeys required them to face fear and attempt to live their best lives as they understood them as God's will for them. This chapter reveals the myriad ways these womenpriests nurtured their connection with the Holy One, the Spirit, Mother/Father God of the universe. Teilhard de Chardin also observed: "We are not human beings having a spiritual experience, we are spiritual beings having a human experience."[3] Our questions teased out how these women sustained their journeys through accessing their spiritual beings.

St. Paul writes to the Galatians (5:18) "Brothers and sisters, if you are guided by the Spirit, you are not under the law." He then lists the myriad ways that hinder the faithful in their living in Spirit—licentiousness, idolatry, sorcery, hatreds, and the like. He follows that list of obstacles with a list of fruits by which we recognize those who are following the way of Jesus's spirit: love, joy, peace, patience, kindness, generosity, faithfulness, gentleness, and self-control. He affirms that there is no law against these fruits of the Spirit, and indeed encourages all of us to practice the way of Christ's spirit as a result of our dying to self and rising in Christ through baptism. Vatican II affirmed this teaching. The Decree on the Apostolate of Lay People (*Apostolicam Actuositatem*) reiterated that all Christians are called to a life in the Spirit through their baptism. Citing Paul's letter to the Colossians, this document further encouraged lay people to "a continuous exercise of faith, hope and charity. Only the light of faith and meditation on the word of God can enable us to find everywhere and always the God 'in whom we live and exist (Acts 17:28)'; only thus can we seek God's will in everything, see Christ in everyone . . . make sound judgments on the true meaning and value of temporal realities both in themselves and in relation to our final end."[4] In this spirit, we asked questions about each womanpriest's practices of prayer and discernment in life that reflect a disposition toward God.

Christine responded almost in the same way Paul wrote when she expounded: "I think you have to . . . as a spiritual person, open eyes and ears . . . it also depends on what do I allow to come into my brain? Do I play, all the time, terrible games with people shooting or whatever? Or do I drink all the time alcohol? Or do I use drugs? Or do I share hostile jokes against women? What do I speak?" Dianne says similarly, "If we are opening our hearts, and opening our minds, and opening our whole being to the Spirit of life, the Spirit of love that flows through everything, then we can trust that." Like Paul, these two women spoke about how Christ blesses them with "every spiritual blessing in the heavens . . . to be holy and without blemish before him" (Eph 1: 3–4). None of the women claimed to be without blemish, but they did reveal gratitude for their many blessings.

We asked the womenpriests how they nurtured their life in God. We wanted to know how they opened their minds, hearts, and being to God. We questioned them about spiritual practices, people and texts that sustained and nurtured their lives in God. We inquired about their decision-making and discernment processes. In other words, we asked how they "persevere[d] in prayer, being watchful in it with thanksgiving" (Col 4:2). This chapter considers several themes that emerged from their responses: traditional practices, embodied rituals, and spiritual discernment processes.

Traditional Practices

Lay people are encouraged to pray daily, even as St. Paul urged the Thessalonians to "pray without ceasing"(1 Thess 5:17). The major Catholic traditional prayer practices include, first and foremost, participation in liturgy. Daily prayer takes many forms, including the monastic liturgy of the hours. Some take time away from normal activities to spend extended time in prayer and contemplation. They often call this practice a retreat. Many find reflection on scripture important and use a variety of practices including *lectio divina* and daily lectionary contemplation. The womenpriests spoke about sustaining their lives integrating these five traditional practices: liturgy, daily prayer, liturgy of the hours, retreat, and scripture reflection and spiritual reading.

Liturgy

As chapter 2 revealed, most of the women experienced God's presence in a very significant way through Catholic liturgy. Dagmar celebrates Mass with her community; she also "participates in EWTN's televised Mass and then does a meditation before, and some spiritual reading afterwards." For her it is simple and obvious. These are the ways of the tradition. Juanita exclaimed "Eucharist is my life!" Jean confirms this in her own practice of stopping in and praying in the chapel. She reflected that "even as a little girl I always felt like I had a connection to the divine." Morag confessed that she always went to Benediction and liked it. Even before she became Catholic, Benediction attracted her to a deeper place with God. As we have seen, Celie also found the Host of the Eucharist "shimmer" and recognized it as God before she could conceive of being Catholic. Now she spends time each day in the chapel pondering the Eucharist in the tabernacle as a way to sustain her faith and practice as priest.

The Constitution on the Sacred Liturgy states that the goal of the Council is to "intensify the daily growth of Catholics in Christian liturgy; to make more responsive to the requirements of our times those Church observances which are open to adaptation; to nurture whatever can contribute to the unity of all who believe in Christ; and to strengthen those aspects of the Church which can help summon all of mankind [*sic*] into her embrace."[5] The next paragraphs highlight the importance of the Eucharist, through which "the work of our redemption is exercised."[6] As women who experienced aspects of Vatican II, the womenpriests naturally attended first to their lives in the sacramental reality of the Catholic experience.

Christine stated her Benedictine point of view: "The liturgy is highly regarded." She thinks one needs to know lots of the speaking prayers and gestures by heart so one can celebrate and bless. She contends that "the liturgy has to be part of the life of the priest because otherwise it is only a job she or he does." Dagmar affirms this and builds on it. She acknowledges, as does Vatican II, that Baptism is the sacrament that initiates and reconciles us to God. She continues that Eucharist and liturgy help people to evolve as Christians. Agreeing with both, Juanita and Celie simply "celebrate Mass every day." Others celebrate Mass with their communities once a week, twice a month, or as often as "two or more gather together." Kathy noted that she was one of the first to do Eucharistic liturgy on zoom so that people could participate during Covid.

Celie brings additional insight to the discussion. She believes, "Yes, God is absolutely and truly present in the bread and in the cup. I also believe that God is absolutely present in the people gathered." She speaks about "just sitting with the Eucharist and having a very deep relationship with the Eucharist as a parishioner." As a presider when she lifts the bread she reflects, "This is us, this is the people offering themselves and everything that they're bringing with them . . . I always pause in the air, because I think of the Eucharist as ourselves and becoming the Body of Christ." Jane affirms this when she speaks of encouraging people to "go back to church. Go back because you need this." She acknowledges that "I can't live without it." Similarly, Helen recalls her life as a vowed religious in a community that practiced perpetual adoration for over one hundred years. As a lay minister she oversaw the practice in several parishes to which she was assigned. She reflected that "the Eucharist, the Mass, is very important to me. That is where I get a great deal of my strength. . . . For me adoration is about presence. And that is what Eucharist is for me. It is presence." Pat consecrates hosts and visits those who cannot come to Mass. She notes that she sits with people and together they talk about spiritual things, "about life after death and so many unknowns, and then we talk about the beauty of this world and the things we don't see because we don't open our eyes to see." Then they receive.

Several womenpriests visit people in hospitals. They bring Eucharist, reconciliation, and anointing to those who are suffering. Paula notes "I always bring the Spirit with me and ask the Spirit to speak to the person through me. To let them know they are loved just the way they are."

Interpreting the document on liturgy with the broadest understanding, Dagmar wondered why any sacrament would be limited to only some? She exclaimed "we have seven sacraments and we act like one of them has this aura of really hierarchical superiority to it. I don't think that's the way Jesus operated in his life . . . I think every Roman Catholic should claim every sacrament. Why not?"

Daily Prayer

Joanna uses words from spiritual writers when she exclaims, "I need to show up! Pay attention! Tell the truth! Let go of the outcome!"[7] To do this, she reflects daily (for over twenty years) on the work of God's love and peace in our lives and world. Helen's time in the convent taught her to "pay attention to the sanctification of every moment." Every day she repeats the prayer she learned in the novitiate: "Live my Triune God. So live in me that all I do is done by Thee." Similarly, Donnieau recalled a Jewish friend who told her that life is prayer. She revealed that she tried to make her life a prayer, to remember frequently that her life is offered as a prayer. "So all these little pieces, the contemplative in the busiest of moments, my spiritual prayer practices in the morning, they help to remind me that I am trying to offer it the best prayer that I ever could." Dagmar, Paula, Esperanza, Maureen, Donnieau, Olivia, Diane, Jeanette, Suzanne, Dana, and Gabriella all named their daily meditation as essential to their spiritual lives. Donnieau spoke about the "intentional slowing down, the slowing down just of the body in order to really be more present and more focused . . . it allows me to center myself and be ready to face whatever the day brings." Jane and Victoria also practice meditation, and they incorporate Buddhist practices as well as centering prayer. Dana writes about integrating all these into her practice of centering prayer imaging the Mystical Heart of Jesus.[8]

Chava reveals, "I light my candles, pray, and spend time journaling. I try to make sure I have time for prayer and spiritual reading every day." Like Chava, Celie tries to "begin the day in silence, in a contemplative way, either with just a candle or before my little altar at home. I just try to be present and listen and kind of let myself rest in God." Paula also uses the language of presence. She says, "Part of my prayer is just being present, just being present and trying to be present to whomever I am with . . . every day I try to connect with God within . . . sometimes I write."

Christine, as a Benedictine, named hospitality as essential to her practice of prayer. She acknowledged that one must be able to be alone with God to sustain an inner life. Many linked prayer to exercise. Juanita walks while praying the rosary and reflecting on Scripture. Paula walks and asks God to speak to her. She often finds herself listening to someone she meets on the path. Judy walks outside close to the lake near her property and listens to nature reveal God to her. Jane and Victoria do yoga. Dagmar says the rosary during her daily swim and Suzanne studies and prays in the bathtub. In fact, she said, two bishops have blessed the tub.

Liturgy of the Hours

Since so many of the womenpriests had some experience with vowed religious women, either in schools or in some aspect of vowed religious life, they also retained a love of the liturgy of the hours. The Constitution on the Liturgy devoted an entire section to the importance of this spiritual practice in forming ministerial lives. The document states firmly that "the church, by celebrating the Eucharist and in other ways, especially the celebration of the divine office, is ceaselessly engaged in praising the Lord and interceding for the salvation of the entire world."[9] Christine recalled that St. Benedict encouraged new religious to live in community before trying to live alone. In that path, she noted one prayed the "prayers of the hours every day, so that eventually you learn it by heart." Juanita affirms this practice as she describes her early morning prayer to start every day. Jane rewrites the prayers as she prays them, so they open more images of God and are more inclusive to all people. She says, "gratitude is a big portion of my prayer . . . and I try to stay awake long enough to do night prayer." Chava attended Compline on Sunday nights and reflected that "it was Compline that brought me back to the church."

Retreats

Diane remembered that she led charismatic renewal in her college small group. This community of prayer opened her to her call to ministry. Maureen and Juanita pursued a thirty-day retreat with the Jesuits in California. Chava, on the other hand, spent time in Mexico and El Salvador on retreat with liberation theologians and small ecclesial communities. She treasures the work of St. Oscar Romero. Others have pursued retreats in shorter and more communal ways. Diane, Dagmar, Joanna, Juanita, and others attend retreats as ways to renew their spiritual lives. Shanon "spent a month with Hildegarde" in Bingen, Germany and leads annual retreats for her community and others. They all agree with Juanita's summary: "What is important for me is to have that time away from everything. That quiet time. And to really continue my spirituality."

Some participated in pilgrimages as a way of retreat. Diane spoke about her journey on the Camino. She described the experience: "I heard that you walk by yourself, you know? I didn't know that . . . I not only have a tattoo that shines and says 'Talk to me. I'll listen to you,' but I mean, I think my whole body was shining." She then lamented a bit, that people actually talked to her and she was hoping for more quiet solitude as she journeyed. Shanon described her month-long retreat in Bingen as a pilgrimage, and Juanita studied with Tibetans in Tibet as well as making pilgrimages to

Jerusalem. Like Shanon, Juanita organizes retreats and pilgrimages with her communities almost annually.

Scripture and Spiritual Reading

Chava makes time every day for prayer and spiritual reading. She notes her extended library and reflects that she is currently working on a text by Thomas Merton. She and Esperanza reflect on St. Juan Diego and St. Oscar Romero. Esperanza adds Franz Jägerstätter to her list of saints because he offered his life for another. Morag considers the lay women of the Beguines, the desert mothers, and the spirituality of Brother Charles de Foucauld. She is particularly drawn to saints and others who spoke for the option for the poor, the equality of women, and interreligious understanding. Bishop Suzanne reads current literature as well as theologians such as Elizabeth Johnson and Joseph Martos. Dagmar expands her reading beyond seminary requirements when she lists Mary Daly and reading on the spirituality of the Yoruba women. She notes, "the gods don't have any gender" and she continues to pursue larger and more inclusive images of God in her prayer. Joanna recommends Richard Rohr and Thomas Berry as they include creation and ecology in their work. Paula shares new books with her husband every day and they read in depth while they drive to see grandchildren. Esperanza has discovered Celtic and Black spiritualities as she continues to appreciate her own Latina liberation spiritualities. Christine admitted that even though she respects St. Francis very much, she needs more infrastructure: "I need my books. I need space."

All the women mentioned special Scripture passages. Indeed, each chose passages for both their ordination to the diaconate and to the priesthood. Pat spoke about reading Scripture with such enjoyment it was like eating candy. She further explains, "I daily read the *Living with Christ*. I have to walk the talk." Teresa is inspired by the story of the bent over woman and how she was healed and able to stand erect. She also reflected on the story of the talents, and her own commitment to "not be the person who shows up with dirty hands and a thousand talents and says, 'All I did was bury it.'" She continues, "my fear was that if I didn't do something that would be me, I would not have done what I needed to do with the gift that was given to me by God. So it was time to get those talents working, to be an upright and erect woman!" Jane follows Jesus the Rabbi and connects to Jesus as teacher and spiritual leader. She, Joanna, and Jean relate to Mary of Magdala, the first Apostle, identifying with her courage and faith.

Kathy and Shanon both ponder the contributions of Hildegard of Bingen. Noting that Hildegard's antiphons and music are written in honor of wisdom, Shanon reflects on wisdom literature. For her, this literature is a source of the feminine image of God in the Scriptures. She reflects: "one of the passages in scripture which was sort of life changing for me is in Wisdom, where she talks about what the human race—the whole of salvation history even—is all in the feminine . . . So, Wisdom literature for sure has been very formative, as has been the Gospel of John . . . I love the garden imagery of the vines and branches." Celie picks a different book of Wisdom literature: "the scripture I have open now is the Song of Songs, which is always my favorite. In Advent especially, I suppose I've been cherishing it. Advent is my favorite liturgical season. I like that there's something invigorating about waiting. That's what my bible is open to at the moment."

Juanita prays the Road to Emmaus passage from the Gospel of Luke. "I try to bring the women in. And I try to show them that the woman is the wife of Cleopas. Every time I teach scripture, if I can squeeze a woman in there somehow, because even there it is so obvious. Mary, the mother of Jesus, at the foot of the Cross and Mary the wife of Clopas at the foot of the Cross.[10] There are so many beautiful Scriptures: 'I am the bread, I am the way. Come to me all who are hungry . . . Unless you eat my body and drink my blood you shall not have life within you.' There are so many." She continues, "I love the Old Testament and Jesus fulfilled so many passages in the Old Testament . . . I'm working on Sunday's gospel right now—the Good Shepherd. It's hard for us to think of shepherds, because we don't have any sheep around here." She then speaks of her travel to Tibet and Jerusalem, and the images and understanding that those experiences offered her in her preaching and prayer.

Kathleen admits to using commentaries to see how others under-stand scripture passages. She then speaks about how her prayer takes her to new understandings. She used her work on Pentecost to clarify that while many speak about the power of tongues, she was emphasizing that year the power of listening to understand. Similarly, Marina Theresa often finds alternative texts for her own prayer and for her work with marginalized peoples. For instance, she explored the Hagar texts as those concerning a Black woman. She thinks of Hagar as beautiful and healthy and nice. She identifies with the implied objectification that results from people in power (Abraham and Sarah) using another (Hagar) as property. She further reflects that Hagar "had no connection to the Hebrew religion, and nothing to do with Christians . . . God speaks to her. God gives her an announcement. This is very, very important for me because I see that God is not only for men, God is God for all persons." She moves from her understanding of Hagar to her work with the book of Exodus. She notes the power the women have in the text. She lists several women that sustain her work: Shiprah and Puah, Deborah, Ruth, Judith, Naomi, the woman who bled. And she speaks of her own prayer with her reading: "I say, I pray, I cry, and 'Yes, I accept.'" She admits "I do not have the same courage as the women in the Scripture, but I decide to say yes and I am here."

Donnieau reads Scripture and studies it as well. Like many liberation theologians, she looks at the human condition before she reads. She sometimes ponders what is going on in the world and observes the social reality: "I try to become reflective as much as I can, not only in morning Scripture but any Scriptures that I read to create a homily. There's something about living it . . . and trying to understand how it applies to us today. I've always been very fortunate to speak to the lived experience of how the Scripture was striking for me or what I've noticed for how it could be striking for others." Judy confesses: "I have one hundred bibles in English and Spanish. I try to understand Aramaic, in order to understand where Jesus comes in terms of his culture . . . I try to get at all the meanings. I read the Scriptures and I try to read different versions in Spanish and in English because I understand something different in Spanish than in English . . . Reading the Scriptures and praying by my little body of water feed me. That's my spirituality." Vikki notes how people are transformed through their interaction with Jesus, and also how the Samaritan woman and the Syro-Phoenician woman challenged and expanded Jesus's ministry.

As Vatican II people, these women accepted the challenge of *Dei Verbum*, the document that opened Scriptures to contemporary scholarship and exploration. That text relates the study of Scripture to living a life in Christ. Reflecting on "the obedience of faith" as one's response to God (Rom 16:26), the passage continues: "by faith one freely commits oneself entirely to God, making the full submission of intellect and will to God who reveals, and willingly assenting to the revelation given by God."[11] As demonstrated above, the womenpriests readily name Scripture stories and practices of exegesis and prayer that form their lives to God. Moreover, their rituals of ordination, Mass texts, and prayer celebrations witness to the depth and breadth of their reliance on Scripture.

Womenpriests' liturgies of ordination and prayer, as found in the archives at Marquette University, reveal over fifty-five images for God. Like the Israelites, they sought to expand images rather than limit them. Knowing deeply the passage of Exodus 3:13–14, when Moses asks for and receives God's name, these women recover biblical images for the divine such as an eagle, the woman who searches for coins, the hen, the mother who protects her children, Spirit, and many feminine evocations of the divine including Ruah and Sophia. They include Jesus and the Father but refuse to limit imagination to literalize specific names as though they are God. We obtained lists of Scripture passages they used in special liturgies and found passages from almost every book of the Bible. At the same time, their weekly liturgies follow the liturgical cycles of the Roman Catholic Church. It's true they translated many passages in more inclusive language, yet their prayer lives remain steeped in the tradition which they claim and in which they have ministered for most of their lives.

Embodied Rituals

Rooted in traditional practices, the womenpriests expanded their spiritual practices. As the *Sacrosanctum Concilium* invited, the women grounded themselves first in the sacraments and, as we have seen, in daily prayer as well. Further, they found God in many places. They described practices that revealed "there is scarcely any proper use of material things which cannot thus be directed toward people's sanctification and the praise of God."[12] This section, then, explores the womenpriests' prayer practices in creation, art and music, and social justice.

Creation

Vikki and Judy speak of their homes being close to places of nature that draw them to prayer. Vikki says, "We have beautiful foliage and lots of birds. I go and sit and be." Judy thanks God for allowing her to live in a place that faces onto a lake: "So I meditate outside. I go out and feed the ducks and turtles and cat. I also just stand there and say 'Thank you God.'" Joanna affirms these experiences as she describes nature as "God's cathedral." She experiences "the theology of oneness, that we're all part of a greater" way of being in the world.

Teresa takes her spirituality in nature to a different level. She's served groups as a guide on rivers in the Northwest. She reflects, "With a partial bloodline of being Native American, sometimes I find the silence and then putting my hands in soil, being deeply rooted in the soil or the river has been a tremendous mentor and friend over years and years." She described that process as an immersion in the creation. Kathleen has also put her hands in soil to grow gardens that have fed her family and others for many years. She works with local farmers and makes food from scratch to serve those she feeds. She knows the satisfaction of "watching people at the tables who smell real flowers" and who share organic fresh food. She describes gardening as "therapeutic" and the practice of gardening combined with feeding others a deep spiritual practice. Marina Theresa prays a prayer of unity in the style of St. Francis of Assisi. She ponders: "I think we should get rid of the dualism and promote the respect for the environment and for the healing for our bodies within. We need to promote initiatives in the community that go with unity in nature, because when we care for nature we care for ourselves." Indeed, she concludes, "We are one with the universe, we are in communion with the earth."

Art and Music

Chava declared "I've discovered I need to play! Covid is hard and I'm buying Legos and keeping them to build and create things. Creativity is essential."

Kathleen's group includes dances and sacred music, and she marveled at the sounds a woman made with "all her twenty-five different singing bowls and gongs!" Like Jane and Myra, Diane exclaimed "I love to sing! It's part of my spirituality." Jane and Judy fell in love with chanting, vestments, color, and movement in liturgy. Jane appreciated the symbolism and the opportunity to move from her logical left-brain self to a more right-brain, symbolic appreciation of the holy. Maria also appreciates the symbolism and beauty of fabric, especially in the stole. Like these women, Victoria states that music and yoga allow her to go into more depth. Now her work as a playwright and performer informs her spiritual life. As an artist, she uses "the imagination that moves her forward." It is her imagination that she "keeps listening to." Indeed, she says, "the arts in general are avenues for me to experience Spirit and to understand how God is working in and through us." Dana names her "early background as a visual artist as a pathway to the deepening of my relationship with God."[13]

Kathy translates her spirituality into quilts. She links her material art to her priesthood. "When I'm working on a sermon, if I have a quilt I can get onto the machine and kind of get into a zen and then I can write more sermon. I spend a lot of time on my sermons." She demonstrated some examples hanging on the walls in her home. "I'll do Pentecost and here's my flame. That's a very spiritual thing for me." She further describes, "It can be very mind cleansing, it's almost a meditation, a Zen."

Vikki also explores her spirituality through visual art. She meditates as she paints. "I'm kind of ADHD so a more active kind of prayer is my way. I pray throughout the day." She further expands "I want to paint endangered species. I've done forty-four of them so far . . . I pray for the earth and for the species. Not just the animals but moss, trees, everything." When she's really upset, she confesses she writes poetry.

Prayer through Social Justice

Kathleen brings her centering prayer to fruition in her work for justice. Catherine of Siena wrote that her call to service came when she heard Christ tell her to "walk on two feet": love of him and of neighbor. Like Catherine of Siena, Kathleen centers herself in a special prayer chapel built on property she owns and uses for her ministry. She describes how "on Fridays, people are coming and going into the tiny house for prayer." She notes that they have used Thomas Keating's centering prayer and Ilia Delio. She also reveals that nine women who work in Catholic worker style with her start once a week in a more monastic style. They include an hour of sacred sounds, dances for universal peace, and work in the large garden that feeds the hungry in their neighborhood. These women then go to Los Angeles once a month to clean the feet of those living on the streets. Kathleen declares that the moments with the people on the streets are the holiest moments in her days. Similarly, Judy speaks of her deep connection to those who suffer from lack of housing and economic resources. She celebrates the times she assists and interacts with people in the name of God's love for them. Jen, Olga, Marina Teresa, Donnieau, Victoria, Vikki, and Esperanza each name working with those who are relegated to the margins in societal structures. Their work with marginalized peoples constitutes a significant part of their spiritualities. Morag stated that her ordination is an act of poverty, a stance of accompaniment in the vein of St. Francis and St. Charles de Foucauld.

Spiritual Discernment

All these women knew early in their lives that God called them to a relationship that would challenge them to roles of leadership, evangelization, and sacramental celebration. As other chapters delineated, each confronted the reality that what they thought God called them to do was forbidden to them by the canon law of the Church. From 1976 through 1996 several authoritative ecclesial documents reiterated the ban on women's ordination.[14] Therefore, as chapter four identified, the women sought to serve in multiple other Church-approved ways.

The final statement issued under Pope John Paul II's signature but clearly written by then Cardinal Ratzinger (now deceased Pope Emeritus Benedict XVI), attempted to close discussion of the topic under pain of sin and potential excommunication.[15] From 1996 through 2000 these documents and warnings successfully quieted discussion among theologians and others. The emergence of the pedophilia scandal in 2000 combined with priest shortages in the US and Canadian churches, and multiple other significant events propelled the church into a new reality. In that milieu, three bishops agreed to ordain women on the Danube River. As noted, seven were ordained, and quickly after that, two were consecrated as bishops.

As researchers we were curious about the decision-making processes that guided these women. As scholars deeply immersed in Jesuit traditions, we asked about their processes of spiritual discernment. We anticipated that they would agonize over the decision to suffer excommunication from a religious tradition they had served for most of their lives. We learned that they actually celebrated with joy as they found ways to answer a call they found impossible until they moved toward the choice of ordination. Discernment involves prayer, a willingness to respond to God, a desire to know God's will, and a love for God's people.

Many of the womenpriests were previously vowed religious women. Helen says, "I learned a lot about discernment when I was in community. Discernment was a way of life for us." She reflected on her current situation and admitted that with the death of her husband and her retirement from paid ministry, she again was discerning next steps in life. "So, I really went through discernment" to move. Like Helen, Paula was required to have a spiritual director so she could discern her next steps as a vowed religious woman. Her director at the time said, "I think you need to pray about it" and Paula entered a retreat opportunity. Since then, she left the community and married her husband. He is now the most important counselor she consults. Together they visit a vowed religious in a nursing home who claims the couple are her spiritual directors. They take this seriously and assist each other in living lives in Christ.

Donnieau states the process of discernment in concrete terms. She says, "There has always been this stirring inside of me that I can never quite describe. I like to say that is part of the discernment. I really do believe that it is something that I have always had as part of my life. Since I was able to recognize that I am a living human breathing individual with thoughts and wants. It just so happens that my desire is to understand this divine, this divinity." Christine describes her turn to discernment in cases of "inner or outside conflict." She tries to "slow down everything. Go, stop a moment, and then speak slowly. Go slowly. Wait with acting and then act in a secure way." She admits that at times she acts on the wrong decision, and then she relooks at the decision to see if a new way emerges. She says, "My experience was, when the problems were too big, we went forward until the door closed, and then the doors opened and it was like cutting butter." As a Benedictine she attended to prayer and silence and patience in waiting for an answer or a path for action. She searched for possibilities that "made the situation a little bit better . . . my best solution is to find common ground everybody can live with."

Christine wanted to ensure no one was hurt in major decisions, and Joanna spoke about discernment as a process of overcoming fear with love. Like Christine, Joanna asks "How is this affecting the greater whole?" Jean adds that trust in God is essential to discernment. For her, trust overcomes fear. She states, "fear is paralyzing" and it "gets you nowhere." She spoke about moments of fear in her life—choosing to have another child after losing two; choosing to go to theological school as a divorced single mother; choosing to work with AIDS patients when the stigma was at its highest. Ultimately, she said discernment is "trust in the Spirit moving. If you are listening and paying attention to the Spirit then anything can happen."

The chapters on call and journey demonstrated how these women experienced God and desired to know God's will for them. The previous section of this chapter illuminated their commitment to constant prayer as a way of knowing God's will for them. These womenpriests relied on multiple methods of discernment: Community, Spiritual Directors, Dreams, and signs. The next sections explore the impact of these discernment processes.

Community

Not one of these women chose ministry as a singular endeavor. Each found a way to the priesthood through various paths of service and in consultation with broad groups of people. One of the tenets of spiritual life includes attention to community. While the documents of Vatican II supported personal conversion and journey with God in Christ through the Spirit, some Christians could assume that meant a personal journey with just "me and Jesus." As Lazar noted, Gustavo Gutierrez criticized this singular focus, insisting that "spirituality is a community enterprise. It is a passage of a people through solitude and dangers of the desert as it carves out its own way in the following of Jesus Christ."[16] Karl Rahner builds on this insight and notes that there is power in the community, *koinonia,* and he finds that specifically in Base Christian Communities.[17] Several participated in vowed religious communities, others in lay ecclesial ministries, and some in professional organizations. In each case, the communities around them impacted their decisions to pursue ordination.

Chava recalled, "People were randomly coming to me and saying 'Do you feel a call to priesthood? Because we see it in you.'" She wasn't there yet but was asked to preach in her parish. "There was a realization for me when I first put on a stole. We all put on stoles for our ministries in liturgy as a sign of our universal baptism. As I put it on, I had an inner certainty that kept growing. And people were saying to me 'Are you called to the priesthood?'" Myra chuckled as she remembered that no matter where she went people would tell her their life stories and ask her to pray for them. Christine affirmed the group process. "Groups give feedback and form the candidate," she said, "Because faith as service as a priest has something to do with a group." Maria received feedback from her community when she complained about the revised Roman missal. She said to the group, "You don't understand what is happening!" and they challenged her: "Well, why don't you show us." She partnered with another person and demonstrated how the sacramentary worked in prayer and liturgy. Then, the community had a decision to make. "I said, as a community we have a choice to say no to this. And they were afraid. But there were some who said: 'You know, the answer of course is that you become a priest.' And I said, 'You must be kidding!'" She chuckled as she remembered that she was seventy years old at the time. Yet, the community insisted: "You know we want you to become our priest." She gave in and she now serves them in a little church as they gather for Mass. She recalled, "the community made it very clear, and I understood what they said. I was reluctant and I made my reluctance clear. As a result, I didn't sleep for three months." When she finally said Yes, she "slept like a baby!"

Suzanne had a similar experience. She was working in a parish as a pastoral associate and nearing retirement. A speaker came to the area to meet with people about the ordination of women. A group of people wanted to go and invited her to go with them. She said she wasn't interested and would meet with them after the event. While they went to hear the speaker, Suzanne went about her business and said to herself and God that she would only ever consider ordination if the community called. Shortly after that prayer, they called and invited her to dinner. At dinner they asked her to get ordained so they could have a priest. She laughed at their invitation while admitting it was a sign in response to her prayer.

A community in New York called Victoria. Literally on the phone, they asked her to say Mass outside St. Patrick's cathedral on Fifth Avenue. "I stood beside an out gay priest in January 1988!" They concelebrated Mass there for several years. She speaks of the protests that subsequently occurred and of the ecclesial disobedience they conducted. She said, "Afterwards we would all lay down on the ground and be arrested. Of course, the cops knew about it ahead of time and they would take us to the judge in the paddy wagon. And the judge would say 'You did this, congratulations!'" She speaks of that work as her first ordination, the ordination of the people.

Helen also resisted the call to priesthood. While working in her parish community several heard about a speaker in a city close to them. They went together and heard about the Roman Catholic womenpriests movement. When they drove back to their homes, they stopped for a shared dinner. She affirmed that all baptized are copresiders and priests, and that the community she shared with them was collaborative. Yet, she admitted that some would say "Helen you are my priest." It was at their shared dinner that the group urged her to pursue priesthood for them. They wanted her to lead their community. Even in her retirement, the new community saw her spirituality and called her forth. "I have led the liturgy," she admitted.

Jean first served the most marginalized community in the 1980s and '90s: those suffering with AIDS. Her work she said, "created a kind of kindred bond. I still get texts and emails from some of the guys." She reflects further, "all through my hospice ministry, it was confusing for many patients. They would ask 'Why do you have to call the priest? You're coming!'" Similarly, Marina Theresa admits "I took this position because the community told me, yes, we approve you are a priest. They said you are a priest, you will be a priest, you will celebrate with us, no other church." When she was in Colombia at a gathering of almost a hundred people led by now bishop Olga, the people were asked if Marina Theresa should become a priest. She recalled that every person except one shouted yes, she should be a priest. Vikki described a similar experience in which all in the group she consulted urged and affirmed her movement to priesthood. Only one abstained and that was in fear of losing a volunteer for her justice program—something Vikki still sustains as a priest. An early bishop, Patricia claims that "we are called in the first place as a community: we are church, the people of God, we are a community called to follow Jesus in a church of communion. And as a church, we are all on our long walk to freedom."[18]

Spiritual Direction

While in preparation and formation, all future womenpriests sought spiritual direction. Moreover, most had consulted with spiritual directors for much of their lives. Spiritual directors, serve as community members who mirror God's work in peoples' lives back to them so they can make choices of continued progress in their spiritual journeys. In other words, these men and women accompany those who "want assistance and support as they discern the will of God"[19] in their lives. We were interested in their processes before the decision to become priests, since that seemed the most consequential decision in our study. Since all had consulted with these guides of God's activity in life, we chose just a few stories to highlight in this section.

Christine said, "I asked every single member to have a spiritual director from outside. I did this for myself too, with the following condition: the person had to be older than me, to have a little more life experience." She specifically looked for a priest—a male priest—since he would have travelled the path she set out for herself. She stated, "He always brought me forward. He asked me only questions. He never gave directions. He was very, very careful." She mentioned that she wanted for herself and others the accountability that comes with priesthood. Chava met a man from El Salvador at a Catholic Worker gathering in Las Vegas. She calls him her partner in ministry. Diane actually became a spiritual director through a charismatic community in Pecos, New Mexico. She had always valued the practice and wanted to be a better guide as a lay ecclesial minister before the opportunity to become ordained presented itself. Indeed, she had a feeling of call to priesthood while she was an undergraduate student. Even then she consulted a spiritual director. She recalled, "I was talking about it in spiritual direction. I had no idea what it meant, because anytime I asked 'Well what do I do about the Church?' The answer was, 'I don't know, just stay on the road you are on.'" She served as a lay ecclesial minister for over thirty-five years before being ordained.

Dagmar worked with a Franciscan sister for over twenty years. She says, "I was committed to a spiritual path, but I wasn't really interested in being part of the hierarchy." Helen and Paula both worked with spiritual directors while they were vowed religious women. Both left their communities with the help of their spiritual directors. Kathy said her spiritual director of seven years helped her see nature more and that led to taking more time in contemplation. Pat talked about Anglican priests serving as mentors while she did fieldwork for her theology degree. She was encouraged by feedback and "loved it. I didn't want to leave." Vikki consulted with male priests, friends, and the superior of her vowed order. In speaking of her spiritual director, Donnieau summarized what most of the others testified about their spiritual directors. "[She] helped me become more still and really allow the presence of God into my life."

Dreams

The Christian Church recognizes two Josephs who depict how one determines God's call to action through dreams. Joseph, son of Jacob and Rachel, dreams about how to save Egypt from starvation during famine. He is noted for interpreting dreams and secures a position of authority due to his ability. This sets up the salvation of the Hebrews, the followers of God, Elohim, El Shaddai. The other Joseph dreams about accepting Mary even though she is pregnant. He then dreams how to save them from annihilation due to Herod's fear of a Messiah being born. The depth psychologist Carl Jung taught that dreams communicate the deepest desires, fears, and loves to people while they sleep. Many have taught how to interpret the dreams that seek to teach and inform. Indeed, "in the Judeo-Christian tradition dreams have been aptly referred to as the forgotten language of God."[20] Several womenpriests found their dreams taught them how to move forward.

Sleeping in an overflow homeless men's shelter, Kathleen experienced a major dream. She described:

> *I was sleeping on the church floor with all of these homeless people and just going "Okay, God, you've got to give me some guidance*

here. I don't know what to do." And in my dream, I was in the church, in the back of the church trying to get all my RCIA kids—we always sat together because we did Dismissal . . . and I couldn't find my kids, and I walk into the church to see if they're there. The church is all packed and the priest is on the altar, and I looked at all their faces, and the faces were gone. They were just white ovals. And it was dead. They were all just sitting there with a white oval face. And I'm walking around the church and . . . it's like I couldn't find anything. And there's a woman in the back, and she's wearing priest robes. And she's waving at me to come. She's waving at me to come! So I go. I go to her and she ushers me into this room, and I turned into a deacon, and she was the priest, and this room was a huge baptismal font. It must've been like twelve feet by twelve feet deep and all around on the perimeter of the baptismal font were children waiting for me to initiate them and baptize them.

While this dream and others eventually led her to her ordination as a womanpriest, she commented that she "sits with things. I hold them in my lap. I ask for dream-answers." She acknowledged that it sometimes takes her years to discern the next step.

Jane recalled a dream she had of "someday founding a parish of driven-away Catholics like my husband, fallen-away Catholics like my children, and married and remarried Catholics who didn't have an annulment. Catholics like so many of my colleagues at work, LGBTQ Catholics like many of my friends, and for people who like myself can no longer worship in a canonical Catholic church with integrity. My dream was to someday have a parish like that." Maria's dreams disturbed her sleep. She was reluctant and made her reluctance clear to all. Then, as we've seen, she didn't sleep for about three months. She continued, "but I had dreams and all kinds of things. So, I finally said to the Spirit: 'OK, I'll do it.' And I slept like a baby after that!"

Signs

When God called prophets, God often gave them a sign to use with the people. Sarah received the promise that she would be mother of a great nation whose people would outnumber the stars. When she was in her nineties, she hadn't had a single child. Upon offering three messengers hospitality, she received a sign that she was pregnant. She laughed at the sign until she gave birth to the reality. Mary was given a sign that God could indeed create her pregnancy when Gabriel told Mary her older cousin Elizabeth was also pregnant. Mary went to her cousin to confirm the sign and received *another* sign—the babe in Elizabeth's womb leapt for joy as it recognized Emmanuel in Mary's womb. Similarly, Zechariah was struck dumb for all to witness while Elizabeth carried John to birth. Until Zechariah named the child John he was not able to speak. The sign of the right name and new belief was proclaimed in a beautiful hymn we attribute to him thanks to Luke's gospel (Luke 1:67–79). Stars, angels, pillars of fire, thunder, clouds, the ark of the Covenant, and Moses's face shining after an encounter with God all constitute signs of God's presence in human reality. Womenpriests are steeped in the Scripture stories and named their own signs as they discerned what to follow in accordance with their understanding of God's will.

Dagmar confessed that she really didn't want to be ordained at the time. An Austrian immigrant to the United States, wife of a past Ohio governor, a mother and grandmother, she sought a more contemplative lifestyle. She had completed her master's degree at the nearby United Methodist seminary. Despite the promise of an immediate position as pastor in a struggling congregation, she turned down offers to be ordained in the Methodist ecclesial community. She kept communicating with friends in Germany and Austria and admits she was surprised when Christine called her and asked her if she wanted to be ordained a priest. She really didn't, but she had studied theology and they wanted someone from the United States. So, she packed her bags and went to Austria. When she arrived, she discovered that the airlines had lost her bags. She "called Christine and said 'Look, I'm here, but everything that you wanted me to bring is not.'" Dagmar was hoping that the lost bags were a sign for her to not participate. Christine shrugged it off and made an appointment for Dagmar to meet the male bishop who had agreed to ordain the first womenpriests. This process was the last in the formal discernment of whether a person was of good fit for priesthood. Dagmar thought, "He will decide whether or not it's a good idea to get ordained. And the bag never came. And I spent time with the bishop and he wanted me to move ahead." With the bishop's approval, she acknowledged one more sign confirming her readiness for ordination. Still, Dagmar wasn't convinced. Then she said: "I discovered that the ordination was going to take place on the Danube. I was raised on the Danube. First communion, I even was married on the Danube. So, you know, it seemed like the right thing to do." All the signs aligned for her, in spite of roadblocks she tried to create.

Shanon, who would be ordained much later, also on the Danube, waited upon God for signs of next steps in responding to God's call. She wanted to wait until the Church approved ordination for women. She remembers hearing God say "No, no, no." She felt confused so she "got on a plane and went to Germany for two weeks to spend time with Hildegarde [in Bingen]. I cried. I felt like my whole world was coming to an end. I came back. When I got back, I felt it was time for me to apply for ordination." As she reflected on her path, she was able to recognize the elements that prepared her for ordination: her service as a lay ecclesial minister, her circuitous educational path, her ability to earn a doctorate in theology and in ministry, her work for her diocese, and her oversight of a retreat center.

Juanita told God "It's in your hands!" She pursued her theological credentials and was surprised when her previous work was accepted toward her final degree with Global Ministries. "It all fell into place," she recalled. Yet, she wondered why she would even think to make this change after her career in nursing and teaching at Kaiser and DeAnza. She thought to herself "This is crazy!" Still she applied, offered herself to God, and rejoiced when she heard back from Bishop Patricia "Yes! Apply." She then shrugged and said "everything opened up. When I let go and let God take over, everything just fell into place."

Maureen and Jean also relied on signs throughout their ministries. Jean remembered feeling vulnerable and uncertain as she finished her undergraduate degree in the middle of a divorce. She was the single mother of daughters and she read a memoir about an Episcopal woman who was ordained to the priesthood. She identified with the woman, saying to herself "This is like my story!" She recalled that she was assigned an advisor who turned out to be an Episcopalian going on to divinity school. She said "I just happened to meet my faculty advisor who just happened to have an MDiv from Union Theological Seminary. So, I said 'OK God! I guess I can talk about this now!

There is a place for me to explore this.'" She eventually applied to Weston Theological School and asked for major transcript and financial exceptions. She was turned down initially and said again—"God this is yours." A few days later, the dean called her offering the opportunity to study and scholarship assistance!

In a similar way, Maureen found herself entering an undergraduate program on the other coast. She encountered a Dominican vowed religious woman who taught a Scripture course as part of her undergraduate work. She was invited to continue her studies at the Graduate Theological Union. The first day of class in her graduate studies began with a Mass and she found herself in the chapel "looking at the Dominicans and all I saw were white robed men walking in. I literally paused and I remember saying to myself 'Really? Here? Here? You don't really want to do this.' Then she looked again at the course catalogue and said 'Yes! Yes!'" She switched to the Jesuit school where the Jesuits were "really great" to her and gave her a scholarship. She revealed that the signs to continue sustained her even as she felt pain upon graduation. She worked with her spiritual director who helped her acknowledge her call to priesthood and encouraged her to follow her call.

Donnieau also recounts stories of looking for and interpreting signs as one way to inform her decisions. She remembered her deep sadness when the parish priest turned her joy into despair as he said "You can't be a priest! You're a girl!" She recalled how even as she turned a vowed religious woman stood behind her and affirmed her, saying "You can be anything God calls you to be." Thus, from the time she was seven or eight she listened to both kinds of voices. She heard of the Catholic Womenpriests later in her life and she recalled "I felt like my whole internal insides were on fire, but it wasn't a fire of agony, it was a fire of extreme ecstasy. I felt like literally I was on fire but in a good kind of ecstasy type way." She was with a vowed religious who was celebrating her fiftieth Jubilee and living in senior housing. This woman who was her spiritual director encouraged her to choose the path God revealed to her. She recounted, "These women really helped me to make these dynamic shifts. From Sister Attracta, my beloved sister . . . to my spiritual director."

Esperanza admitted she received signs throughout "my whole life." She was approached by Episcopalians and said "No it's not possible, I don't want to be an Episcopal priest. I don't want to be a minister in another denomination. If God really wants this to happen, God will find a way, and I will just wait." Later she discovered the RCWP organization and heard about the bishops who ordained the first seven on the Danube River. "I said I would only do this if there is apostolic succession, and then RCWP showed up. And I thought 'OH MY GOD!'" She reflected on this practice of recognizing God's activity in signs. "It's hard to describe. It's being aware of what is around me. Trying to have a sense that it's not just my five senses, it's not just myself, my eyes, not just my hearing, not just that. But in using my five senses, opening so that something else comes through—whether I want it or not. Testing it, to see if there is some type of a peace after I follow what I sense. Peace doesn't mean that everything is wonderful like a trip to Disneyland, no, no. Sometimes, what has to be done is asking 'You're kidding! Right God? You're kidding me.'" But the peace is 'All right, I have to do this, otherwise I will be waking up at two o'clock in the morning thinking about this over and over again.' And to me this is the Spirit." As Esperanza spoke she laughed a little and thought about how much suffering comes from trying to listen to God in the midst of the mixed messages she received as a woman called to priesthood. She called God cruel, saying "God, I don't know why you created me, a woman, and put this in me. That's very cruel! But fine! Yes, I'll do it!'" She noted "I've slept perfectly well ever since I made that decision." She amplified this with an example "I can understand the prophet being called, waking up and saying 'Here I am.'" And someone saying God's not calling you. But someone is calling me! I can understand, 'I'm going to avoid this, I'm going to avoid this.' And then God saying 'I'm going to send a whale until you pay attention to me.' I can understand all of that. I can also understand 'Why me?' God sends the least likely person. God sends who God sends. And you go and do it and it's done."

Summary

This chapter on Roman Catholic womenpriests' spiritual practices demonstrates their deep commitment to walking with God in the Spirit. From early in their lives, each woman chose to follow a God of love and possibility. They have prayed, acted for justice, and discerned in love with patience and gentleness, caring for one another and for the people of God. As Vatican II people they strove to live the documents, particularly those major constitutions that impacted a change in understanding that all baptized are called to holiness through liturgy, reading the signs of the times, and understanding the word of God. The next chapter examines how their commitment, fueled by their call, journey and prayer, leads them in action with and for the people of God, including some of their surprising contributions to the Church.

❧ 6 ❧

PRIESTLY LEADERSHIP[1]

"You are a chosen race, a royal priesthood, a holy nation, a people of God's own, so that you may announce the praises of the one who called you out of darkness into God's wonderful light."

—1 Peter 2:9

WE REVIEWED THE answers the womenpriests offered in response to our questions about their priestly ministries, their understanding of priesthood, and their relationship with the hierarchical church. Our next step was to organize their reflections into categories that mirror those of other ordained ministers throughout the Christian community. It is important to note that ecumenical and Catholic documents name four leadership ministries: *kerygma* (proclaiming the word of the gospel), *koinonia* (gathering people into communities of care), *diakonia* (offering their communities and others service), and *leiturgia* (celebrating and remembering the presence of God in their midst).[2] Some contemporary documents also list *martyria* and teaching. At this point in time, the womenpriests we interviewed are not dying for their faith (*martyria*), although their journeys have charted great pain and suffering. For practical purposes, we have followed the current practice of linking teaching to kerygma.

While these four leadership functions describe much of what the womenpriests revealed, they do not adequately frame the totality of the womenpriests' insights. As we pondered how to frame the additional information they revealed, we organized their comments according to three other major aspects of forming and sustaining ecclesial communities: enlarge the space of our tents, embody communion (Eucharist), and collaborative leadership (open oneself to mission). Thus, this chapter is divided into two major sections: the four basic Christian marks of leadership and three additional ecclesial leadership practices. Each of these two major sections is supported by subsections.

The Four Basic Christian Marks of Leadership

Kerygma: A Stole with a Fiery Motive[3]

Ten women named teaching as their main joy and gift in the leadership that accompanies ordination. Since Peter's first proclamation after Pentecost, people who are ordained claim preaching and teaching the word of God as central to their call. Pat says simply, "My priestly ministry is to first and foremost keep the story of Jesus alive theologically." Teresa speaks about how people hear the word of God anew as others proclaim the readings from sacred Scriptures. Thus, she invites many in her community to proclaim the word. Diane, Pat, Jean, and others speak about preparing conversation starters and questions to spark shared homilies. They claim their communities enjoy the opportunity to share insights with each other.

Naming teaching as her primary gift, Jane created a new inclusive language translation for all three cycles of the Catholic lectionary.[4] Diane also claimed teaching as a primary gift. Having spent over thirty years in parish ministry as a director of religious and adult education with responsibility for sacramental preparation, Diane participated in a local TedX conference in Olympia.[5]

Many of these women are highly educated and several have earned doctoral degrees. Shanon, like Diane, emerged from years of religious education experience both at the parish and at the diocesan level. She uses her PhD and DMin degrees to ground her writing and her preaching. She conducts pilgrimages to Hildegard of Bingen's original abbey in Germany. With a PhD in counseling, Donnieau teaches her community to share power and insight. She speaks eloquently about her work in helping members understand their baptismal call as taught through the documents of Vatican II.

Others share the word through art, music, and drama. A university professor, Victoria started with street theatre and communal Mass celebrations outside St. Patrick's Cathedral in New York. She now works on bringing people in Scripture to life through drama, presenting reflections on Mary, Martha, and others to faith communities throughout the West coast. Similarly, Kathy creates quilted art to highlight aspects of liturgical feasts such as Pentecost, or to depict specific women saints as guides for her community. The proclamation of the Word remains core to the function of the priestly vocation for each of these womenpriests.

Koinonia: All Are Welcome

During our study we observed several liturgical celebrations conducted by womenpriests. Attendance at these services ranged from twenty-five to over one hundred and fifty participants. The priests and people welcomed everyone. Throughout the celebration of Eucharist, they invited the whole community to read the prayers together. The whole community blessed the bread and wine. All were invited to the table as evidenced in one liturgy of ordination during which the priest said: "We have all been blessed and called to this table which is the altar of Jesus Christ. All are welcome to approach this table to receive communion."[6]

During lunch with congregants in California, one woman stated, "We are the church for those dispossessed by others." Another at the table agreed and indicated that their community welcomed divorced and remarried Catholics, people of all faiths or even no faiths, LGBTQIA+ persons, and folks of every economic status. As we shared lunch provided by the hands of those gathered around the table, we recalled the stories of Jesus at table with the marginalized and dispossessed of his time.

Jesus, the Spirit, Ruach, Creator, Love, Mother/Father God—all are names invoked in addressing God.[7] The womenpriests believe, as Paul instructed in 1 Corinthians 12, that each of them contributes gifts given for the upbuilding of the community. For example, Teresa noted that her main leadership style was that of facilitating gifts. As pastor she paid attention to the people, learned who they were, encouraged them to claim the power of their baptism and their distinctive gifts, and facilitated their contribution in the communal reign of God to which each has been gifted for the edification of the entire Body (1 Cor 12:7).

Unlike those surveyed in a recent study by the Barna Group, in which 56 percent of practicing Christians believe that their calling is a solo journey, we found that RCWP communities claim close communal connection.[8] Those we visited testified to their desire to come together to celebrate and support each other along their journey of faith. While the womenpriests and their communities easily identified obstacles and sufferings that got in their way, they also readily named allies and communities that supported them. Even the journey to ordination involved communal sharing directed by spiritual directors and companions. The evidence suggests that theirs is a thoroughly relational spiritual path.

Like most Protestant pastors, womenpriests typically serve small congregations. Sociologist of religion Mark Chaves discovered that while 75 percent of all Protestant congregations consist of seventy-five people or less, these congregations dedicate themselves to fostering rich and vibrant communities.[9] Given the small communities that most womenpriests serve, Teresa summarized the RCWP commitment to developing koinonia: "I do believe that the ministerial priesthood allows for that focus to form community to happen. I think that's part of what I do: my presence in the community really does form community."

Diakonia: The Basin and the Towel

The Roman Catholic womenpriests have emerged from a long tradition of service through various ministries in the Church. It should be no surprise, then, that most of them see themselves as servant leaders who offer personal outreach and justice leadership. Akin to the early church's decision to call women to the diaconate,[10] the RCWP name diaconal ministries as core to their priesthood: visiting the sick, listening to people and their pain, spiritual counseling, reconciliation, attending demonstrations for justice issues, and championing those who are otherwise ignored.

As priests, the women we interviewed continued their outreach and advocacy after ordination. For example, when Victoria moved to California, she continued her work in parks ministering to those who would otherwise not be welcome in the church buildings. Like her, sociology professor Judy and her partner Judy began ministering to the homeless by housing them and helping them secure a more predictable future. When they moved their ordained ministries from the Northeast to Florida, they housed people and established a feeding program. In addition, they made multiple trips to Columbia to share their experience. Olga and Marina Theresa worked tirelessly to serve the poorest in Colombia, including people of African descent. Now ordained, Marina Theresa works specifically with people of African and Latin American descent in Florida, while Olga serves as a bishop and currently oversees multiple priests and those in priestly formation.[11]

Other priests have lived in Catholic worker communities and carried lessons of shared responsibility into their priesthoods. Kathleen focused on food sustainability and grew food, taught others to do the same, and her congregation now manages a garden and feeds people every month of the year. She exclaimed that nothing brings her closer to God than working with those who are homeless![12] Monthly, she and others in their community take their towels and basins to the Los Angeles area to minister to folks while caring for their feet. Vikki[13] continues to work in a Catholic Worker house and to share housing with those who are needing some assistance. Their housing and work with the poor in their neighborhood support the work of the congregation she leads and centers their spirituality.

One womanpriest works specifically with undocumented Latinx migrant workers. Her parish worships, proclaims the gospel, feeds, and houses several people throughout the year. She also lobbies for immigration reform. Naturally, her name remains hidden to protect the people she serves. Another, Jen, was reared in a family that valued the union movement and pacifism. She remembers, "I learned Catholic social teaching and helping somebody out. If somebody doesn't have a place to stay, letting them sleep on the couch. It meant, you know, you were being church to that person."

Many womenpriests have been nurses and public health professionals in their prior lives. They continue to reach out to those who are shut in, suffering or ill as part of their priestly ministry. Morag recited the list of people she regularly contacts by telephone and explained their isolation during the Covid-19 pandemic. She knows from her years of experience as a public health nurse that these people suffer emotionally and psychologically as well as spiritually. Thus, she ensures connection through her telephone calls and by bringing Eucharist. Juanita consecrates multiple hosts in her house church and takes them to people who are homebound.

Joanna simply states, "I'm here for them. If someone is ill, I'll call them. I'll go visit." She also joins protests when the community wants to support others for the common good. Marina Theresa agrees, "We visit people. I visit Hispanic people. I celebrate Mass and pray for the sick." Paula notes that she has done several anointings. She further confides that when she visits in the hospital, several people have "felt disconnected from the church and have held guilt. I have been able to help them see that God is so much bigger than what they learned about. And that God is so loving and loves them so dearly and wants them to know that." Jeanette uses similar words to describe how she is there for the people in her community. She states, "somebody winds up in the hospital, you make food, you make sure you visit, you know, you do all this stuff . . . It's really important . . . you need to be there."

In the same vein, Esperanza states she is available for someone to call her and let her know what has been happening in their lives. She starts by listening. She describes her frame of mind: "I am talking to them about what God is here for and to help them see [what is possible] in the position they are in." Similarly, Judy simply says, "My happiest days are those when I can reach out to somebody that is broken, totally broken, and help them put themselves back together with God's help. And people would say, you do things nobody else could do, and I reply that it is easy, that God did it. God gave them this chance to become whole."

Leiturgia: Come and Rejoice

The sacramental life of the Roman Catholic Church constitutes a major source of spiritual care. Given the word proclaimed and community formed to reach out to the world, the members return to renew and refresh. As recorded in 1 Corinthians 12, the community gathers to tell the story and offer the meal through remembering Christ's actions as the last supper. Roman Catholic womenpriests embrace the sacramental and liturgical aspects of their ministries. Each of them spoke of their work in eucharistic celebrations, anointing of the sick and dying, reconciliation, and baptism. They officiate at weddings and burials. The *leiturgia* of the church is the work of the liturgy, the rituals that accompany all aspects of communal life.

Our observations of liturgies included ordinations and weekly Masses. We were struck by the predominance of women at the altar. Each liturgy followed the familiar Roman Catholic rite. Yet, each is creatively expressed in more inclusive ways.

Jean reflected that she listens carefully to what people say during the prayers of the faithful and the shared homily times. She follows up with individuals after the celebration because of her deep listening. Similarly, Kathleen notes who is there and who is missing, and she makes visits or calls during the week to ensure that people are well and cared for.

Jane reflected, "Much to my amazement it turns out I have some liturgical gifts . . . so I exercised liturgical leadership that I think was very important." She established a liturgical commission that eventually functioned without her input. She translated the rituals from the sacramentary so they would reflect inclusive language and multiple images of God. She worked with the song leaders to amend male-only wording so that music, action, and preaching all reflected a liturgical wholeness.

While some congregations led by Roman Catholic womenpriests celebrate weekly liturgies, others manage bimonthly or monthly liturgies. They all commit to using a reworked and more inclusive version of the Roman Catholic lectionary to guide their liturgical celebrations.[14] Kathleen describes her commitment to leading and participating in weekly eucharistic celebrations:

> *I think it's more like what Ron Rolheiser writes—it's—the eucharist and sacraments are God making love to us. Yeah. Jesus . . . I believe Jesus was already present and Christ was present in the wheat that was ground. And it's blessed even more by all of us together, gathered to become more of that, and—and by participating—but we're in that eucharistic prayer. It's also us that gets blessed and transformed. It's not the bread and the wine. It's the community gathered. And so you become more of what you eat. And it's also our lives broken and shared. If, you know, you go out to your field hospitals, like Francis calls it, and then you come back, you're kind of broken down, and you share each other and the eucharist as food, as strength for that journey, to go back out.*

Kathleen and Diane's community celebrate weekly Eucharist, prayer in a small chapel, and centering prayer at least once a month. They then go out to care for homeless peoples' feet and share food from their garden. As Kathleen observed, what they do during the liturgy is embodied in everyday life.

In Ohio, Shanon admits to being a pretty "traditional" ordained minister. She ensures that Hildegard Haus, the community of St. Hildegard, celebrates weekly Mass, liturgy of the hours, weekly Bible study, rosary, and vespers. She wears vestments, and other women and men take on roles of reading, preaching, and leading devotionals. Similarly, Juanita confides she is more liturgically centered. She created an altar in her house which focuses the house church to celebrate weekly Eucharist. The community shares prayer, reading, homily, and consecration. She maintains that the ordained priest has the gift of gathering and consecrating just as a doctor has the gift of healing. Likewise, Maureen speaks about the attention she pays to liturgical work because of her training at Jesuit School of Theology in Berkeley. Using her background in sacramental theology, she invites others to worship. She asserts that the priest's presence is essential in the liturgical celebration, but simultaneously maintains it is "the community at work in our liturgies." In Colombia, Olga, a bishop, notes that she is not in competition with the masculine clergy. Rather, "I am a presbyter serving the Church, announcing with joy the kingdom of God, eradicating sexism, marginalization, inequality, present sins that harm the church."

Forming and Sustaining Ecclesial Communities

Many Catholics embraced the teaching and vision found in the documents of Vatican II. After the close of the council Catholic communities and dioceses all over the world experienced liturgies in the vernacular, newly revised rituals, and expanded roles for lay leaders. Seminaries developed new curricula and Catholic universities offered master's programs in theology and ministry to lay people. The Latin American Church moved forward in a collaborative way, gathering bishops, priests, and lay leaders in synods. *Communidades des Bases* gathered lay people to reflect on Scripture, news events of the day, and life. Latin American bishops and theologians discovered a new way of contemplating Scripture and life through liberation theologies. This created a movement of discipleship that was mirrored in the continent of Africa synods and countries, Asian synods and countries, and the United States and Canada.

Since the documents of Vatican II had summoned lay believers to learn more about Christ, to embrace the work of the Spirit in their lives, and to conform their lives to the work of God in them, lay leaders around the world began to teach, preach, serve in various roles at the altar, and seek justice in the world and the church. The council introduced a notion of the Church as the pilgrim people of God. It sought to empower lay people as equal partners in the Gospel by recognizing baptism as the initiation to God's community of believers. The Church was identified as a group of learners on a journey to full life in God. Each baptized person became a disciple of the risen Lord in the spirit of God.

The womenpriests and their communities seem to be expanding the conversation currently invited by Pope Francis' synodal process. We clustered additional reflections from the womenpriests using terms emerging from the national synodal documents: enlarge the space of your tent, embody communion (Eucharist), and collaborative leadership (open oneself to mission).[15] The next sections articulate womenpriests' reflections on their own priesthood in light of these areas of the synod on synodality.

Enlarge the Space of Your Tent[16]

This phrase, citing Isaiah 54:2 "enlarge the stretch of your tent, stretch your tent curtains wide," emerged as a theme within the synod on synodality effort in the church. Our conversations and encounters with the womenpriests and their congregations documented their combined efforts to open their work to as many as possible. We saw and heard them speak of including a larger ecumenical group, people currently refused sacraments, and those who are defined as objectively disordered. This section reflects womenpriests' attempts to expand the tent in each of these areas.

As we observed our first ordination, we heard the womenpriests invite the community to pray the prayers of consecration together. While there were many womenpriests and several women bishops participating, they joined the laity and invited all to pray together. In addition, they invited everyone to receive the Eucharist, acknowledging that some were of other Christian traditions, of Jewish faith, or atheist. We were startled as we watched people receive. These womenpriests invited everyone to the table.

Since the ordination of women in mainline Protestant churches, Vatican officials worried that ecumenical dialogue would suffer. While some discussions at the highest levels may have stalled, the experience on the local levels seems to contradict hierarchical fears; at least that is the testimony of the RCWP, their congregants, and their hosts as we connected with them.

Theological education is a good example of the serendipitous ecumenicity of women's journey into priesthood. While Roman Catholic institutions of higher education offer advanced theology degrees, many are located in places that remain geographically or theologically inaccessible.[17] Thus, many women shared master of divinity education with Protestant counterparts. At some moment during their educational experience, most of the women were asked to shift their Christian allegiance from Roman Catholicism to another ecclesial community. Dagmar describes her experience in being invited to preach and then preside at a United Methodist congregation prior to her graduation. Morag admits that Episcopalians and United Church of Scotland faculty and colleagues invited her multiple times to join their institutions so she could serve as ordained minister. Indeed, one of our RCWP revealed that during a visit with her bishop prior to her ordination, he suggested she change ecclesial allegiance to prevent excommunication!

Like those identified through the writings of the early church, these womenpriests lead small congregations. By choice, they gather people who are looking for a place to find community, belief, and service. Unlike their ecumenical women peers, however, Roman Catholic women literally freed themselves to live outside the institution. With a few exceptions, they are not dependent on the smaller congregations to provide a living wage, retirement, and advancement opportunities. This freedom encourages them to explore options of language, God-image, and ministry that ecclesial institutions may discourage.

The ecumenical tent expansions include the pastors of many Protestant churches who have risked offending Roman Catholic archbishops by offering their facilities as places of ordinations and collaboration. The RCWP movement is dependent on these ecumenical relationships for worship space, community gathering space, joint efforts in relation to social justice issues, and even shared worship on various occasions. On some occasions, Protestant and Jewish women and men have risked retribution from the Roman Catholic community as they opened their doors to events that resulted in automatic excommunication for all the Catholic participants. As Elsie writes, "Archbishop Burke, famous for facing down prominent Catholics (i.e., John Kerry), was ill-prepared for resistance from a 'mere' Jewess and Board members who supported the idea of this socially active inclusive place of worship and welcome."[18]

Recalling the ecumenical communion she experienced through her long struggle, Teresa commented,

> *I continue a relationship with the local Catholic parishes, parish members and our local Inter-Religious communities. However, there are new relationships and possibilities that manifest themselves because RCWP priesthood and our communities cannot be contained (and not welcomed by those who hold authority and power over the Church) within the traditional and hierarchical institution. We want to be led by Christ and the Holy Spirit to form communities of inclusion and welcome that offer service and companionship to all we encounter.*

Similarly, Dagmar remembered a time when she hosted her weekly agape meal on Friday evenings. She had a variety of people participating. She recalls that during her first year after her ordination, she celebrated Mass around her table: "And this woman . . . who was Presbyterian . . . just burst into tears. And we kind of stopped and asked, 'What's happening?' And she said, 'Oh my God, I just experienced an encounter with Jesus!'" Dagmar continued, "There was all of us Catholics who had not had that profound an experience. And here was this Presbyterian woman who had never experienced this, and she experienced that reality of Jesus." She concludes her story asking, "How open do you keep the sacrament, the celebration, so that people experience whatever it is that God wants them to experience, as opposed to what you think they should experience." Morag agrees that the Mass and holy communion should be open to all Christian believers . . . The other Christian churches give communion to all who are Christian, I do this too."

Shanon broadens the expansion to include those baptized Catholics who feel unwelcome in their home parishes. She states: "We don't ask if people are baptized. Most of the people are Catholic, and those coming to the table are in second marriages or other circumstances where they wouldn't be able to receive communion in a traditional parish." The congregants we interviewed from two parishes in California revealed similar inclusion. They welcomed those hurting from a variety of exclusions from the sacraments: cultural and gender identities, pedophilia wounds, and remarried situations. Recall that Jane's dream in her discernment envisioned a community that welcomed all those who felt rejected by judgement in their former parishes. She saw people being loved and welcomed in her church of Mary Magdalene the Apostle.

Victoria began her ministry in the streets with the homeless, hungry, and outcast. She described Eucharist as "any moment people come together over food of some kind and share it. When we come together . . . this is intentional. Being part of the Jesus Jewish tradition, and Ramadan starting today with iftars, etc. There are many ways to understand Eucharist, for me it is intentionally understanding the goodness of God's gifts to the world. It's not about atonement. It certainly recalls the suffering we all go through. I don't lionize Jesus as the focus of the Eucharist." Jean concurs. She exclaims, "Everyone is welcomed, no one is excluded. When we do the breaking of the bread, we have little ones who come and do the breaking with us. This is not something that cannot be touched by everyone and anyone. I just go back to the Last Supper—you know, the inclusive one with the women. Can you imagine Jesus saying: 'No I'm sorry not you, just pass it on. Skip him!' It just doesn't fit!"

Jean further recalls how she was inspired by an article many years ago in the Maryknoll magazine. She described how she cut out a little piece and put it on her refrigerator for about twenty years. She said it read: "Lord make me your bread, and then break me up and pass me around." She has used that as her mantra even before she went to theological school, entered decades of lay ministry, and became ordained.

Jen contended with feeling excluded herself, as a woman and as a queer person. She asked, "What does it mean to be part of an institution that says the very being of a me as a queer person is not right? . . . and the oppression of women, I struggle with it." As a result, she opens her community to action and living out the Eucharist through "walking alongside the hotel workers who are fighting for their rights, or the poor, the truck drivers and the poor. I think we need to create the church in some other way." Paula concurs. She states, "If you come and pray with us, then you can eat with us. And that's what people do. Whether they are divorced or remarried and don't have an annulment . . . They are welcome to pray with us and come eat with us." Maureen asked:

> *where in the world is the bread not being broken? Not being shared? You know that's where you can look and say in the poor, in the injustices, in the wealth of the small percentage. The bread needs to be broken in and amongst all of our society until we recognize that the dignity in each human being. Do you know I was just reading a quote from Martin Luther King Jr: 'You know we're looking for people to be lovestruck not colorblind.' And I think that was a very profound statement that's really applicable in this world we live in right at the moment. That's a whole spiritual level that again the spirit of God is always trying to find ways to enter into the world again and again . . . Eucharist is always the encounter with the other.*

The womenpriests share an openness to expanding the tent as they include believers and interested people together. Their practices and postures follow Jesus's invitations to tax collectors, sinners, and women to eat together.

Their commitment to inclusion mirrors that of some bishops within the Roman Catholic hierarchy. Cardinal McElroy, for example, has written and spoken about inclusion of historically marginalized Catholics. He encourages the church to "embrace a eucharistic theology that effectively invites all the baptized [Catholics] to the table of the Lord, rather than a theology of eucharistic coherence that multiplies barriers to the grace and gift of the eucharist."[19] His invitation reflects Mark's gospel account of Jesus challenging the food and purity practices of the scribes and pharisees who accused Jesus's followers of ignoring the traditions of purity by not washing their hands before eating and drinking (Mark 7:1–3). Mark has Jesus say, "Nothing that enters one from outside can defile that person; but the things that come out from within are what defile (Mark 7:15)." Like

Cardinal McElroy, Pope Francis declared, "I have never denied communion to anyone."[20] He encouraged the bishops of the United States to reconsider their desire to deny Catholic politicians access to the Eucharist. At the same time, the regional and continental summaries of the synodal processes conducted from 2020 to 2023 clearly support expanding the tents in much the same way the womenpriests have done in their communities. The expansion of tents, as Pope Francis invites, challenges some traditions and exclusionary practices and attitudes.

Embody Communion

The Constitution on the Sacred Liturgy (*Sacrosanctum Concilium*) recognized that Christ is present in many ways: the elements of bread and wine, the priest who ministers the sacrament, the word of God as it is proclaimed, and the people themselves.[21] At the same time, the same document describes the Eucharist as "the divine sacrifice of the Eucharist."[22] Further, the document notes that daily Eucharist builds up the people of God, "making of them a holy temple of the Lord, a dwelling-place for God in the Spirit (see Eph 2:21–22)."[23] Then the document speaks of the will of God "that all be saved and come to knowledge of the truth."[24]

With the tent extended to such a large group ordinarily excluded from Roman Catholic Eucharist, we wondered what Eucharist meant to Roman Catholic womenpriests. After our first interview, we added a question about the meaning of Eucharist to our list of prepared questions. We returned to our first interviewee and asked her to answer the question as well. We sought to understand what womenpriests signified when they celebrated eucharist in an enlarged tent. This section looks at how the womenpriests described their beliefs. It includes notions of embodying or living communion with God.

Within the Roman Catholic church we were aware of many variations of belief in transubstantiation that impacted all in the Church. While some bishops denied Communion to Catholic politicians in their parish or diocese, other bishops argued that the Eucharist is not a weapon but an invitation to community. In 2019 Pew Research found that just one-third of US Catholics agreed with Church teaching that the Eucharist is the body and blood of Christ.[25] In 2021, as we were compiling our research, the US

Conference of Catholic Bishops approved a new document, *The Mystery of the Eucharist in the Life of the Church*,[26] to educate Catholics about this sacrament. Clearly, the teaching on Eucharist and liturgy is being clarified even as the womenpriests reflected.

Sacrosanctum Concilium proclaimed, "The liturgy is rightly seen as an exercise of the priestly office of Jesus Christ. In the liturgy the sanctification of women and men is given expression in symbols perceptible by the senses and is carried out in ways appropriate to each of them."[27] It also states that Christ is "present when the church prays and sings, for he has promised 'where two or three are gathered together in my name there am I in the midst of them' (Matt 18:20)."[28] In the next few sections, the document invites all baptized believers to participate and also warns that priests/celebrants must prepare the faithful for their responsibility in being ready to receive.[29] Womenpriests also use many symbols: table, meal, sacrifice, music, art, drama, bread and wine, and liturgical vestments.

Teresa answered first when she said: "We all celebrate Eucharist together and consecrate together. We all share in homilies and reflections. We all share if we do an anointing and in the anointing action or laying on of hands on an individual." Diane follows with "We are the body of Christ. We, the community, are the body of Christ. And in this ritual action that we do together, we help each other believe that Christ is present in all creation and that creation is what nurtures us. And this meal reminds us of Jesus . . . God present with us as we feed each other, as we eat together." She also admits: "I'm very careful about the consecrated bread and wine . . . This ritual action . . . is an invitation to come and eat, come and experience God's incarnation in creation, in this bread and wine, in our potluck meal, in each other." Shanon also attends to the ritual and sacredness of the elements as does Juanita. Christine furthers the understanding when she details: "Gather, remember, share bread and wine. This is the short formula I always use." Her pithy summary mirrors theologian John Shea's notion of "gather the folks, tell the story, break the bread."[30]

At the same time, the womenpriests reflect on the multiple ways Christ is present to the community and to the cosmos. Kathleen invited, "If you're hungry come and eat. For some people that's a conversion experience!" She further reflected, "the food is in the symbol of bread and wine, but we are

also the food. We are also Eucharist. We become what we eat . . . Jesus is
food for our journey. It's the cosmic stuff that Ilia talks about."[31] Maria agrees
with her. Her conversion and call story center on a priest setting out the
altar. She knew it was a table, asked for whom he prepared the food, and
recounts that he immediately said, "Oh child for everyone!" Having known
profound hunger as a child, she knows Eucharist now as "the power of love
in action . . . always food involved, always an invitation to whomever is
there, the poor and the hungry."

Donnieau agrees that Eucharist is about being fed: "You can be fed
by word, you can be fed by communion bread, you can be fed by your
morning meditation. That is our daily bread . . . I have expanded it. We are
fed when we are comforted. We are fed when there is a need and it is met."
For Donnieau it goes beyond the "sanitized altar." She experienced Eucharist
with "one of my kid runaways. When I used to work in social services and I
would just sit on the corner with them and I would just be in that moment
in the throes of their dilemma." She wants to expand the ways people think
and act about being fed, because for her, "Eucharist could be truly so much
more!" Christine confirms: "The sacrament has something to do with the
person and with God . . . you need a ritual to make the invisible visible for
others . . . So the priest does the ritual to make visible what God does."

Jane moves the discussion further when she reflects on the elements
themselves. Borrowing an image from her colleague, retired professor Gary
Macy, she recalls how each bottle of wine is unique: "It will never exist again."
She relies on people in the community to bake the bread and notes how it is
baked and shared in love. She tears up a bit when she describes how "we take
it into our physical bodies and we all metabolize it. And for a little while we
are chemically, biologically connected in a way we wouldn't be otherwise."
As a theologian and Scripture scholar, Jane addresses the issue of transubstantiation. "It's a Greek concept that goes with Greek philosophy . . . I
don't think Greek philosophy fits life in the modern world and I'm more
connected to process theology. Neither is wrong. It's just what fits in a particular time." In line with the Vatican II documents, she values the multiple
ritual actions of the liturgy: liturgy of the Word, the homily and teaching,
deepened spirituality that emerges from the shared word, music, liturgical
colors and robes, the eucharistic prayer, and circumambulation as people

move to receive, return to their places, and go into the world changed by the body of Christ. She believes the "consecration is about the faithfulness of the people coming together to engage, not just stand around and think the bread and wine are holy. They themselves participate in the consecration of the bread and wine under the leadership of someone who is trained."

Joanna expands the notion of transubstantiation in her practice. She asserts, "We take the power within ourselves as baptized people and we say we are honoring Jesus in his wishes and we are accepting it and we are becoming it, so we take it into ourselves when we ingest it . . . we transform it into the living body of Jesus the Christ, into who we are becoming or evolving." Maria confesses that "sometimes I am not able to speak for a while because of the incredible power and simplicity of what the gift that Jesus gave us . . . It is the food that we need to not only exist but to be." Jean exclaimed, "I always liked the doctrine of transubstantiation! I like the word! I like the feel of it! I think we are all changed. We are part of it. We are all changed when we sit around that table together and pray together. I feel my heart changing when I'm there. I notice there are parts of me that are broken and yearning to be healed."

Esperanza thinks the literal sense of the word transubstantiation doesn't do it justice. She looks to Mary for inspiration. She recalls a poem about Mary that "when she gives birth says, 'this is my body, this is my blood.'"[32] She reflects: "It's the offering of oneself. It is the gift of one's self. That very life. When I hear people say Jesus came to die for us, I think 'You got it wrong. Jesus didn't come to die for us, he came to live for us, to show us how to live.'" These womenpriests reflect theologies of Eucharist similar to "sixty-three percent of the most observant Catholics—those who attend Mass at least once a week— [who] accept the church's teaching about transubstantiation."[33]

Womenpriests make clear statements of belief on both ends of the continuum between sacrifice for those who are worthy and meal for all invited to participate. Dagmar speaks of taking "bread and wine and turning it into something more than bread and wine, whatever faith opens up to you." On the other hand, Juanita reflects that to be priest is to break bread. She acknowledges that she acts *in persona Christi* when she, not the community, consecrates the elements. She consulted with a Jesuit priest about her understanding. He said, "It's not just the words, it's the whole eucharistic prayer." As she pondered this more, she recognized that "Jesus sat down with the women and the men at the Passover meal. He took the bread and broke it and passed it around very casually and said, 'This is my body and this is my blood—share it with everybody.'" She reiterates after this reflection that while some womenpriests believe the community consecrates, it is not her belief.

Helen recognizes the sacrifice elements of the Eucharist: "I see it as a life lived with a debt undertaken for us." She notes that as a Sister of the Precious Blood she pondered the death and suffering of Christ. "I think that is deep in me." While she doesn't really think endlessly about sin and hell, she does acknowledge that "God leads us to heaven in his mercy." She prays the prayer of St. Michael, "Defend us in battle, protect us from the wiles of the devil." At the same time, she reflects, "Who's to say this English muffin did not become Jesus? Or at least Jesus's presence? For me, Eucharist brings Jesus's presence to me, even though I can't explain it."

Pat recalled her discomfort when she submitted her reflection on Eucharist to the bishop. "I remember I handed in a unit on Eucharist and there was a side question on the atonement." When she received comments back, the reviewer noted that Pat had ignored the issue in her paper. Pat confessed that she "was not a big fan of atonement." When she met the person three years later, the womanpriest took her aside and admitted "Pat, I'm not a big fan of atonement either." Pat reflected more on the feeding of the five hundred, the meals Jesus shared with so many, and food for the journey.

Marina Theresa agrees. She considers the community as sign of God's invitation to be present "whenever two or more gather together." She continues "I believe the kingdom of God is inside. I believe it is not conquered but it is encountered . . . the transubstantiation is not me. It is through the whole community, not only through me because I believe the Holy Spirit is in many different people. I think we are equal; all human persons are equal." Similarly, Paula remarks "there's nothing magical about these hands, in the consecrating, I'm not doing this, but the Holy Spirit is. And I along with the community call on the spirit to change us and to bring the spirit within us that we may be the body and blood. And this bread and wine that we're going to eat, the body and blood of Christ, so that it will change us to be like Jesus."

Essentially, Eucharist is our response to Jesus's invitation to remember him through the breaking of the bread and the drinking of the cup. As Miriam Therese Winter writes, Paul contributed to the shape and theological insight of Eucharist. Paul encouraged the community in Corinth (1 Cor 11–12) to gather, remember, share the elements, and say the words. He attributed his formula to the testimony of others, that which we find in Luke's Gospel (Luke 22:19): "Do this in remembrance of me." Winters notes that it is Paul who linked the night when Jesus was betrayed to "the sacramental meal of the Corinthian community."[34] She describes this movement in the community as a "radical reorientation of existing understanding."[35] She notes that it is about a meal, as so many of the womenpriests articulated. She develops the notion that Paul links this meal in community to "transforming the community into the body of Christ."[36]

The womenpriests noted how the reception of communion brought Christ's presence to the community in such a way as to transform them, just as the Constitution on the Sacred Liturgy described: "In the liturgy, the sanctification of women and men is given expression in symbols perceptible by the sense and is carried out in ways appropriate to each of them . . . public worship is performed by the Mystical Body of Jesus Christ, that is by the Head and his members."[37] The women call communities to discipleship, a journey of following Christ. As the document encouraged, "in order that sound tradition be retained, and yet the way remain open to legitimate progress, a careful investigation—theological, historical, and pastoral—should always, first of all, be made into each section of the liturgy which is to be revised . . . and care must be taken that any new forms adopted should in some way grow organically from forms already existing."[38]

The question we asked on Eucharist opened a deep and extremely Catholic spirituality rooted in the experience of these womenpriests who moved through Vatican II into leadership of their communities. Their emphasis on inclusion and widening the tent combined with their almost universal focus on feeding and becoming food for the world provided a theological reflection on becoming a living communion. This communion required leadership adaptations that form the third response to priestly leadership reflecting a synodal influence: collaborative leadership.

Collaborative Leadership

A disciple follows a leader, learns from that person, and imitates the model of the leader. Christian disciples follow Jesus in the Spirit guided by the Triune God of many names. Jesus often challenged the status quo of his Jewish leaders and is considered a prophet for his time. Womenpriests, like Jesus, challenge the status quo of their religious leaders. They choose to be prophets in their time. The major shift they embody resides in their collaborative style of leadership.

Donnieau sought to educate the people in her community so they could function without her as leader. Helen affirmed this style of leadership and moved away from her first community, trusting her work as leader had equipped them to be a community of believers without her. Teresa regularly encourages her community to accept their own leadership initiated through their rite of baptism.

Maria described her ordination to the diaconate as one of her most important and transforming spiritual experiences. As she lay prostrate before the altar and the cross, she gave herself totally to God and to Jesus as disciple and leader of the Spirit's people. She found herself transported to a unitive and mystical experience. She knew she was not dedicating herself to loyalty to an institution or to a male hierarchy. She wasn't taking a vow of obedience to her female bishop. She was dedicating herself to God and the people who came forward to lay hands on her to affirm her role, acknowledged this very act of prophetic reform in the Catholic tradition.

Rites of women's ordination stand in stark contrast to the current ordination rite of male priests, during which the men prostrate themselves to the bishop and take a vow of obedience to the bishop. Ordination of women is an echo of the divine call to all the gathered, a call to holiness and full participation as the people of God. No longer, the ritual declares, does the fullness of faith reside in a single ordained religious leader assigned to a geographic location. Indeed, the faith is ever growing and developing as the people of

God are pilgrims, disciples, learners of the person of Jesus, his parent and the spirit that enlivens all.

These moves in language, ritual, and inclusiveness change the culture of the community. As leadership scholar, Ronald Heifetz asserts:

> *The politics of inclusion are not faint-hearted efforts at making everybody happy enough. Inclusion means more than taking peoples' views into account in defining the problem. Inclusion may mean challenging people, hard and steadily, to face new perspectives on familiar problems, to let go of old ideas and ways of life long held sacred. Thus, inclusion does not mean that each party will get its way. Even the most well-crafted efforts at inclusion can rarely prevent the experience of loss by some. As a result, one often cannot shield oneself from the outrage of those parties who must face loss and are unwilling to change.*[39]

Women priests and bishops intentionally implement rituals that signal a shift in organizational structures. Bishops Christine and Suzanne speak about intentionally working with and educating male bishops in the church. They claim prophetic obedience and note, in the words of Bishop Patricia Fresen, that the hierarchy can "jail the resistors but not the resistance."[40] Indeed, even as they struggle for position within the institution, some question the need for ordained leaders.

Helen reflected that her ordination as priest really emerged from her baptism. "I've thought much of this through my ordination. I needed to be ordained for the community to form . . . I think the community needed an ordained person . . . But since then I have grown to see that we are all priests. I'm not sure I would be ordained today. That's not to say I would give it up . . . but I think if people are properly formed, is ordination necessary? Are we not all co-presiders?" Victoria reflected somewhat similarly. Noting that she had founded and nurtured several congregations and had successfully handed them to other leader womenpriests, she ruminated, "I've been on a progression of understanding what ordination is, and what my response to it is." She presently does not serve a congregation but turns her energy to theater as a director and writer. Teresa muses, "I think my role is as a transitional person. I believe someday in the future whatever the priesthood is will look different than what I am presenting, but I want to advance that . . . I want that priestly ministry to look different and that people would assume their rightful place as the baptized in its fullest sense of how they minister to one another and celebrate the eucharist with one another."

As Vatican II women, these womenpriests articulate some of the theological ponderings of others in the Church. As a past seminary rector, Donald Cozzens wrote about the dichotomy between the traditional belief in a church divided into castes—clerics and lay—and those who embrace the post-conciliar notion of the church as a society of equals. He noted that even in the 1980s the US bishops recognized that the church is first and foremost a gathering of those whose "primary reality is Christ in the assembly of the People of God."[41] By 2017 when Cozzens wrote this text, he acknowledged the deep divide between those who asserted allegiance to pre–Vatican II understandings and those who embraced the challenge of synodality as Pope Francis invited. Other ordained men such as George Wilson SJ seek ways to dismantle clericalism.[42] Massimo Faggioli documents this ongoing division as he describes signs of the times for the Catholic Church. Noting the public criticism of Pope Francis after Pope Benedict XVI and Cardinal Pell of Australia died, Faggioli acknowledged that Josef Cardinal Ratzinger (Pope Benedict XVI), "became the symbol of the Vatican's regaining control over the energies that the Council had unleashed."[43] Observing that leadership following any major council ordinarily redefines itself, Faggioli documented how the combined papacies of John Paul II and Benedict XVI "steered the Church away from the sirens of progressivism and responded to the anthropological challenge coming from biopolitics and the secularization of legislation and ethics . . . ultimately produced a new model of bishops designed to put the brakes on post-conciliar Catholicsim . . . they ended up in an open conflict with their local churches—and in the last few years, also in declared opposition to Benedict's successor on the Chair of Peter, Pope Francis."[44]

Clearly, tensions remain within the continuum of belief in the Roman Catholic Church. Patricia names this a "*kairos* time 'when the church is called to return to its authentic, deeper self.'"[45] She continues that "for the sake of credibility and also as a matter of justice, these women [womenpriests following those ordained on the Danube in 2002] are ordained in apostolic succession . . . ordained in the same way, in the same tradition as men. At this early stage of women's ordination it is important even essential to claim this right. The sacrament of Orders is founded on baptism not on gender."[46] Fresen then proposes that this movement shifts from the hierarchical laying on hands of one bishop to another to the community laying on of hands, that "would fit the communitarian model."[47] Thus, she concludes that rather than leave the Roman Catholic Church, ordained women "need to reform the church structures from within . . . going outside of official church structures, we can achieve nothing. We are already excluded, and leaving would intimate that we accept our exclusion. By ordaining women, we are reimagining, restructuring, reshaping the priesthood and therefore the Church."[48]

Walter Brueggemann describes prophetic leadership as one that evolves out of deep connection to the community, usually situated in a smaller subcommunity. The community and its prophetic spokespersons speak truth to the dominant community. This truth emanates from pain that is experienced and somewhat alleviated through attention to the tradition and renewal of that tradition in a new time. The subcommunity works together to change the oppression of the dominant community.[49]

As we have seen, RCWP emerged from deep connection to the Roman Catholic church. When asked why they stayed, each one named the deep love they have for the people of God within their ecclesial tradition. In fact, they located this connection in their very DNA! Their journeys reflect pain, ostracization, and even excommunication from the institution they served for decades. Now, their subcommunities of faith offer the dominant Catholic community a vision of more equal participation within the baptized. The RCWP embraces their collective task as prophets within the larger Christian and specifically Roman Catholic Church.

Teresa summarizes here what others have said, as well:

> *Yes, we priests and our communities are prophetic. Our existence*
> *challenges the structures of our Church that have oppressed us.*
> *We refuse to live in a muted and false sense of our baptism, our*
> *confirmation and our Eucharist. . . . There's a sense that somehow*
> *we're trying to reform from the outside, but for me I always found*
> *that within the structure of the Church, that's where reformation, I*
> *think, truly happens.*

Indeed, she speaks to the embodied reality of the womanpriest even as Ivone Gebara writes about the challenge theologically. Positing that the shift to full inclusion for women is actually cultural, Gebara argues that all theology needs renewal. Given that there is a shift in philosophy, additional understanding of what it is to be human, and a broader notion of multiple cultures within the Christian and Catholic cultures, Gebara suggests that women are trying to deconstruct traditional theology so as to move beyond the hierarchical and sexist structures of our inherited patriarchal religion.[50]

Brueggemann argues that prophetic leadership emerges from those who deeply understand the tradition and have suffered as a result of power and wealth placing oppression in the hands of a few. In the biblical times during which Brueggemann situates his thesis, power resided in the monarchy and priests. In the Roman Catholic Church, power resides in the hierarchy. Teresa called for reformation of the hierarchy itself: "I have been and continue to be more inclined to live and work within structures as I call for change and transformation. For me, as a Roman Catholic womanpriest, I know I am living outside of the traditional, hierarchical structure of the Church but only because of the inability of that traditional and hierarchical structure to live into its own highest good."

The hierarchy relies on its interpretation of tradition. Rodriguez and Fortier link tradition and culture. Like Brueggemann, they assert that "traditions pass on a world of meaning."[51] Like Gebara, they place theological traditions in cultural contexts. They distinguish between the process of tradition, that is, the handing on of the tradition, and the product or the content. They document how "narratives, rituals, and historical and collective memories function as a human wall of resistance to annihilation and a means to ensure survival."[52] Together in community womenpriests resist the hierarchically claimed power to determine that males only can be ordained for priestly service to God and the community.

Early in the RCWP movement, theologians Müeller and Raming named the resistance as *contra legem*. After the 1998 publication of Ratzinger's "Commentary on *Ad Tuendeam Fidem*," anyone who talked about ordaining women was threatened with excommunication. Müeller and Raming asked themselves: "How can Catholic women free themselves from this spiritual prison made up of definitive declarations and prohibitions?"[53] As priests, they write about their own commitment to pursue resistance and claimed a tradition that overruled the authority of the hierarchy. "We committed ourselves to Action Against Current Church Law [Canon 1024]. . . . For us the scripture provided the authoritative guidance 'One must obey God rather than men' (Acts 5:29)."[54] Just as the prophets Brueggemann described, these two women named their ordination as a threshold. "Behind us was a path along which we had tortured ourselves with oppressive church law, against which we had struggled without effect. In front of us was a path free of this burden, but still presenting a very uncertain future. That we had now freed ourselves gave us an uplifted feeling and filled us with joy."[55]

Brueggemann contends that prophets must experience pain, which chapter 4 on these women's journeys attests. He then argues that out of prophets' pain, in collaboration with a community, they emerge in hope. The stories of the women we interviewed consistently reflected this movement. Indeed, they all ended with what Helen asserted: "No one can excommunicate me from God." To a person, they have rejected the excommunication.

At the same time, they offer alternative ways of being church. Their commitment to systemic change results in public websites, multiple articles, books, and their universal willingness to be interviewed and documented. Womenpriests see themselves as critical yeast for the change in the church they embody.[56]

The renewed liturgies model in a symbolic way a new openness to recognizing Jesus, as Juanita claims, *in persona Christi*. Womenpriests and bishops intentionally implement rituals that signal a shift in organizational structures. They are standing firm in the face of hierarchical resistance. Christine and Suzanne, as bishops, speak about intentionally working with and educating male bishops in the church. They claim prophetic obedience and note, in the words of Bishop Patricia Fresen, that the hierarchy can "jail the resistors but not the resistance."[57]

Summary

Most women we interviewed and studied lived through Vatican II and embraced its call to discipleship. Each heard a call to ordained priesthood, and for many years attempted to answer the call. What they now offer is a type of leadership that rejects hierarchical, patriarchal obedience. Rather, they see themselves as facilitators, educators, and convenors; they accompany the people of God on their journeys of faith. These shifts demonstrate different styles of leadership and accountability.

Reform in the Roman Catholic Church takes time. It took five hundred years for most of the reforms Luther called for in 1517 to become natural in the Roman Church.[58] These women recognize that reform comes from within the organization as well as from outside it. Like leaders described by Donna Markham, these women link spirits and allow for the wonders that only a community of spirits can accomplish. They are committed to balancing individual and communal transformation.[59] They help their people "confront the contradictions in their lives and communities and adjust their values and behavior to accommodate new realities."[60] They offer their communities a "sanctuary to restore a sense of purpose, regain courage and heart."[61] They are full of mission, and free from their own fear of reprisal because they have faced that fear and accepted institutional consequences.

Standing on the shoulders of women and men who have gone before them, these womenpriests "generate courage and the belief that as long as persons are connected and unified in single-minded commitment to the mission that is yet hazy and amorphous, the swirling and fuzzy vista ahead is filled with possibility and potential."[62] Filled with the Spirit's charisms and sustained by practices that continue to deepen their spirituality, these womenpriests conform to the four tasks of the Gospel as delineated in the Acts of the Apostles. Those tasks of *kerygma*, *koinonia*, *diakonia*, and *leiturgia* move through the tension of institution and spirit/charism toward equipping disciples as the pilgrim people of God. Margaret Mead is attributed as writing: "Never doubt that a small group of thoughtful, committed, citizens can change the world; indeed, it's the only thing that ever has." Their determination as thoughtful citizens is exemplified by Jen who said, "I love the Catholic Church. It is who I am. I will never leave."[63]

EPILOGUE

Challenge? Renewal?

WE STARTED OUR research because we were curious about the phenomenon of women claiming to be legitimately ordained in a church that canonically rejects that status. Knowing some of the women who were lifelong lay ecclesial ministers, we sought to understand their choice. We suspected that deep spiritual grounding and connection guided their passage from respected lay leaders in Catholic parishes and organizations to excommunicated ordained leaders of mostly smaller communities. We hoped to discover what that spiritual experience was and how it influenced, supported, and guided their journeys of faith.

As women in the Catholic Church, we have at times questioned some inherited interpretations of Scripture and accepted traditional practices. Thus, we acknowledge our own status has at times been perceived as "challenge." We also see renewal in the Church as mostly positive and consider ourselves part of the Vatican II pilgrim people of God who choose to follow Christ in the Spirit as best we can. In this section we pose a few final observations about the stories of these Roman Catholic womenpriests related to the topics of spirituality, ordination, and excommunication; are they challenge or renewal? It really is up to each of us to decide how to understand and respond to this movement and these women and men.

Spirituality

Gilberto Cavasos, OFM, defines spirituality as "all about relationship, for no one can live an authentic human life without relating to the 'other,' with God and neighbor."[1] He cites Gustavo Gutierrez's definition of spirituality as "a walking in liberty according to the Spirit of Love and of life."[2] He uses the word *corazón,* defined as that heart and love which enlivens one to serve, to relate to another and to the cosmos, to be touched and transformed.

Each of the women we interviewed spoke about her relationship with God. They used over fifty words to describe God in their prayer. They expanded their relationships with people and reached out to develop ever-widening circles. They spoke about their liberty and their joy at following the call they wrestled with most of their lives. Like Jacob, they carry the wounds of their journey, and they climbed the ladder to the heavens and proclaimed God's goodness and reconciliation to their people.

These women reflected on Christian and Hebrew scripture texts, admired male saints and teachings, and intentionally focused on the many women saints upon whose shoulders they stand. They spend time in daily prayer, spiritual reading, mindfulness, eco-spiritual practices, and social justice efforts. They celebrate and participate in Eucharist and consult communities of faith and spiritual directors as they discern next steps in relation to the sacred. Their practices led them to new theological and ecclesial choices. We ask you to consider the women you met in this text. Are they challenge? Renewal? Both? Neither?

Ordination

Influenced by Vatican II ourselves, we wondered how these womenpriests would describe the difference between the priesthood of all believers through baptism and the priesthood of ordained ministry. Maybe one answer, from Dagmar, illuminated us more than we could imagine. She exclaimed that she wanted all the grace she could get! Why not all the sacraments? As chapter 6 delineated, the womenpriests emphasized different aspects of leadership through ordination. Their own gifts determined the emphases they preferred. Thus, Suzanne, Joanna, Olivia, Mary Ellen, Gabriella, and Kathleen sought to embrace more spirituality in their daily lives, practice of liturgy, and weekly offerings. Teresa, Helen, and Donnieau spoke about ensuring the people of God could lead themselves, without a priest. At the same time Shanon, Juanita, and Jane highlighted the role of priest as presider while Chava, Olga, Vicki, Judy, Andrea, and Marina Theresa focused on leading social justice efforts in various communities.

Of all the womenpriests we interviewed or studied, Bishop Fresen addresses this issue most directly. In a talk she gave to a group of people in Olympia, Washington she outlined the explicit need for ordination of women.[3] Fresen responds to other women critics who object to joining the patriarchy that has oppressed them. She asserts that "we need to reform the church structures from within." To that end, she outlines major differences that the womenpriest movement offers as reform: no power structure, rather a "discipleship of equals"; differentiation of ministries based on gifts and talents; no obligatory celibacy; no promise of obedience to the bishop(s); intentionally embracing the status of worker-priests thus financially independent of the church; no titles—no Father, Reverend, and the like; simple vestments and stoles; and communitarian and inclusive celebration of Eucharist.

As we interviewed the womenpriests and some of their congregants, we witnessed elements of each of the characteristics Bishop Fresen named. We also noted that the womenpriests are not perfect, and they have serious disagreements about requirements and preparation for priesthood. A split resulted in two groups sharing a single website and claiming unity in diversity. In response to the division, a subgroup met regularly to pray for their unity as they continue to work through disagreements about "order" in their flattened hierarchy of equals. Recently, a BBC documentary featured a newly ordained womanpriest who is intentionally claiming the title Father and wearing clerics to signal a definite challenge to Church practice. Indeed, when Jeanette witnessed Juanita wearing the Roman collar during her trip to Turkey and Greece, it inspired her curiosity and led to our pursuing this topic. Despite their claim to eschew trappings of current male priests, then, some embrace titles, clothing, and authority as ways to reform the Church.

As we studied these womenpriests and reviewed their stories, we agreed with theologian Ilia Delio, OSF, that spirituality is potentially the future of theology. As the womenpriests struggle with their own journeys and their priesthood, they offer insight into shifting theologies. Delio cites the rise of spirituality as a theological discipline in the theological curriculum and quotes theologian Jean Danielou who wrote that it isn't possible to consider theology without a spiritual life. Spirituality, Delio argues, is based on one's experience. We started our exploration with the womenpriests experience.

Many models of theological reflection encourage people to start with experience rather than using theological or Scripture texts to prove their points and validate their experience. To start with experience and ask the question "Where is God in this?" leads one to discover God ever revealing God's self. Delio notes that this process reflects the *ressourcement* that has led to renewal of both spirituality and theology in the last century. She relies on her own Franciscan heritage to link these two avenues of seeking to understand God in life. Relying on her understanding of Bonaventure, she suggests he integrated "faith and reason, intellectual and spiritual, speculative and symbolic, knowledge and love."[4] Thus, *ressourcement* springs from *aggiornamento*, the new or renewed experience of different peoples in evolving ages. Just as Vatican II relied on the two movements, so too do these movements play an important role in the discussion of ordination that arises from the womenpriests' lived experiences and spiritual journeys.

When one refers to the Decree on the Ministry and Life of Priests, *Presbyterorum Ordinis*, one can recognize the council father's tension between situating the priest in the hierarchy and in the daily life of the Church. On one hand, for instance, the document acknowledges that "the very unity of their consecration and mission requires their hierarchical union with the order of bishops."[5] On the other hand, the document declares "priests while being chosen from the midst of humanity and appointed to act on its behalf in what pertains to God, to offer gifts and sacrifices for sins, live with the rest of humanity as with brothers and sisters."[6] Priests, then, are in hierarchical union while also encouraged to live among people, and to be kind and generous.

The Vatican II document on the life of priests also highlighted the centrality of Eucharist. After listing the sacraments of baptism, penance, and anointing of the sick, the document states "the other sacraments, and indeed all ecclesiastical ministries and works of the apostolate are bound up with the Eucharist and are directed towards it. For in the most blessed Eucharist is contained the entire spiritual wealth of the church."[7]

When we recall the early call stories of our womenpriests, we remember how many of them recognized the deep presence of God in the Eucharist. Celie recognized God through the shimmer of the raised Host; Joanna knew she belonged to God's family; Donnieau went running in excitement to proclaim her call after receiving Eucharist; Maria knew her place at the table through her hunger. Janos Glaser affirms that "given the radical changes in the world, the Church has to change; as the institution of the Eucharist is the 'decisive event' in the life of the Church, those aspects of its life that need to be adapted and the nature of the changes to be accomplished are to be defined by the meaning of this event and not by tradition."[8] Theologies are shifting as a result of deep spiritual experience and reflection.

Olivia wrote about her understanding of being ordained within the tradition as part of a "cosmic shift." She continued that this shift is "a challenge; but it is one filled with much joy and peace as well as opportunity for growth."[9] Mary Ellen wrote that "acting on this prophetic call has brought challenges. . . . With each new challenge comes new grace and strength to be present, celebrate, anoint and love whomever God sends."[10] Speaking from a place of deep immersion in the mystery of the sacred, Dana, wrote about how womenpriests are "reclaiming the table ministry of eucharistic celebration and our apostolic authority as servant leaders. This *anamnesis*, whereby the past is made present again in this time and this place, is a revivification of the early Church when women were priests, deacons, and bishops in full apostolic authority."[11] Clearly, these womenpriests' spirituality evolved into new theologies of church, priesthood, sacraments and especially Eucharist, discipleship, and relationship to the sacred.

Wanting to be a saint since she could remember, Dagmar considered how mystics accept a way of life that is not understandable on a practical, daily practice. Seeking to deepen her relationship to the sacred, she notes that "mystics are difficult to coral and control; they are led by the Spirit . . . Mystics help humanity to evolve."[12] Lavinia Byrne, then a vowed religious, wrote several texts documenting women's spiritual journeys. In 1994 her work advocating ordination of women appeared shortly after Pope John Paul II's apostolic letter closing discussion of the topic. Clearly arguing for ordaining women, she relied on a feminist methodology which she described as "the bonding experience of shared storytelling, the political and social agenda of sisterhood"[13] which asserts "the importance of solidarity in relationships."[14] She further links this process to theological insight because it "invites us to remember our story and to share the patterns which emerge as we reflect on the way in which God has dealt with us."[15]

We continue to ponder the stories these womenpriests have shared in the context of our post–Vatican II Church and world. We consider the polarities evidenced in news stories about Bishop Thomas Paprocki of Springfield, Illinois criticizing Robert McElroy of San Diego[16] while others pit Australia's now deceased Cardinal George Pell against Pope Francis.[17] We ask: Are these womenpriests a challenge to the Church? Renewal? Both? Neither?

Excommunication

As discussed in chapter 4, excommunication is a legal term that prohibits a person from full participation in the sacramental life of the Catholic Church. Excommunication is considered a medicinal practice intended to call the offender back to full participation in the Church. As Anna Terpin outlines, excommunicated people are prohibited from celebrating and receiving the Eucharist and other sacraments but are not prohibited from participating in these.[18] During the Renaissance in the fifteenth and sixteenth centuries, Martin Luther, King Henry VIII, and Galileo were excommunicated during a time of great cultural, religious, social, and scientific upheaval and change. Eventually, five hundred years later, the Catholic Church rescinded the anathemas that accompanied Luther's and Galileo's excommunications. In other words, when Helen says simply "no one can excommunicate me from God," she is right. At the same time, as she described, her priest can legitimately deny her communion and burial rites in the church because of her excommunication.

While womenpriests reject their excommunication we found no one who took it lightly. During our interviews each spoke about grappling with the repercussions of being rejected by the very communities they had served for their lifetime. At the same time, they argued that the magisterium can make decisions but the *sensus fideli,* or will of the people, must affirm the decision for it to be valid. Indeed, the womenpriests argue that the three-fold braid that constitutes the traditional argument against ordaining women and supports Canon 1024 deserves additional consideration theologically and spiritually. Christina Gringeri and Alexandra Himonas describe these strands as: "the magisterium, or teaching of the Pope and bishops; the canonical scripture; and the apostolic tradition."[19] The womenpriests draw upon their Vatican II practices of *resourcement* and *aggiornamento* to reframe the underpinnings of the three strands.

Andrea wrote "in obedience to the gospel of Jesus Christ, I have now disobeyed this unjust law, Canon 1024, through valid but illicit ordination as a Roman Catholic womanpriest during the summer of 2007. Given the overwhelming reasons to stand for justice, how could I not do this?"[20] Reflecting on her own work as a therapist toward healing and reconciliation, Gabriella pondered her decision to pursue ordination in spite of excommunication. She named as her first reason for acting *contra legem*: "the failure of the institutional church to protect children from assault by priests and the subsequent cover-up by the institutional bishops, the failure of the institution to understand, with compassion, the pain involved in trying to put the pieces of one's life back together."[21] Finally, Olivia wrote "this action born of my faithfulness to God, is my positive and loving response to the deepest place of union with the Holy Trinity within me . . . and it is my offering not only of all that I am as gift to God, but it also is a pouring out of myself with love, for the good of the Church and the world. I can make no other response than to take the risks, including the risk of painful losses of precious friendships inherent in my decision to be ordained to the priesthood . . . Even before I was formed in my mother's womb, I am becoming who I will become."[22] Each womanpriest confronts the law and chooses to break it. Bishop Fresen likens this resistance to the stance against apartheid she and others took in South Africa. These womenpriests refuse to recognize their excommunication status, and many attend liturgies and receive sacraments anonymously as well as publicly. Many male celibate priests support these womenpriests, even as others enforce the law. So we again ask: Challenge? Renewal?

The Nature of Change—Challenge or Renewal?

Prior to Vatican II, everyone's role seemed defined and accepted. The early to mid-1950s experienced a rapid economic growth and recovery from two world wars and a major economic depression. Lay people fulfilled their roles: Pray, Pay and Obey. Yet, as Kenan Osborne documents, as early as 1889 some laymen called for a congress of lay people.[23] The bishops sought to control aspects of the gathering, nevertheless it was held and Bishop Ireland wrote to others, "Tell them that there is a mission open to laymen."[24] In 1893 a second congress took place in Chicago. A large number of women attended and, according to Osborne, Rose Hawthorne Lathrop urged them to "arise and defend your rights, your abilities for competition with men in intellectual and professional endurance."[25] Osborne further notes that the congress also appealed to the church leadership to recognize and "respect the rights of native Americans . . . Black Catholics and colored people [*sic*]."[26] This Chicago congress also addressed the arms race and peace. Osborne summarizes that there were no more congresses after that Chicago gathering, because they were opposed by the conservative reaction of the bishops. He continues, "The ramifications are typical of two issues: (a) the pressure which Catholic lay people, well-educated and well trained brought to bear on Catholic life and (b) the slow-but-sure negative response of most of the higher clergy."[27] Locating the movement of lay people toward more effective discipleship, Osborne reflects, "In case after case such forms of lay activity in the structuring of the church were met by church leadership with negativity, and even at times with reprisals. Two world wars and a number of lesser wars may have focused national and international attention on issues other than the church and its relationship to the modern world, but in spite of such wars and even more importantly because of such wars, the issue and relevance of gospel discipleship in the present age has become increasingly more acute."[28]

When Pope Francis names women as a challenge of the church, then, what does he mean? How do we respond? Diane Kennedy spoke to this issue. In 2013, as a vowed religious woman who was an academic dean of a highly regarded Dominican School and seminary, she wrote: "For Roman Catholic women leaders, there is an inherent irony at the core of their ecclesial leadership. They serve as CEOs of hospitals, leaders of congregations and presidents of universities, but no offices of the Church are open to them. Although they are the largest organized non-clerical body in the Roman Catholic Church, they have no official place in the system."[29] She acknowledged the impact of Vatican II in opening opportunities for women in the Church yet mourned the struggle women faced in the ongoing "gender bias that perpetuates the imbalance of power and authority within a men-only hierarchy."[30] Similarly, another vowed religious woman leader, Simone Campbell, recalled the resistance of the bishops to emerging leadership among vowed religious sisters. She noted the recruitment process of bishops toward securing vowed religious women to come to the United States in the nineteenth century. She then recounted how the sisters would advocate for supplies, building materials, salaries, and policies that respected their contributions to the evolving church. She confessed that "when they questioned policies, however, the male hierarchy punished them by silencing them."[31]

Vowed religious women responded immediately to the call to renewal based on the documents of Vatican II. By the 1970s the vowed religious women's orders collaborated on several fronts. They formed the Leadership Conference of Women Religious (LCWR) and a social justice effort called NETWORK. As Campbell described they "incorporated feminist values such as participation, shared leadership and collaboration." She further noted that these women had been accustomed to obey "without question whatever was decided by Bishops or others in the power structure."[32] As these movements gained traction and influence, Theresa Kane, a Sister of Mercy and then president of the LCWR addressed Pope John Paul II at the Basilica of the National Shrine of the Immaculate Conception during his visit to the United States in 1979. She admonished:

> *As I share this privileged moment with you, Your Holiness, I urge*
> *you to be mindful of the intense suffering and pain which is part of*
> *the life of many women in these United States. I call upon you to*
> *listen with compassion and to hear the call of women who comprise*
> *half of humankind. As women we have heard the powerful messages*
> *of our Church addressing the dignity and reverence for all persons.*
> *As women we have pondered upon these words. Our contemplation*
> *leads us to state that the Church in its struggle to be faithful to*
> *its call for reverence and dignity for all persons must respond by*
> *providing the possibility of women as persons being included in all*
> *ministries of our Church. I urge you, Your Holiness, to be open to*
> *and respond to the voices coming from the women of this country*

*who are desirous of serving in and through the Church as fully
participating members.* "[33]

Placed against the backdrop of the civil rights movement in the 1960s and
'70s, and the second wave of the feminist movement in the 1970s, these
efforts drew concern from the more conservative and mostly Western European hierarchy and papal leaders who were attempting to keep a unified
church after a major global council that highlighted the need for change.
Women became targeted as "challenges" to a church that wanted to remain
true to traditional practices it had enforced since the 1200s.

Still thinking the discussion was open, Lavinia Byrne questioned:

*Whose images work? Whose images are valid? . . . Some would see
the ordained ministry of women in history as essentially heretical
and deviant; whilst others would see it as a lost gift. Some want
to tie it to pagan origins as a way of condemning it; whilst others
are not quite so dismissive and would be interested to examine the
pagan origins of all priesthood. Two ways of making theology clash
over this question; one of which assumes that Christian revelation
is fixed and unchanging, the other of which values process and
disclosure.* [34]

After thirty-five years as a vowed religious who considered women's spiritual journeys and argued for women's ordination, she left her order in 2000
under pressure from the Vatican to resign.

During his ten years in office, Pope Francis has appointed Dr. Raffaela
Giuliani as Secretary of the Pontifical Commission of Sacred Archaeology,
Professor Antonella Sciarrone Alibrandi as Undersecretary in the Dicastery
for Culture and Education, Professor Luca Tuninetti as Secretary of the
Pontifical Academy of St. Thomas Aquinas, and Salesian Sister Alessandra
Smerilli as the number two position at the Dicastery for Promoting Integral
Human Development, the highest post ever held by a woman at the Vatican.
As Carol Glatz recorded, the pope addressed a group of women on Interna-
tional Women's Day in 2023. She reviewed the progress made during his
papacy (2013–2023). According to her findings, women currently constitute

23.4 percent of the Vatican workforce. Within the curia, "five women hold the rank of undersecretary and one is ranked as Secretary."[35] She noted that these women are full members which allows them to vote. She summarizes that Pope Francis not only brought more women to the table, he "opened up new ways for women's voices to be heard."[36] In her article, Glatz noted that several organizations are currently seeking women's input in anticipation of the synod to be held in fall 2023 and 2024. Maria Lia Zervino, one of three women appointed to the Dicastery for Bishops urged the pope and others to consider the words submitted for synodal reflection. She also quoted Pope Francis: "The church cannot and should not remain just with words," and added that she "believed the time for concrete action has come."[37]

Christine, one of the Danube seven and the first woman bishop, spoke about the task of change. She compared the journey to an "attempt to climb up a mountain of 25,000 feet for the first time."[38] She knew ordination for her was a political act, and she confessed surprise and encouragement when she heard from a high church official who expressed "Oh, now I see you are not only talking about, but you are actually going to do something."[39] She confessed that she wanted to encourage the "many women and men to follow God's call to priestly ordination. I wanted to show the legislators of the church that the Holy Spirit is acting in the church by persuading bishops to ordain women and persuading women to receive ordination."[40] Like Christine, Bishop Fresen supports the taking of concrete prophetic action "to break down the sexism that is so rampant in our hierarchical structures."[41] Womenpriests as a group have taken the concrete action Pope Francis called for in other contexts.[42]

As the womenpriests lived through the hope inspired by Vatican II, followed by a perceived retrenchment, followed by potential new hope, they were part of the vowed religious and lay leadership that lobbied for a more collaborative and inclusive church. We have shared with you their spiritual calls, practices, journeys, decisions, resilience, suffering, and leadership. Their spiritualities reflect their shifting theologies. The current process of synodality in the Roman Catholic Church suggests that the shifts reflected in the womenpriests' stories are more universal than particular. Now we ask the same questions with which we started this process of discovery. Do the womenpriests represent challenge? Renewal? Both? Neither? Something else?

Appendix 1

DEMOGRAPHIC DATA

Table 1. Ages of Significant Moments in Womenpriest' Journeys

Age	3–10	11–30	30–50	51–70	71–85+
Age of first call to priesthood	12	7	2	1	–
Age at time of ordination	–	–	9	22	3
Age at time of interview	–	–	4	11	16

Table 2. Years of Experience in Ministry Other Than Ordained

Years of experience	3–10	11–29	30–49
As lay minister	16	12	8
As vowed religious	3	5	1
In health care	–	5	–

Table 3. Level of RCWP Education

	Doctorates	Master's degrees	Bachelor's degrees	Other
	14	21	2	1

Not all people we interviewed gave us all the information we asked. Some people served in multiple roles: lay ecclesial ministers, lay volunteers or vowed religious women. Thus, the numbers overlap. Since doctoral degrees require master's level degrees, the numbers on this chart do not include additional master's degrees earned by womenpriests who have earned a doctorate. The numbers do not include multiple doctorates or master's degrees earned by a single individual, although several womenpriests have earned multiple doctorates and master's degrees.

Appendix 2

INTERVIEW QUESTIONS
AND SUBJECTS

Name:

Date Ordained:

Community Serving:

Demographic data related to community:

Numbers in community:

Breakdown: (w)_____ (m) _____ Children _____ Age range _____

Describe your priestly ministry.

How old were you when you heard your first call?

When you heard the call, how did it come to you? How did you recognize it?

What was your initial affective response to this call?

What were some of the barriers you immediately confronted when trying to respond to the call?

Describe any hesitation you had as you tried to understand your own response to the call you felt.

Did you share your call with anyone? With a male priest? How did those with whom you shared respond? How did you respond back to them?

Did you receive support? From whom? Describe the support you received.

What practices sustained you on your journey? Is there any scriptural passage, image, saint, theologian, or other companion that impacts/directs/guides/supports your journey?

Describe your process of discernment.

What was your relationship with the institutional church?

Describe your current relationship with the institutional church.

(Added after First Interview) Describe your theology of Eucharist.

List of Women Interviewed

Teresa Gregory

Suzanne Thiel (Bishop Suzanne)

Kathleen Bellefeuille-Rice

Diane Whalen

Christine Mayr-Lumetzberger

Jeanette Love

Suzanne Dunn

Jennifer O'Malley (Jen)

Dagmar Celeste

Jane Via

Joanna Truelson

Mary Theresa Streck

Bridget Mary Meehan

Maria Etz

Shanon Sterringer

Helen Umphrey

Jean Marchant

Maureen Mancuso

Donnieau Snyder

Judy Lee

Morag Liebert

Victoria Marie (Vikki)

Patricia Cook (Pat- deceased 2022)

Chava Redonnet

Celie Katovitch

Myra Brown

Olga Lucia Alvarez

Kathy Bean

Ezperanza

Paula Hoeffer

Victoria Rue

Juanita Cordero

Marina Teresa Sanchez-Mejia

Nine RCWP Cited Through Use of Their Written Work

We included nine women by accessing their written materials. Each of these women have a chapter in:

Hainz McGrath, Elsie, Bridget Mary Meehan, and Ida Raming, eds. *Women Find a Way*. College Station, TX: Virtualbookworm.com Publishing, 2008.

Their individual chapters and page numbers are listed under their names. Additional written or published material is included under each name. We used these materials to augment our understanding of these earliest ordained womenpriests.

Doko, Olivia

Doko, (Merlene) Olivia. "From Resentment to Peace," 144–151.

Meehan, Bridget Mary, Olivia Doko, and Victoria Rue. "A Brief Overview of Womenpriests in the History of the Roman Catholic Church." https://romancatholicwomenpriests.org/pdf/RCWP_Resource.pdf

Patricia Fresen, Bishop, South Africa.

Fresen, Patricia. "A New Understanding of Priestly Ministry," 28–35.

———. "Ordained Ministry as envisioned by RCWP and by the Dutch Dominicans. Two Models of Priesthood: Convergences and divergences," 2008. http://www.rk-kerkplein.org/home/themas/ Kerk-zijn/ambten/roman-catholic-women-priests-en-de-nederlandse-dominicanen-in-hun-visie-op-het-gewijde-ambt/index07a0.html? language=en Accessed April 5, 2023.

———. "A Long Walk to Freedom: A Woman Bishop Speaks." An unpublished talk delivered in Olympia, WA.

Gisela Forster

Forster, Gisela. "The Start," 9–13.

McGrath, Elsie

McGrath, Elsie. "The Road Less Traveled by: Canonical Disobedience in St. Louis," 108–114.

Hinman, Kristen. "The Church Ladies: Two St. Louis Women Will Soon become Ordained Catholic Priests—And in a Jewish Synagogue, No Less," *Riverfront Times.* St. Louis, MO. Nov. 07, 2007.

Müeller, Iris

Müeller, Iris. "My Story, Condensed," 19–20.

Raming, Ida and iris Müeller. *"Contra Legem"—A Matter of Conscience: Our Lifelong Struggle for Human Rights for Women in the Roman-Catholic Church.* Piscataway, NJ: Transaction Publishers, 2010.

Raming, Ida
> Raming, Ida. "Situation of Women in the Roman Catholic Church," 21–26.
>
> Raming, Ida and iris Müeller. *"Contra Legem" —A Matter of Conscience. Our Lifelong Struggle for Human Rights for Women in the Roman-Catholic Church.* New Piscataway, NJ: Transaction Publishers. 2010.

Reynolds, Dana
> Reynolds, Dana. "The Mystical Heart of Table Community," 37–42.

Robertson, Mary Ellen
> Robertson, Mary Ellen. "My Story," 115–121.

Ward, Gabriella
> Ward, Gabriella Velardi. "Draw Me, We Shall Run," 68–75.

NOTES

Foreword

1 See https://romancatholicwomenpriests.org
2 Can. 1024: A baptized male alone receives sacred ordination validly.
3 Richard A. Schoenherr and Lawrence A. Young, *Full Pews, Empty Altars*, University of Wisconsin Press, 1993 https://tinyurl.com/3wu6uzwj
4 Over the years the FutureChurch mission has evolved so that today the organization "seeks changes that will provide all Roman Catholics the opportunity to participate fully in church life and leadership https://futurechurch.org
5 Stephen Huba, "Catholic Priest Ordinations Not Keeping Pace with Retirements," *TribLive* Westmoreland, Tarentum, PA August 23, 2017. https://tinyurl.com/srx7mxs
6 Center for Applied Research in the Apostolate. "Frequently Requested Church Statistics," Georgetown University. https://tinyurl.com/hny7vet3
7 Center for Applied Research in the Apostolate. "Frequently Requested Church Statistics."
8 Stan and Eileen Doherty, Informal Statistical Study (Part II): Roman Catholic Archdiocese of Boston 08/17/2004 www.futurechurch.org/Doherty.pdf. Of seventy-seven suppressed parishes, 34 percent (n=26) were located in towns whose income was classified as low (less than $30K per year) with another 26 percent (n=20) in towns whose household income was moderate ($30K–$40 K).
9 Michael O'Malley, "Cleveland Catholic Diocese Announces Church Closures," *Cleveland Plain Dealer*, March 28, 2009, https://tinyurl.com/wk2pt9vb; David Briggs, "Diocesan Reorganization Hits Ethnic, Minority Parishes," *Cleveland Plain Dealer*, July 13, 2008. https://tinyurl.com/2zvdt6zx
10 Andrew DePietro, "US Poverty Rate by City in 2021," *Forbes*, November 26, 2021. https://tinyurl.com/mte3b66p
11 Jessica Ravitz, "Catholic Faithful Face Church Closures," *CNN*, March, 2009. https://tinyurl.com/2pum2wda
12 Center for Applied Research in the Apostolate, "Frequently Requested Church Statistics."

13 Center for Applied Research in the Apostolate, *Research Review: Lay Ecclesial Ministers in the United States,* February, 2015. https://tinyurl.com/4scavusuf

14 Tricia C. Bruce, PhD with Cella Masso-Rivetti and Jennifer Sherman, "Called to Contribute: Findings from an In-depth Interview Study of US Catholic Women and the Diaconate," 2021. https://www.calledtocontribute.org

15 Courtney Mares, "Pope Francis: The Holy Spirit Reforms the Church through the Saints," *Catholic News Agency,* January 15, 2022. https://tinyurl.com/v79ubxmu

16 Vatican Synod of Bishops, *Synod 2021–2023, For a Synodal Church Preparatory Document,* 2–3. https://tinyurl.com/5ey8usu8

17 Vatican Synod of Bishops, *Synod 2021–2023,* 9.

18 Pope Francis, "Address at Ceremony Commemorating the 50th Anniversary of the Institution of the Synod of Bishops," October 17, 2018. https://tinyurl.com/4uz2wspwl

Chapter 1

1 This translation of Genesis 1:1 invokes a beginning. All books start with an idea, an experience, a notion, a nudge from the Spirit. The very act of research and writing puts order into the impulse. Throughout this book, the reader will encounter the ongoing dynamic between Spirit and order.

2 Pope Francis. *Evangelii Gaudium (The Joy of the Gospel).* (Vatican City: Vatican Press, 2013), 104.

3 We have permission from all but one of our interviewees to include their names as we write. To keep names of bishops, ally priests, and communities of faith protected from repercussions, we have decided to use first names for everyone in the text, except authors of published books, since their names are already publicly attached to their writing. We have changed some first names for double protection.

4 Dr. Carolyn Osiek led a study group to Greece in Fall 2015.

5 Osiek, 2015.

6 E. Kinerk SJ, "Toward a Method for the Study of Spirituality," in *Psychology and Religion,* ed. M. Goran, Gorman (New York: Paulist Press, 1986), 320.

7 Iris Müeller and Ida Raming. *"Contra Legem"—A Matter of Conscience.* trans. Harry Radday. (Piscataway, NJ: Transaction Publishers, 2010). These theologians, now Roman Catholic womenpriests, write about

this stance of protesting church law rather than defying Doctrine of the Church. RCWP uses their arguments throughout their own teachings and writings.

8 Patricia Fresen, "A New Understanding of Priestly Ministry." in *Women Find a Way*. ed. Elsie Hainz McGrath, Bridget Mary Meehan, Ida Raming (College Station, TX: Virtualbookworm.com, 2008), 31–32.

9 Roy Lazar, *Christian Spirituality, Roman Catholic Perspective* (Academia. edu), 1. https://www.academia.edu/17812589/Christian_Spirituality_ Roman_Catholic_Perspective

10 B. Jroeschel, *Spiritual Passages. The Psychology of Spiritual Development* (Bangalore, India: Claretian Publications, 2003), 4.

11 John W. Creswell, *Qualitative Inquiry and Research Design. Choosing among Five Tradition* (Thousand Oaks, CA: Sage, 2008), 18.

12 Creswell, *Qualitative Inquiry*, 15.

13 Jill Peterfeso, *Womanpriest: Tradition and Transgression in the Contemporary Roman Catholic Church* (New York: Fordham University Press, 2020).

14 N. K. Denzin and Y.S. Lincoln, *The SAGE Handbook of Qualitative Research* (Thousand Oaks, CA: Sage, 2011), 5.

15 Elsie Hainz, et al., ed., *Women Find a Way*. (College Station, TX: Virtualbookworm.com, 2008). The stories that more completely revealed material related to our interview questions included those by: Olivia Doko, Mary Ellen Robertson, Elsie McGrath, Iris Mueller, Ida Raming, Patricia Fresen, Dana Reynolds, and Gabriella Ward, and Gisela Forster. Other stories in this book expand understanding but did not have all the elements of spiritual journey we were researching.

16 Many thanks to William Fliss and others at Marquette University archives, Milwaukee, WI.

17 Creswell, *Qualitative Inquiry*, 6–17.

18 Creswell, *Qualitative Inquiry*, 19.

19 Creswell, *Qualitative Inquiry*, 19.

20 We rely on St. Paul here, as he asserted that he did not rely on the communities he served for his livelihood, but rather on his skill as a tentmaker. Acts 18:1–4.

21 Carol Christ, *Diving Deep and Surfacing: Women Writers on the Spiritual Quest* (Boston: Beacon Press, 1980), 1.

22 In October 2021, Pope Francis announced through his homily at Mass that the Roman Catholic Church would gather a synod of bishops in Fall 2023. He reminded the bishops that they and the people of God they serve are expected to meet and encounter Jesus. He urged them to listen to one another about what Jesus asks of them in today's world.

Then he asked them to discern together what the spirit of God is calling the people of God to live in the twenty-first century. Each country's bishops and others gather the reflections in their locales, and compile reports to submit to the Vatican prior to the universal meeting of the bishops. The process is ongoing throughout the world and has required bishops to listen to the people as they prepare to discern what God is calling the Church to do and be.

23 *GS*, 2.

24 Early in our process, we identified these first chapters of "call" and "context" as essential beginnings within a person's spiritual journey. These two foundational aspects of spiritual journeys framed our interview questionnaire, our process of ethnographic immersion in different contexts, and our insistence on including womenpriests from all the countries and contexts we could. After we began, Jill Peterfeso published her landmark history of the womenpriest movement. Interestingly, she too began with "call." Her work consistently analyzes the process and is a source of deep understanding of the movement. Ours refrains from analysis as much as possible so as to allow the women to speak their own realities in their own words, relying on their own resources.

25 *SC*, 12.

26 *Lumen Gentium*, 2.

27 Lazar, *Christian Spirituality*, 8.

28 Lazar, *Christian Spirituality*, 15.

Chapter 2

1 "Message to Humanity." 1962. In *The Documents of Vatican II*. Ed Walter M Abbott, S.J. Trans Ed Very Rev. Msgr. Joseph Gallagher. New York: Guild Press, 1966, 1.

2 "Declaration on Religious Liberty." *Dignitatis Humanae*. 1965, 1

3 "Declaration on Religious Liberty." *Dignitatis Humanae*, 3.

4 "Declaration on Religious Liberty." *Dignitatis Humanae*, 3.

5 Raming, Ida and iris Mueller. *"Contra Legem"—A Matter of Conscience. Our Lifelong Struggle for Human Rights for Women in the Roman-Catholic Church* (Piscataway, NJ: Transaction Publishers, 2010), 69. *The Code of Canon Law in English Translation*, Prepared by the Canon Law Society of Great Britain and Ireland in Association with the Canon Law Society of Australia and New Zealand and the Canadian Canon Law Society (London: Collins, 1983). Canon no. 1024.

6 Osborne, Kenon R. *Ministry: Lay Ministry in the Roman Catholic Church* (New York: Paulist Press. 1993).

7 *As One Who Serves: Reflections of the Pastoral Ministry on Priests in the United States.* Bishops Committee on Priestly Life and Ministry. (United States Catholic Conference, Washington, DC, 1977); *A Shepherd's Care: Reflections on the Changing role of Pastor.* Bishops Committee on Priestly Life and Ministry. (United States Catholic Conference, Washington, DC, 1987).

8 Bond, Louise C. *An Evaluation of the Effectiveness of Lay Ministry Training in the Roman Catholic Church of the United States.* Diss. The Catholic U of America, 1990. (Ann Arbor: MI, 1990); D'Antonio, William, James Davidson, Dean Hoge and Ruth Wallace. *American Catholic Laity in a Changing Church* (Kansas City: Sheed, 1989); Murnion, Philip J. *New Parish Ministers: Laity and Religious on Parish Staffs* (Cincinnati: St. Anthony, 1993).

9 Bridget Mary Meehan, Olivia Doko, and Victoria Rue. "A Brief Overview of Womenpriests in the History of the Roman Catholic Church," 1. https://romancatholicwomenpriests.org/pdf/RCWP_Resource.pdf

10 CARA (Center for Applied Research in the Apostolate) "Frequently Requested Church Statistics. Accessed 4/19/22. Access at www.georgetown.edu

11 CARA, "Frequently Requested Church Statistics."

12 Murnion, 1993; Bond, 1990; Callahan, Sharon. "The Roman Catholic Lay Leader," in *Religious Leadership: A Reference Handbook*, ed. Sharon Henderson Callahan (Los Angeles: Sage Reference, 2013); Fox, Zeni, *New Ecclesial Ministry: Lay Professionals Serving the Church* (Kansas City, KA: Sheed and Ward, 1997).

13 *Co-Workers in the Vineyard of the Lord: A Resource for Guiding the Development of Lay Ecclesial Ministry* (Washington, DC: United States Conference of Catholic Bishops, 2006).

14 Zikmund, Barbara Brown, Adair T. Lummis, Patricia Mei Yin Chang. *Clergy Women an Uphill Calling* (Louisville, KY: Westminster John Knox Press, 1998); Lehman, Edward C. *Women's Path into Ministry: Six Major Studies* (Durham, NC: Duke Divinity School, 2002); Chaves, Mark. *Ordaining Women: Culture and Conflict in Religious Organizations* (Boston, MA: Harvard University Press, 1997); Houston, Sheila M. *Gender Bias in the Leadership of Protestant Churches.* Diss. Seattle University. 2018. D

15 Chaves, Mark. *American Religion: Contemporary Trends* 2nd ed. (Princeton, NJ: Princeton University Press. 2011); *Congregations in America* (Cambridge, MA: Harvard University Press, 2004).

16 Hahnenberg, Edward. *A Concise Guide to the Documents of Vatican II.* Cincinnati, OH: Franciscan Media, 2007, 17.

17 In September 2021, we visited the archives of RCWP and ARCWP at Marquette University and studied the liturgies used for priestly and diaconal ordinations, prayer services, and Sunday celebrations. We documented over fifty names for the sacred, heard the word read in a very inclusive language text translated by Scripture scholars who are womenpriests. We witnessed two ordinations of priests and three Sunday liturgies. Even song texts were altered to make them more inclusive in reference to the Holy.

18 *SC*, 60.

19 *SC*, 61.

20 *DH*, 1.

21 *DH*, 1.

22 *DH*, 2.

23 *DH*, 3.

24 *DH*, 3.

25 "Biblical Commission Report Can Women Be Priests?" in *Women Priests. A Catholic Commentary on the Vatican Declaration*, ed. Leonard Swidler and Arlene Swidler (New York: Paulist Press), 348–346.

26 *The Order of Priesthood. Nine Commentaries on the Vatican Decree Inter Insigniores*. An OSV Source Book. (Huntington, IN: Our Sunday Visitor, 1978).

27 *Code of Canon Law*, 1024.

28 Karis, Robert J. O.F.M. "The Role of Women according to Jesus and the Early Church." In *Women and Priesthood: Future Directions*. A Call to Dialogue from the Faculty of the Catholic Theological Union at Chicago, 1978. Edited by Carroll Stuhmueller, C.P. (Collegeville, MN: The Liturgical Press), 56.

29 Apostolic Letter *Ordinatio Sacerdotalis* of John Paul II to the Bishops of the Catholic Church on Reserving Priestly Ordination to Men alone, 1994.

30 McBrien, Richard. "Infallibility on Women's Ordination in Question." In *National Catholic Reporter*. June 13, 2011. https://www.ncronline.org/blogs/essays-theology/infallibility-womens-ordination-question accessed 12/30/22.

Chapter 3

1 Wilkie Au and Noreen Cannon Au, *The Discerning Heart. Exploring the Christian Path* (New York: Paulist, 2006), 21. Citing Marcus Borg, *The Heart of Christianity: Rediscovering a Life of Faith* (New York: HarperCollins, 2004), 73.

2   Georgina Zubiria, "Mi Corazon Me Dice Que te Busque (Sal 26,8)," (trans. My Heart Tells Me to Look For You). In *Diabonia Servicio De La Fe Y Promocion De La Justicia*, trans. Jeanette Rodriguez (Managua : Centro Ignaciano de Centroamerica, 2001), 61–65.

3   Zubiria, "Mi Corazon," 60.

4   Zubiria, "Mi Corazon," 61.

5   Au and Au, *Discerning Heart*, 51.

6   Zubiria, "Mi Corazon," 61.

7   Zubiria, "Mi Corazon," 62.

8   Olivia (Merlene) Doko, "From Resentment to Peace," in *Women Find a Way*, ed. Elsie Hainz McGrath et al. (College Station, TX: Virtualbookworm.com Publishing, 2008), 144.

9   Reynolds, Dana. "The Mystical Heart of Table Community," in *Women Find a Way*, ed. Elsie Hainz McGrath et al. (College Station, TX: Virtualbookworm.com Publishing, 2008), 37.

10 Reynolds, *Mystical Heart*, 37.

11 Reynolds, *Mystical Heart*, 37.

12 Andrew Greeley, *The Catholic Imagination* (Berkeley, CA: University of California Press, 2000), 45.

13 Greeley, *Catholic Imagination*, 1.

14 Greeley, *Catholic Imagination*, 1.

15 *SC*, 2.

16 *SC*, 2.

17 Gabriella VelardiWard, "Draw Me, We Shall Run," in *Women Find a Way*, ed. Elsie Hainz McGrath et al. (College Station, TX: Virtualbookworm.com Publishing, 2008), 68.

18 Meehan, Bridget Mary. "Holy People, Holy Music, Holy House Church," in *Women Find a Way*, ed. Elsie Hainz McGrath, et al. (College Station, TX: Virtualbookworm.com, 2008), 89.

19 Reynolds, *Mystical Heart*, 39.

20 Pfatteicher, Philip H. *The Liturgical Spirituality* (New York: Bloomsbury Academic, 1997), 4.

21 Doctrine of Vatican II, volume V, Commentary, 134.

Chapter 4

1   *AA*,4.

2   *AA*,4

3   *AA*,4

4   *AA*,4

5   Appendix 1 depicts some of the demographic data of our sample.

6 Joseph Campbell, *The Hero with a Thousand Faces* (Princeton: Princeton University Press, 1968). First published in 1949 this text influenced subsequent work related to both women and men in describing their journeys.

7 Alice H. Eagly and Linda L Carli, *Through the Labyrinth. The truth about How Women become Leaders* (Boston, MA: Harvard Business School,2007), 2. Eagly and Carli acknowledge K. Klenke as the one who introduced Labyrinth as a better metaphor for women's journeys to leadership. Klenke, K. 1997. "Women in the leadership and the information labyrinth," in *Women in Leadership* 1:57–70.

8 Eagly and Carli, *Through the Labyrinth*, 2.

9 Eagly and Carli, *Through the Labyrinth*, 2.

10 Eagly and Carli, *Through the Labyrinth*, 3.

11 Anne E. Patrick, "Studies on Women Priests," in *Women Priests: A Catholic Commentary on the Vatican Declaration*, ed Leonard Swidler, and Arlene Swidler (New York: Paulist Press, 1977), 70.

12 Patrick, "Studies on Women Priests," 74.

13 Müeller, Iris. "My Story, Condensed." in *Women Find a Way*, 20.

14 John Donohue, "A Tale of Two Documents," in *Women Priests: A Catholic Commentary on the Vatican Declaration*, ed. Leonard and Arlene Swidler (New York: Paulist Press, 1977), 25.

15 Donohue, "A Tale of Two Documents," 25.

16 Donohue, "A Tale of Two Documents," 25.

17 Pope Paul VI, *Declaration Inter Insigniores on the Question of Admission of Women to the Ministerial Priesthood* (Vatican: 1976).

18 Patrick, "Studies on Women Priests," 72.

19 Jane Via, "Response 1 to Rosemary Radford Ruether: 'Should Women Want Women Priests or Women-Church?'" *Feminist Theology*, 20 (2011):73, https://doi.org/10.1177/0966735011411815.

20 Ilia Delio, O.S.F. "Is New Life Ahead in the Church?" *Global Sisters Report: A Project of the National Catholic Reporter*, (September 5, 2018), https://www.globalsistersreport.org/column/spirituality/new-life-ahead-church-55350

21 Bridget Mary Meehan, Olivia Doko, and Victoria Rue, "A Brief Overview of Womenpriests in the History of the Roman Catholic Church." https://romancatholicwomenpriests.org/pdf/RCWP_Resource.pdf

22 Meehan, Doko, and Rue, "A Brief Overview of Womenpriests," 1

23 Meehan, Doko, and Rue, "A Brief Overview of Womenpriests," 1.

24 Meehan, Doko, and Rue, "A Brief Overview of Womenpriests," 1.

25 Barbara Brown Zikmund, Adair T. Lummis and Patricia Mei Yin Chang, *Clergy Women. An Uphill Calling* (Louisville, KY: Westminster John Knox Press, 1998).

26 George B. Wilson, *Clericalism. The Death of the Priesthood* (Collegeville, MN: Liturgical Press, 2008).

27 Gisela Forster, "The Start," in *Women Find a Way*, 9.

28 Forster, "The Start," 10.

29 Forster, "The Start," 11.

30 Eagly and Carli, *Through the Labyrinth*, 5.

31 Eagly and Carli, *Through the Labyrinth*, 6.

32 Eagly and Carli, *Through the Labyrinth*, 6.

33 Lauren Artress. "Finding my Soul's Path," in *The Spirit of a Woman: Stories to Empower and Inspire*, ed. Terry Laszlo-Goadze (Santa Monica: Santa Monica Press, 2010), 204.

34 Center for Applied Research in the Apostolate (CARA). Frequently Requested Church Statistics. http://cara.georgetown.edu/frequently-requested-church-statistics

35 Margaret Wheatley, *Leadership and the New Sciences* (San Francisco: Berrett-Koehler 1992).

36 Au and Au, *Discerning Heart*, 16.

37 Joshua McElwee, "Maryknoll: Vatican has dismissed Roy Bourgeois from order." National Catholic Reporter, November 19, 2012, http://ncronline.org/news/people/maryknoll-vatican-has-dismissed-roy-bourgeois-order

38 Tom Dickey, "Labyrinth Provides Path for a Spiritual Journey," the Presbyterian Record, 11 (2002),1. http://www.proquest.com/magazines/labyrinth-provides-path-spiritual-journey/docview/214358070

39 Patricia Fresen, "A Long Walk to Freedom: A Woman Bishop Speaks." An unpublished paper delivered to a group in Olympia, WA, 1.

40 Fresen, "A New Understanding of Priestly Ministry," 31.

41 Fresen, "A New Understanding of Priestly Ministry," 31.

42 Fresen, "A New Understanding of Priestly Ministry," 33.

43 Fresen, "A New Understanding of Priestly Ministry," 34.

44 https://religiondispatches.org/vatican-equates-womens-ordination-with-priest-pedophilia/. Mary Hunt. Religion Dispatches. July 15, 2010. "Vatican Equates women's ordination with pedophilia?"

45 *EG*, 1.

46 Barbara Reid. Commentary (August 1–6. 18th week in ordinary time. Pp 14–15, August 2022).

47 Forster, "The Start," 12.

48 Forster, "The Start," 13.

Chapter 5

1 Pope Francis Sunday Angelus Address (Oct 2019)

2 Teilhard de Chardin, "Joy is the Infallible Sign of the Presence of God." *Lafourche Gazette*, Aug 30, 2019, updated Feb 3, 2020. https://www.lafourchegazette.com/opinion/columnists/teilhard-de-chardin-joy-is-the-infallible-sign-of-the-presence-of-god/article_11e53d25-fedf-5eff-b83c-51203dffd0de.html.

3 de Chardin, "Joy," 1.

4 AA, 4.

5 Walter M. Abbott, general Editor. *Sacrosanctum Concilium, The Documents of Vatican II* (New York: The America Press, 1966), *SC* 1.

6 *SC*, 2.

7 Angeles Arrien, *The Fourfold Way: Walking the Paths of the Warrior, Teacher, Healer, and Visionary* (New York: HarperOne, 1993). Joanna did not cite this source when she was speaking, but the source identifies these actions with each of the paths. The warrior shows up physically, emotionally, mentally, and spiritually; the visionary tells the truth without blame or judgment; the teacher is open to possibilities without attachment to the outcome; the healer pays attention to what has heart and meaning.

8 Reynolds, *Mystical Heart*, 39.

9 *SC*, 83.

10 Juanita draws on many current scripture scholars who equate the Mary wife of Clopas found in John's Gospel (Jn 19:25) with the Mary of Cleopas on the road to Emmaus (Luke 24:18).

11 Abbott, Dei *Verbum*, 1965, 5.

12 *SC*, 61.

13 Reynolds, *Mystical Heart*, 37.

14 Pope Paul VI. 1976. Declaration *Inter Insigniores* on the Question of Admission of Women to the Ministerial Priesthood; 1976. Commentary on *Inter Insigniores*; 1983. The New Code of Canon Law, specifically §1024; 1988, Pope John Paul II, Mulieris Dignitatem; 1988, Pope John Paul II, *Christifidelis Laici*; 1996. Catechism of the Catholic

Church, §1577; 1994. Pope John Paul II, *Ordinatio Sacerdotalis*; 1995. *Responsum ad Dubium*, and Letter by Cardinal Ratzinger, commentaries on the infallibility of *Ordinatio Sacerdotalis*; 1998. Commentary on *Ad Tuendam Fidem* (Ratzinger) which held that those who hold women could be ordained priests are "no longer in full communion with the Catholic Church"; 2002. *Monitum*, (Ratzinger) warning regarding the attempted ordination of Catholic women; 2002. Decree on the attempted priestly ordination of women, an affirmation of excommunication of the women who "attempted to receive ordination." (Ratzinger); 2008 General Decree to impose automatic excommunication on those who ordain women to the priesthood.

15 *Ordinatio Sacerdotalis* of John Paul II to the Bishops of the Catholic Church on Reserving Priestly Ordination to Men Alone, May 22, 1994; Congregation for the Doctrine of the Faith, *Responsum Ad Propositum Dubium Concerning the Teaching Contained in "Ordinatio Sacerdotalis*," Joseph Cardinal Ratzinger, Prefect and Tarcisio Bertone, Secretary, October 28, 1995.

16 Lazar, *Christian Spirituality*, 5.

17 Lazar, *Christian Spirituality*, 5.

18 Fresen, "A Long Walk to Freedom," 7–8.

19 Au and Au, *Discerning Heart*, 204.

20 Au and Au, *Discerning Heart*, 167.

Chapter 6

1 Parts of this chapter were printed in an early publication of our findings: Sharon Henderson Callahan and Jeanette Rodriguez, "Gospel Leadership: Roman Catholic Women Priests," *Journal of Religious Leadership* 21, no.1 (Spring 2022): 5–30.

2 R. Banks and B. M. Ledbetter, *Reviewing Leadership: A Christian Evaluation of Current Approaches* (Grand Rapids, MI: Baker Academic 2004); Avery Dulles, *Models of the Church* (New York: Image-Doubleday, 1987); Knud Jørgensen, "Biblical Perspectives on Kerygma and Diakonia," in *Evangelism and Diaknoia in Context*, Regnum Edinburgh Centenary Series, Vol 32. ed. Rose Dowsett, et alii. (Oxford, UK: Oxford Centre for Mission Studies, 2016), 7–18; Isabel Apawo Phiri, "The Imperative of Diakonia for the Church and Theological Education," *Ecumenical Review* 71, no. 4 (Oct 2019): 482–491.; Stephanie Dietrich, "'Mercy and Truth Are Met Together; Righteousness and

Peace Have Kissed Each Other' (Psalm 85:10): Biblical and Systematic Theological Perspectives on Diakonia as Advocacy and Fight for Justice" in *Diakonia as Christian Social Practice*. ed. Stephanie Dietrich, Jørgensen, Korslien and Nordstokke (Oxford: Regnum Books International, 2014), 34; John Stott, *Basic Christian Leadership, Biblical Models Of Church, Gospel, And Ministry* (Downers Grove, IL: InterVarsity, 2002); "The Unity of the church as koinonia: gift and calling," *The Canberra Statement* (Australia: World council of Churches Commission on Faith and Order, 2001).

3   The names we attached to the headings such as "A Stole with a Fiery Motive" come directly from ordination rituals we examined at the archives at Marquette University Department of Special Collections and University Archives. Thanks to William Fliss for his excellent assistance and cataloguing of materials.

4   Jane Via, and Nancy Corran, *Comprehensive Catholic Lectionary*, https://www.inclusivelectionary.org/

5   Diane Whalen was a featured speaker on the Olympia Washington TedX theme of *Point of No Return*, https://www.ted.com/tedx/events/14091

6   Ordination of Chava (Michelle) Redonnet. May 1, 2010. Marquette University Department of special Collections and University Archives. Series 1.

7   We reviewed twelve ordination liturgies and ten prayer gatherings. We found over fifty names for God used throughout the celebrations.

8   Stephanie Shackelford and Bill Denzel, *You on Purpose* (Barna Group, 2021) https://www.barna.com/research/pc-calling/?utm_source=Newsletter&utmmedium

9   Mark Chaves, Mary Ellen Konieczny, Kraig Beyerlein and Emily Barman, "The National Congregations Study, Background, Methods, and Selected Results," *Journal for the Scientific Study of Religion* 38 no. 4 (1999):458–476. https://www.jstor.org/stable/1387606

10 Phyllis Zagano, *Women: Icons of Christ* (New York: Paulist Press, 2020), 10.

11 Olga is featured in a documentary: "The women fighting to be priests," *BBC World Service, 100 Women*." Produced by Valerie Perasso and Georgina Pearce. Released Dec. 2022. https://www.youtube.com/watch?v=YZ-gA1tfkp4

12 Saul Gonzalez, "Roman Catholic Women Priests." *Religion and Ethics Newsweekly*. (PBS, January 11, 2013) https://www.pbs.org/wnet/religionandethics/2013/01/11/january-11-2013-roman-catholic-women-priests/14476/

13 Appendix 2 lists the womenpriests we interviewed. There is both a Victoria and a Vikki in our interview pool. Victoria is a US womanpriest, while Vikki is Canadian.

14 Jane Via and Nancy Corran, *Comprehensive Catholic Lectionary.* https://www.inclusivelectionary.org/

15 These words are taken from the United States Conference of Catholic Bishops website related to the synod on synodality. https://www.usccb.org/synod

16 General Secretariat of the Synod. *Enlarge the Space of Your Tent.* Working Document for the Continental Stage (Vatican City, October 2022).

17 Many Roman Catholic seminaries refuse to grant master of divinity degrees to women. They substitute other degrees and replace elements of the curriculum reserved to those male candidates preparing to be ordained.

18 Elsie Hainz McGrath, "The Road Less Traveled By: Canonical Disobedience in St. Louis," in *Women Find a Way: The Movement and Stories of Roman Catholic Womenpriests*, ed Elsie Hainz McGrath, et. al, (College Station, TX: Virtualbookworm.com Publishing, 2008), 111.

19 McElroy, Robert W. "Cardinal McElroy on 'radical inclusion' for L.G.B.T. people, women, and others in the Catholic Church." *America Magazine* (January 24, 2023) https://www.americamagazine.org/faith/2023/01/24/mcelroy-synodality-inclusion

20 Gerard O'Connell, "Pope Francis: 'I Have Never Denied Communion to Anyone.'" *America Magazine* (Sept. 15, 2021), 1–6.

21 *SC*, 5–13.

22 *SC*, 2.

23 *SC*, 2.

24 *SC*, 5.

25 Gregory A. Smith, "Just one-third of U.S. Catholics Agree with their church that Eucharist is body, blood of Christ," *Pew Report.* (Pew Research Center. August 5, 2019), 1–5.

26 United States Conference of Catholic Bishops. *The Mystery of the. Eucharist in the Life of the Church.* (Washington, DC: USCCB, 2022). https://www.usccb.org/resources/mystery-eucharist-life-church-0

27 *SC*, 7.

28 *SC*, 7.

29 *SC*, 11.

30 John Shea, "The Religious Mission of the Parish," In *The Parish in Community and Ministry.* Ed. Evelyn Eaton Whitehead (New York, NY: Paulist Press, 1992), 69.

31 Kathleen refers to the theologian Ilia Delio, a Franciscan Sister and theologian who writes and speaks about an emerging cosmology and Christ.

32 We found two poems that use this language that Esperanza is quoting. http://enlightenedcatholicism-colkoch.blogspot.com/2010/04/this-is-my-body-this-is-my-blood.html The first is by Frances Croake Frank and is entitled "Did the Woman Say. The other is by Irene Zimmerman and is entitled "Liturgy". The poem by Frank is cited on Bishop Bridget Mary Meehan's blog: http://bridgetmarys.blogspot.com/2015/03/womans-body-poem-by-frances-croak-frank.html

33 Smith, *Pew*, 3.

34 Miriam Therese Winter, *Eucharist with a small 'e'.* (Maryknoll, NY: Orbis, 2007), 31.

35 Winter, *Eucharist*, 31.

36 Winter, *Eucharist*, 31.

37 *SC*, 7.

38 *SC*, 23.

39 Ronald A. Heitfetz, *Leadership Without Easy Answers* (Cambridge, MA: Harvard University Press, 1998), 239–40.

40 Jules Hart, Dir., *Pink Smoke Over the Vatican: The Voices of These Women Must be Heard.* Produced by Eye Goddess Films. (2011).

41 Donald Cozzens, *Faith That Dares to Speak* (Collegeville, MN: Liturgical Press, 2017), 10.

42 See George B. Wilson, SJ., *Clericalism the Death of Priesthood* (Collegeville, MN: Liturgical Press,2008). See also Garry Wills, *Why Priests? A failed Tradition* (New York: Penguin Books, 2013).

43 Maximo Faggioli, "Signs of the Times: Ratzinger and the Reshaping of Post-Vatican II Catholicism," *LaCroiz International* (Jan 2, 2023., accessed Feb 9, 2023). https://international.la-croix.com/news/signs-of-the-times/ratzinger-and-the-reshaping-of-post-vatican-ii-catholicism/17100

44 Faggioli, "Signs of the Times."

45 Fresen, "A New Understanding of Priestly Ministry," 28. She cites Robert A. Ludwig, *Reconstructing Catholicism* (New York: Crossroad, 1995), 42.

46 Fresen, "A New Understanding of Priestly Ministry," 29.

47 Fresen, "A New Understanding of Priestly Ministry," 29.

48 Fresen, "A New Understanding of Priestly Ministry," 30–31.

49 Walter Brueggemann, *Hopeful Imagination: Prophetic Voices in Exile* (Philadelphia: Fortress Press, 1986).

50 Ivonne Gebara, "ECOFEMINISM: A Latin American Perspective," *Cross-Currents* 53, no. 1 (2003), 98. http://www.jstor.org/stable/24461123.

51 Jeanette Rodriguez, and Ted Fortier, *Cultural Memory: Resistance, Faith and Identity* (Austin, TX: University of Texas Press, 2007), 9.

52 Rodriguez and Fortier, *Cultural Memory*, 8

53 Raming and Müeller, *Contra Legem*, 73.

54 Raming and Müeller, *Contra Legem*, 75.

55 Raming and Müeller, *Contra Legem*, 77.

56 John Paul Lederach, *The Moral Imagination: The Art and Soul of Building Peace* (New York: Oxford University Press, 2005), 91.

57 Jules Hart, Dir. *Pink Smoke Over the Vatican*.

58 Pontifical Council for Promoting Christian Unity and the Lutheran World Federation, *The Joint Declaration on the Doctrine of Justification*. (1999).

59 Donna Markham, *Spiritlinking Leadership* (New Jersey: Paulist Press, 1999), ix.

60 Ronald A. Heifetz, *Leadership without Easy Answers* (Cambridge, MA: Harvard University Press, 1994), 127–128.

61 Heifetz, *Leadership without Easy Answers*, 273.

62 Markham, *Spiritlinking Leadership*, 13.

63 Luc Novovitch, *God's Daughters: Knocking on Vatican's Door* (Global, 2015). http://Godsdaughters.vhx.tv

Epilogue

1 Gilberto Cavasos, OFM., "*Cara y cora corazón* (Face and Heart). Toward a U.S. Latino Spirituality of Inculturation," *New Theology*, May 2004, 49.

2 Cavasos, *Cara y corazón*, 49.

3 We have a copy of an unpublished speech she delivered to the group in Olympia. It was provided to us by Diane Whalen during our visit to her community in 2019.

4 Ilia Delio,O.S.F., "Is Spirituality the Future of Theology? Insights from Bonaventure," *Spiritus* 8, no.2 (Fall, 2008), 148.

5 *PO*, 7.

6 *PO*, 3.

7 *PO*, 5.

8 Janos Glaser, *From 'This is My Body' to the Church in the Twenty-first Century: The Last Supper as the Decisive Moment and Criterion of a Renewed Ecclesiology* (Montreal: Papyrus, 2011), 3.

9 Doko, "From Resentment to Peace," 146.

10 Mary Ellen Robertson, "My Story," in *Women Find a Way: The Movement and Stories of Roman Catholic Womenpriests*, ed. Elsie Hainz McGrath, et al, (College Station, TX: Virtualbookworm.com Publishing, 2008), 117.

11 Reynolds, *Mystical Heart*, 41.

12 Leslye M. Huff, "The Making of an American Mystic: Reverend Dagmar Braun Celeste's Ever-Ascending Spirals on the Journey toward the Beloved Community," *Berkeley Journal of Religion and Theology*. 5, no 2 (2019): 135.

13 Lavinia Byrne, *Woman at the Altar: The Ordination of Women in the Roman Catholic Church* (London: Mowbray, 1994), 68.

14 Byrne, *Woman at the Altar*, 68

15 Byrne, *Woman at the Altar*, 68

16 Fraga, Brian, "Illinois Bishop's Provocative Essay Suggests Cardinal McElroy is a Heretic," *National Catholic Reporter*, March 1, 2023. https://www.ncronline.org/news/illinois-bishops-provocative-essay-suggests-cardinal-mcelroy-heretic

17 Turnbull, Tiffanie. "Late Cardinal Pell called Pope a 'Catastrophe' in Anonymous Memo." *BBC News*. Jan 13, 2023, https://www.bbc.com/news/world-australia-64258319

18 Anna Terpin, "The Nature and Effects of Excommunication in the 1983 Code of Canon Law/ Natura i skutki ekskomuniki wedlug Kodeksu Prawa Kanonicznego z 1983 roku," *Kosciót I prawo* 3, no.1 (2014): 191.

19 Gringeri, Christina, and Alexandra Himonas. "Choreographing the Dance of Dissent: Roman Catholic Womenpriests' Claims to Authority." *Religions* 13, no. 4 (2022): 351. https://doi.org/10.3390/rel13040351.

20 Andrea Johnson, "How Could I Not Do This?" in *Women Find a Way: The Movement and Stories of Roman Catholic Womenpriests*, ed Elsie Hainz McGrath et al, (College Station, TX: Virtualbookworm.com Publishing, 2008), 66.

21 Gabriella Velardi Ward, "Draw Me, We Shall Run." in *Women Find a Way: The Movement and Stories of Roman Catholic Womenpriests*, ed Elsie Hainz McGrath, et al, (College Station, TX: Virtualbookworm.com Publishing, 2008), 74.

22 Doko, "From Resentment to Peace," 148.

23 Osborne, *Ministry*, 504.

24 Osborne, *Ministry*, 504.

25 Osborne, *Ministry*, 505. He cites. Hennesey, 1981, 90.

26 Osborne, *Ministry*, 505.

27 Osborne, *Ministry*, 505.

28 Osborne, *Ministry*, 507.

29 Diane Kennedy, "Roman Catholic Women Leaders: By Their Fruits You Shall Know Them," in *Religious Leadership: A Reference Handbook*, ed Sharon Henderson Callahan (Thousand Oaks, CA: Sage, 2013), 327.

30 Kennedy, *Roman Catholic Women*, 328.

31 Simone Campbell, "Women Religious for Social Justice," in *Religious Leadership: A Reference Handbook*, ed Sharon Henderson Callahan (Thousand Oaks, CA: Sage, 2013), 359.

32 Campbell, *Women Religious*, 361.

33 Schenk, Christine, CSJ. *To Speak the Truth in Love* (Maryknoll, NY: Orbis Book, 2019), 266.

34 Byrne, *Woman at the Altar*, 52.

35 Carol Glatz, "Women's Way: Pope Opens Path for More Women at Vatican, in Church." United States Conference of Catholic Bishops, March 8, 2023. Accessed April 17, 2023. https://www.usccb.org/news/2023/womens-way-pope-opens-path-more-women-vatican-church, 1.

36 Glatz, "Women's Way," 1.

37 Glatz, "Women's Way," 2.

38 Christine Mayr-Lumetzberger, "Reflections on My Way: God's Call to Me," 16.

39 Mayr-Lumetzberger, "Reflections on My Way," 16.

40 Mayr-Lumetzberger, "Reflections on My Way," 18.

41 Fresen, "A New Understanding of Priestly Ministry," 30.

42 Glatz, "Women's Way," 2.

BIBLIOGRAPHY

Abbot, Walter M., SJ, ed. *The Documents of Vatican II*. Translated by Very Rev. Msgr. Joseph Gallagher. New York: Guild Press, 1966.

Apostolic Letter Ordination Sacerdotalis of John Paul II to the Bishops of the Catholic Church on Reserving Priestly Ordination to Men Alone. 1994. Libreria Editrice Vaticana. https://tinyurl.com/2nb9skmf

Araujo, Dawn Cherie. "Local Fame Comes with Ordination: Kansas City's First Woman Priest is 'Humbled by the Role I'm Playing'." *National Catholic Reporter*, January 16–29, 2015.

Arrien, Angeles. *The Fourfold Way. Walking the Paths of the Warrior, Teacher, Healer, and Visionary*. New York: HarperOne, 1993.

Artress, Lauren. "Finding my Soul's Path," in *The Spirit of a Woman: Stories to Empower and Inspire*, edited by Terry Laszlo-Goadze, 195–204. Santa Monica: Santa Monica Press, 2010.

Au, Wilkie, and Noreen Cannon Au. *The Discerning Heart: Exploring the Christian Path*. New York: Paulist Press, 2006.

Banks, R. and B. M. Ledbetter. *Reviewing Leadership: A Christian Evaluation of Current Approaches*. Grand Rapids, MI: Baker Academic, 2004.

Behr-Sigel, Elisabeth. *The Ministry of Women in the Church*. Crestwood, NY: St. Vladimirs Seminary Press, 2004.

Bernardin, Joseph. "The Ministerial Priesthood and the Advancement of Women." In *The Order of Priesthood: Nine Commentaries on the Vatican Decree Inter Insigniores*. An OSV Source Book, edited by Francis J. Sullivan, 111–125. Huntington, IN: Our Sunday Visitor, 1978.

Berry, Jason. "A Woman's Journey toward Ordination." *National Catholic Reporter*, November 9–22, 2012.

Bishops' Committee on Priestly Life and Ministry. *As One Who Serves: Reflections of the Pastoral Ministry on Priests in the United States*. Washington, DC: United States Catholic Conference, 1977.

———. *A Shepherd's Care: Reflections on the Changing Role of Pastor*. Washington, DC: United States Catholic Conference, 1987.

Bolman, Lee G., and Terrence E. Deal. *Reframing Organizations.* San Francisco: Jossey-Bass, 2008.

Bond, Louise C. "An Evaluation of the Effectiveness of Lay Ministry Training in the Roman Catholic Church of the United States." PhD diss, The Catholic University of America, 1990.

Bonner, Dismas, O.F.M. "Church Law and the Prohibition to Ordain Women." In *Women and Priesthood: Future Directions: A Call to Dialogue from the Faculty of the Catholic Theological Union at Chicago,* edited by Carroll Stuhmueller, C.P., 71–83. Collegeville, MN: The Liturgical Press, 1978.

Borg, Marcus. *The Heart of Christianity: Rediscovering a Life of Faith.* New York: HarperCollins, 2004.

Broccolo, Gerard T. *Vital Spiritualities: Naming the Holy in Your Life.* Notre Dame, IN: Ave Maria Press, 1990.

Brueggemann, Walter. *Hopeful Imagination: Prophetic Voices in Exile.* Philadelphia, PA: Fortress Press, 1986.

Byrne, Lavinia. *Woman at the Altar: The Ordination of Women in the Roman Catholic Church.* London: Mowbray, 1994.

Catholic Church's Pontifical Council for Promoting Christian Unity and the Lutheran World Federation. *The Joint Declaration on the Doctrine of Justification.* Augsburg, Germany, 1999.

Cahalan, Kathleen A. *Introducing the Practice of Ministry.* Collegeville, MN: Liturgical Press, 1999.

Callahan, Sharon. "The Roman Catholic Lay Leader." In *Religious Leadership: A Reference Handbook,* edited by Sharon Henderson Callahan, 136–144. Thousand Oaks, CA: Sage, 2013.

Callahan, Sharon, and Jeanette Rodriguez. "Gospel Leadership: Roman Catholic Women Priests." *Journal of Religious Leadership.* 21, no.1 (Spring 2022): 5–30.

Campbell, Joseph. *The Hero with a Thousand Faces.* Princeton, NJ: Princeton University Press, 1968.

Campbell, Simone. "Women Religious for Social Justice." In *Religious Leadership: A Reference Handbook,* edited by Sharon Henderson Callahan, 359–367. Thousand Oaks, CA: Sage, 2013.

Cavasos, Gilberto. "Cara y Corazon (Face and Heart). Toward a U.S. Latino Spirituality of Inculturation." *New Theology,* May 2004, 46–55.

Center for Applied Research in the Apostolate (CARA). *Frequently Requested Church Statistics*. Accessed April 19, 2022. https://cara.georgetown.edu/.

Chaves, Mark. *American Religion: Contemporary Trends*. 2nd ed. Princeton, NJ: Princeton University Press, 2017.

———. *Congregations in America*. Boston: Harvard University, 2004.

———. *Ordaining Women: Culture and Conflict in Religious Organizations*. Boston: Harvard University, 1997.

Chaves, Mark, Mary Ellen Konieczny, Kraig Beyerlein, and Emily Barman. "The National Congregations Study, Background, Methods, and Selected Results." *Journal for the Scientific Study of Religion* 38, no. 4 (1999): 458–476. https://doi.org/10.2307/1387606.

Christ, Carol. *Diving Deep and Surfacing: Women Writers on the Spiritual Quest*. Boston: Beacon Press, 1980.

Clark, Matthew H. *Forward in Hope: Saying Amen to Lay Ecclesial Ministry*. Notre Dame, IN: Ave Maria Press, 2009.

Clines, Raymond H., and Elizabeth R. Cobb. *Research Writing Simplified: A Documentation Guide*. 8th ed. Upper Saddle River, NJ: Pearson Education, 2015.

Committee on the Laity, United States Conference of Catholic Bishops (USCCB). *Lay Ecclesial Ministry: The State of the Questions*. Washington, DC: USCCB, 1999.

Canon Law Society of Great Britain and Ireland in association with the Canon Law Society of Australia and New Zealand and the Canadian Canon Law Society. *The Code of Canon Law in English Translation*. London: Collins, 1983.

Congar, Yves. *Lay People in the Church: A Study for a Theology of Laity*. Translated by Donald Attwater. Westminster, MD: Newman, 1965.

"Constitution on the Sacred Liturgy: *Sacrosanctum Concilum*, 1963." In *Vatican Council II: the Basic Sixteen Documents: Constitutions, Decrees, Declarations*, edited by Austin Flannery. Northport, NY: Costello Publishing, 1996.

Cordero, Juanita, and Suzanne Thiel. *Here I Am, I Am Ready: A New Model of Ordained Ministry*. Roman Catholic Womenpriests-USA, Inc., 2018.

Cozzens, Donald B. *Faith that Dares to Speak*. Collegeville, MN: Liturgical Press, 2017.

————. *The Changing Face of the Priesthood*. Collegeville, MN: Liturgical Press, 2000.

Creswell, John W. *Qualitative Inquiry and Research Design*. Thousand Oaks, CA: Sage, 2008.

Cunneen, Sally. *Mother Church: What the Experience of Women is Teaching Her*. New York: Paulist Press, 1991.

D'Antonio, William, James Davidson, Dean Hoge, and Ruth Wallace. *American Catholic Laity in a Changing Church*. Kansas City, MO: Sheed, 1989.

de Chardin, Teilhard. "Joy is the Ineffable Sign of the Presence of God." *LaFouche Gazette*. Aug. 30, 2019, updated Feb 3, 2020. https://www.lafourchegazette.com/opinion/columnists/teilhard-de-chardin-joy-is-the-infallible-sign-of-the-presence-of-god/article_11e53d25-fedf-5eff-b83c-51203dffd0de.html.

"Decree on the Apostolate of Lay People: *Apostolicam Actuositatem*, 1965." In *Vatican Council II: the Basic Sixteen Documents: Constitutions, Decrees, Declarations*, edited by Austin Flannery, 209–225. Northport, NY: Costello Publishing, 1996.

"Decree on the Ministry and Life of Priests, *Presbyterorum Ordinis*, 1966. In *Vatican Council II: the Basic Sixteen Documents: Constitutions, Decrees, Declarations*, edited by Austin Flannery, 209–225. Northport, NY: Costello Publishing, 1996.

DeLambo, David. *Lay Parish Ministers: A Study of Emerging Leadership*. New York: National Pastoral Life Center, 2005.

Delio, Ilia, O.S.F. "Is New Life Ahead in the Church?" *Global Sisters Report: A Project of the National Catholic Reporter*. September 5, 2018, https://www.globalsistersreport.org/column/spirituality/new-life-ahead-church-55350

————. "Is Spirituality the Future of Theology? Insights from Bonaventure." *Spiritus* 8, no. 2 (Fall, 2008): 148–155, 260.

Denzin, Norman K., and Yvonna S. Lincoln. *The SAGE Handbook of Qualitative Research*. 4th ed. Thousand Oaks, CA: Sage, 2011.

Dickey, Tom. "Labyrinth Provides Path for a Spiritual Journey," *Presbyterian Record*, 11 (2002): 1–2. http://www.proquest.com/magazines/labyrinth-provides-path-spiritual-journey/docview/214358070

Dietrich, Stephanie. "'Mercy and Truth Are Met Together; Righteousness and Peace Have Kissed Each Other' (Psalm 85:10): Biblical and Systematic Theological Perspectives on Diaknoia as Advocacy and Fight for Justice." In *Diakonia as Christian Social Practice*, edited by Stephanie Dietrich, Knud Jørgensen, Kari Karsrud Korslien and Kjell Nordstokke. 1517 Media, 2014.

Dignitatis Humanae. Declaration on Religious Liberty. 1965 in *The Documents of Vatican II*. With Notes and Comments by Catholic, Protestant and Orthodox Authorities. Edited by Walter M Abbott, SJ. Translation edited by Very Rev. Msgr. Joseph Gallagher. New York: Guild Press, 1966.

"Dogmatic Constitution on the Church: *Lumen Gentium*, 1964." In *Vatican Council II: The Basic Sixteen Documents: Constitutions, Decrees, Declarations,* edited by Austin Flannery. Northport, NY: Costello Publishing,1996.

Doko, (Merlene) Olivia. "From Resentment to Peace." In *Women Find a Way: The Movement and Stories of Roman Catholic Womenpriests*, edited by Elsie Hainz McGrath, Bridget Mary Meehan, and Ida Raming, 144–151. College Station, TX: Virtualbookworm.com Publishing, 2008.

Doohan, Leonard. *Spiritual Leadership: The Quest for Integrity*. New York: Paulist Press, 2007.

Donohue, John. "A Tale of Two Documents." In *Women Priests: A Catholic Commentary on the Vatican Declaration*, edited by Leonard Swidler, and Arlene Swidler, 25–34. New York: Paulist Press, 1977.

Dulles, Avery. *Models of the Church*. New York: Image-Doubleday, 1987.

Dunning, James B. *Ministries: Sharing God's Gifts*. Winona, MN: Saint Mary's Press, 1980.

Eagly, Alice H., and Linda L. Carli. *Through the Labyrinth: The Truth about How Women Become Leaders*. Cambridge, MA: Harvard Business Review Press, 2007.

Faggioli, Maximo. "Signs of the Times: Ratzinger and the Reshaping of Post-Vatican II Catholicism." *LaCroix International*, January 2, 2023. Accessed February 9, 2023. https://international.la-croix.com/news/signs-of-the-times/ratzinger-and-the-reshaping-of-post-vatican-ii-catholicism/17100

Flannery, Austin, ed. *Vatican Council II: The Basic Sixteen Documents: Constitutions, Decrees, Declarations.* Northport, NY: Costello Publishing,1996.

Forster, Gisela. "The Start: The Danube Seven and the Bishop Heroes." In *Women Find a Way: The Movement and Stories of Roman Catholic Womenpriests,* edited by Elsie Hainz McGrath, Bridget Mary Meehan, and Ida Raming, 9–13. College Station, TX: Virtualbookworm.com Publishing, 2008.

Fox, Matthew, ed. *Western Spirituality: Historical Roots, Ecumenical Routes.* Santa Fe, NM: Bear & Company, Inc., 1981.

Fox, Zeni. *New Ecclesial Ministry: Lay Professionals Serving the Church.* Kansas City, KS: Sheed & Ward, 1997.

Fox, Zeni, and Regina Bechtle, S.C., eds. *Called and Chosen: Toward a Spirituality for Lay Leaders.* Lanham: Sheed & Ward, 2005.

Fraga, Brian. "Illinois Bishop's Provocative Essay Suggests Cardinal McElroy is a Heretic." *National Catholic Reporter.* March 1, 2023. https://www.ncronline.org/news/illinois-bishops-provocative-essay-suggests-cardinal-mcelroy-heretic

Francis I. *Evangelii Gaudium (The Joy of the Gospel): An Apostolic Exhortation of the Holy Father Francis to the Bishops, Clergy, Consecrated Persons, and the Lay Faithful on the Proclamation of the Gospel in Today's World.* Vatican City: Vatican Press, 2013.

Freeman, Sue J. M., Susan C. Bourque, and Christine M. Shelton, eds. *Women on Power: Leadership Redefined.* Boston: Northeastern University Press, 2001.

Fresen, Patricia. "A New Understanding of Priestly Ministry." In *Women Find a Way: The Movement and Stories of Roman Catholic Womenpriests,* edited by Elsie Hainz McGrath, Bridget Mary Meehan, and Ida Raming, 28–35. College Station, TX: Virtualbookworm.com Publishing, 2008.

———. "Ordained Ministry as Envisioned by RCWP and by the Dutch Dominicans: Two Models of Priesthood: Convergences and Divergences." *Rk-kerkplein* (blog), January 8, 2008. http://www.rk-kerkplein.org/home/themas/Kerk-zijn/ambten/roman-catholic-women-priests-en-de-nederlandse-dominicanen-in-hun-visie-op-het-gewijde-ambt/index07a0.html?language=en

————. "A Long Walk to Freedom: A Woman Bishop Speaks." An unpublished paper delivered to a group in Olympia, WA.

Gebara, Ivone. "ECOFEMINISM: A Latin American Perspective." *CrossCurrents* 53, no. 1 (2003): 93–103. http://www.jstor.org/stable/24461123.

General Secretariat of the Synod. *Enlarge the Space of Your Tent.* Working Document for the Continental Stage. Vatican City, October 2022.

Glaser, Janos. *From 'This is My Body' to the Church in the Twenty-first Century: The Last Supper as the Decisive Moment and Criterion of a Renewed Ecclesiology.* Montreal: Papyrus, 2011.

Glatz, Carol. "Women's Way: Pope Opens Path for More Women at Vatican, in Church." United States Conference of Catholic Bishops, March 8, 2023. Accessed April 17, 2023. https://www.usccb.org/news/2023/womens-way-pope-opens-path-more-women-vatican-church

Gomes, Sebastian. "A Reflection for Wednesday of the Fifth Week in Ordinary Time." *America Magazine,* February 8, 2023.

Gonzalez, Saul. "Roman Catholic Women Priests." *Religion and Ethics Newsweekly.* (PBS, January 11, 2013) https://www.pbs.org/wnet/religionandethics/2013/01/11/january-11-2013-roman-catholic-women-priests/14476/

Greeley, Andrew. *The Catholic Imagination.* Berkeley, CA: University of California Press, 2000.

Gringeri, Christina, and Alexandra Himonas. "Choreographing the Dance of Dissent: Roman Catholic Womenpriests' Claims to Authority." *Religions* 13, no. 4 (2022): 351. https://doi.org/10.3390/rel13040351.

Groeschel, Benedict. *Spiritual Passages: The Psychology of Spiritual Development.* Bangalore, India: Claretian Publication, 2003.

Hart, Jules, dir. *Pink Smoke Over the Vatican: The Voices of These Women Must Be Heard.* 2011; Eye Goddess Films.

Hahnenberg, Edward. *A Concise Guide to the Documents of Vatican II.* Cincinnati, OH: Franciscan Media, 2007.

Harvey, Peter Francis. "It's a Total Way of Life? Catholic Priests, Women's Ordination, and Identity Work." *Journal for the Scientific Study of Religion* 57, no. 3 (September 2018): 547–566. https://doi.org/10.1111/jssr.12530.

Heifetz, Ronald A. *Leadership without Easy Answers*. Cambridge, MA: Harvard University Press, 1994.

Hennesey, James J. *American Catholics: A History of the Roman Catholic Community in the United States*. New York: Oxford University Press, 1981.

Houston, Sheila Marie. "Gender Bias in the Leadership of Protestant Churches." DMin diss., Seattle University, 2018.

Huff, Leslye M. "The Making of an American Mystic: Reverend Dagmar Braun Celeste's Ever-ascending Spirals on the Journey Toward the Beloved Community." *Berkeley Journal of Religion and Theology*. 5, no 2 (2019): 115–142.

Hunt, Mary. "Vatican Equates Women's Ordination with Pedophilia?" *Religion Dispatches*, July 15, 2010. https://religiondispatches.org/vatican-equates-womens-ordination-with-priest-pedophilia/

Iersel, Bas van, and Roland E. Murphy, eds. *Office and Ministry in the Church*. New York: Herder and Herder, 1972.

Inter Insigniores. Declaration on the Question of Admission of Women to the Ministerial Priesthood. Franjo Cardinal Seper, Prefect of the Sacred Congregation for the Doctrine of the Faith. Approved by Pope Paul VI, 1976. Vatican.

Janowiak, Paul A. "Running to Communion." *America Magazine*, October 27, 2003. https://www.americamagazine.org/issue/457/faith-focus/running-communion

John Paul II. *Apostolic Letter Ordinatio Sacerdotalis to the Bishops of the Catholic Church on Reserving Priestly Ordination to Men Alone*. Vatican City: Libreria Editrice Vaticana, 1994.

Johnson, Andrea. "How Could I Not Do This?" In *Women Find a Way: The Movement and Stories of Roman Catholic Womenpriests*, edited by Elsie Hainz McGrath, Bridget Mary Meehan, and Ida Raming, 63–67. College Station, TX: Virtualbookworm.com Publishing, 2008.

Jørgensen, Knud. "Biblical Perspectives on Kerygma and Diakonia." In *Evangelism and Diaknoia in Context*. Regnum Edinburgh Centenary Series Vol 32. Edited by Rose Dowsett, Isabel Hiri, Doug Birdsall, Dawit Olika Terfassa Hwa Yung, and Knud Jørgensen, 7–18. Oxford, UK: Oxford Centre for Mission Studies, 2016.

Karris, Robert J. O.F.M. "The Role of Women According to Jesus and the Early Church." In *Women and Priesthood: Future Directions: A Call to Dialogue from the Faculty of the Catholic Theological Union at Chicago*, edited by Carroll Stuhmueller, C.P., 47–57. Collegeville, MN: The Liturgical Press, 1978.

Keifer, Ralph A. "The Priest As 'Another Christ' in Liturgical Prayer." In *Women and Priesthood: Future Directions: A Call to Dialogue from the Faculty of the Catholic Theological Union at Chicago*, edited by Carroll Stuhmueller, C.P., 103–110. Collegeville, MN: The Liturgical Press, 1978.

Kennedy, Diane. "Roman Catholic Women Leaders: By Their Fruits You Shall Know Them." In *Religious Leadership: A Reference Handbook*, edited by Sharon Henderson Callahan, 327–330. Thousand Oaks, CA: Sage, 2013.

Kichline, Kathleen MacInnis. *Never on Sunday: A Look at the Women Not in the Lectionary*. Hyattsville, MD: Quixote Center, 2008

Killen, Patricia O'Connell. *Finding Our Voices: Women, Wisdom, and Faith*. New York: Crossroads, 1997.

Kinerk, J. "Toward a Method for the Study of Spirituality." In *Psychology and Religion: A Reader*, edited by Margaret Gorman, 320–324. New York: Paulist Press, 1985.

Klenke, Karin, ed. *Wo67,165men in Leadership: Contextual Dynamics and Boundaries*. 2nd ed. Leeds, UK: Emerald Publishing, 2017.

Klostermaier, Doris. "Two Women Priests: Latest Blow to Roman Catholic Traditionalists." *Journal of Ecumenical Studies* 33, no. 4 (Fall 1996): 573–575.

Kotter, John P. *Leading Change*. Boston: Harvard Business School Press, 1996.

Lathrop, Gordon. *The Pastor: A Spirituality*. Minneapolis: Fortress Press, 2006.

Lawler, Michael G., and Thomas J. Shanahan. *Church: A Spirited Communion*. Collegeville, MN: Liturgical Press, 1995.

Lazar, Roy. "Christian Spirituality: Roman Catholic Perspective." Accessed April 4, 2023. https://www.academia.edu/17812589/Christian_Spirituality_Roman_Catholic_Perspective.

Lederach, John Paul. *The Moral Imagination: The Art and Soul of Building Peace*. New York: Oxford University Press, 2005.

Lehman, Edward C. *Women's Path into Ministry: Six Major Studies*. Durham, NC: Duke Divinity School, 2002.

———. *Women Clergy: Breaking through Gender Barriers*. New Brunswick, NJ: Transaction Books, 1985.

———. *Gender and Work: The Case of the Clergy*. Albany, NY: State University of New York Press, 1993.

Lerner, Gerda. *The Creation of Patriarchy*. Oxford: Oxford University Press, 1986.

Ludwik, Robert A. *Reconstructing Catholicism*. New York: Crossroad, 1995.

Macy, Gary. *The Hidden Story of Women's Ordination. Female Clergy in the Medieval West*. New York: Oxford University Press, 2008.

Macy, Gary, William T. Ditewig, and Phyllis Zagano. *Women Deacons: Past, Present, Future*. New York: Paulist Press, 2012.

Madigan, Kevin, and Carolyn Osiek. *Ordained Women in the Early Church: A Documentary History*. Baltimore, MD: The Johns Hopkins University Press, 2011.

Markham, Donna J. *Spiritlinking Leadership: Working through Resistance to Organizational Change*. New York: Paulist Press, 1999.

Matusak, Larraine R. *Finding Your Voice: Learning to Lead—Anywhere You Want to Make a Difference*. San Francisco: Jossey Bass, 1997.

Martelet, Gustavo. "The Mystery of the Covenant and Its Connections with the Nature of the Ministerial Priesthood." In *The Order of Priesthood: Nine Commentaries on the Vatican Decree Inter Insigniores*. An OSV Source Book, edited by Francis J. Sullivan, 99–110. Huntington, IN: Our Sunday Visitor, 1978.

Martimort, A. G. "The Value of a Theological Formula 'In Persona Christi.'" In *The Order of Priesthood: Nine Commentaries on the Vatican Decree Inter Insigniores*. An OSV Source Book, edited by Francis J. Sullivan, 85–97. Huntington, IN: Our Sunday Visitor, 1978.

McBrien, Richard. "Infallibility on Women's Ordination in Question." *National Catholic Reporter*, June 13, 2011. Accessed December 30, 2022. https://www.ncronline.org/blogs/essays-theology/infallibility-womens-ordination-question.

McElroy, Robert W. "Cardinal McElroy on 'Radical Inclusion' for L.G.B.T. People, Women, and Others in the Catholic Church." *America Magazine*, January 24, 2023.

"Message to Humanity." In *The Documents of Vatican II*, edited by Walter M. Abbott, translated by Joseph Gallagher. New York: Guild Press, 1966.

McGrath, Elsie Hainz. "The Road Less Traveled By, Canonical Disobedience in St. Louis." In *Women Find a Way: The Movement and Stories of Roman Catholic Womenpriests*, edited by Elsie Hainz McGrath, Bridget Mary Meehan, and Ida Raming, 108–114. College Station, TX: Virtualbookworm.com Publishing, 2008.

McGrath, Elsie Hainz, Bridget Mary Meehan, and Ida Raming, eds. *Women Find a Way: The Movement and Stories of Roman Catholic Womenpriests*. College Station, TX: Virtualbookworm.com Publishing, 2008.

McKenzie, Vashti Murphy. *Not Without a Struggle: Leadership Development for African American Women in Ministry*. Cleveland, OH: United Church Press, 1996.

Meehan, Bridget Mary. "Holy People, Holy Music, Holy House Church." In *Women Find a Way: The Movement and Stories of Roman Catholic Womenpriests*, edited by Elsie Hainz McGrath, Bridget Mary Meehan, and Ida Raming, 89–94. College Station, TX: Virtualbookworm.com Publishing, 2008.

Meehan, Bridget Mary, Olivia Doko, and Victoria Rue. *A Brief Overview of Womenpriests in the History of the Roman Catholic Church*. https://romancatholicwomenpriests.org/pdf/RCWP_Resource.pdf

Müeller, Iris. "My Story, Condensed." In *Women Find a Way: The Movement and Stories of Roman Catholic Womenpriests*, edited by Elsie Hainz McGrath, Bridget Mary Meehan, and Ida Raming, 20–35. College Station, TX: Virtualbookworm.com Publishing, 2008.

Murnion, Philip J. *New Parish Ministers: Laity and Religious on Parish Staffs*. Cincinnati, OH: St. Anthony, 1993.

United States Catholic Conference of Bishops. *Together in God's Service: Toward a Theology of Ecclesial Lay Ministry*. Washington, DC: USCCB, 2021.

Novovitch, Luc. *God's Daughters*. Global, 2015. http://www.godsdaughters.vhx.tv.

O'Connor, Karen, ed. *Gender and Women's Leadership: A Reference Handbook*. Los Angeles: Sage Reference, 2010.

O'Connell, Gerard. "Pope Francis: 'I Have Never Denied Communion to Anyone.'" *America Magazine*. September 15, 2021, 1–6.

O'Connell Killen, Patricia. *Finding Our Voices: Women, Wisdom and Faith*. New York: Crossroads, 1997.

Our Sunday Visitor (OSV). *The Order of Priesthood: Nine Commentaries on the Vatican Decree Inter Insigniores*. An OSV Source Book. Huntington, IN: Our Sunday Visitor, 1978.

———. "Occasion and Purpose of the Declaration: Commentary Prepared at the Congregations' Request by a Theologian Expert." In *The Order of Priesthood: Nine Commentaries on the Vatican Decree Inter Insigniores*. An OSV Source Book, edited by Francis J. Sullivan, 21–50. Huntington, IN: Our Sunday Visitor, 1978.

Osborne, Kenan B., OFM. *Ministry: Lay Ministry in the Roman Catholic Church, Its History and Theology*. New York: Paulist Press, 1993.

Osiek, Carolyn. R.S.C.J. "The Ministry and Ordination of Women According to the Early Fathers." In *Women and Priesthood: Future Directions: A Call to Dialogue from the Faculty of the Catholic Theological Union at Chicago*, edited by Carroll Stuhmueller, C.P., 59–68. Collegeville, MN: The Liturgical Press, 1978.

Ostdiek, Gilbert. "The Ordination of Women and the Force of Tradition." In *Women and Priesthood: Future Directions: A Call to Dialogue from the Faculty of the Catholic Theological Union at Chicago*, edited by Carroll Stuhmueller, C.P., 85–102. Collegeville, MN: The Liturgical Press, 1978.

Parvey, Constance F, ed. *Ordination of Women in Ecumenical Perspective: Workbook for the Church's Future*. Geneva, Switzerland: World Council of Churches, 1980.

"Pastoral Constitution on the Church in the Modern World: *Gaudium et Spes*, 1965." In *Vatican Council II: the Basic Sixteen Documents: Constitutions, Decrees, Declarations*, edited by Austin Flannery. Northport, NY: Costello Publishing, 1996.

Patrick, Anne E. "Studies on Women Priests." In *Women Priests: A Catholic Commentary on the Vatican Declaration*, edited by Leonard Swidler, and Arlene Swidler, 70–74. New York: Paulist Press, 1977.

Patton, Michael Quinn. *Qualitative Research & Evaluation Methods*. Thousand Oaks, CA: Sage, 2014.

Perasso, Valerie, and Georgina Pearce. "The Women Fighting to be Priests" *BBC World Service, 100 Women*. Dec. 2022. https://www.youtube.com/watch?v=YZ-gA1tfkp4

Peterfeso, Jill. *Womanpriest: Tradition and Transgression in the Contemporary Roman Catholic Church*. New York: Fordham University Press, 2020.

Pfatteicher, Philip H. *The Liturgical Spirituality*. New York: Bloomsbury Academic, 1997.

Phiri, Isabel Apawo. "The Imperative of Diakonia for the Church and Theological Education." *Ecumenical Review* 71, no. 4 (October 2019): 482–491.

Pontifical Biblical Commission. "Biblical Commission Report Can Women Be Priests?" In *Women Priests: A Catholic Commentary on the Vatican Declaration*, edited by Leonard Swidler, and Arlene Swidler, 346–348. New York: Paulist Press, 1977.

Pope Francis. "General Audience." Saint Peter's Square. Wednesday, April 15, 2015. The Vatican. https://www.vatican.va/content/francesco/en/audiences/2015/documents/papa-francesco_20150415_udienza-generale.html

Pope Paul VI. *Declaration Inter Insigniores on the Question of Admission of Women to the Ministerial Priesthood*. 1976. https://tinyurl.com/5ftka473

Pontifical Biblical Commission. "Biblical Commission Report Can Women Be Priests?" in *Women Priests: A Catholic Commentary on the Vatican Declaration*, edited by Leonard Swidler and Arlene Swidler, 338–346. New York: Paulist Press, 1977.

Quixote Center. *Inclusive Lectionary: Sunday Readings with Responsorial Psalms*. Hyattsville, MD, 2008.

Rademacher, William J. *Lay Ministry: A Theological, Spiritual and Pastoral Handbook*. Crossroads. 1991.

Raming, Ida, and Iris Müeller. *"Contra Legem"—A Matter of Conscience: Our Lifelong Struggle for Human Rights for Women in the Roman-Catholic Church*. Piscataway, NJ: Transaction Publishers, 2010.

Rahner, Hugo, ed. *Saint Ignatius Loyola: Letters to Women*. New York: Herder and Herder, 1960.

Ratzinger, Joseph. "The Male Priesthood: A Violation of Women's Rights?" In *The Order of Priesthood: Nine Commentaries on the Vatican Decree Inter Insigniores.* An OSV Source Book, edited by Francis J. Sullivan, 127–137. Huntington, IN: Our Sunday Visitor, 1978.

———. *Responsum Ad Propositum Dubium Concerning the Teaching Contained in "Ordinatio Sacerdotalis."* October 28, 1995. https://tinyurl.com/bdh26j3a

Reid, Barbara. "Commentary On August 1–6. 18th Week in Ordinary Time." *America Magazine*, August, 2022, 14–15.

Reynolds, Dana. "The Mystical Heart of Table Community." In *Women Find a Way: The Movement and Stories of Roman Catholic Womenpriests*, edited by Elsie Hainz McGrath, Bridget Mary Meehan, and Ida Raming, 37–42. College Station, TX: Virtualbookworm.com Publishing, 2008.

Roberston, Mary Ellen. "My Story." In *Women Find a Way: The Movement and Stories of Roman Catholic Womenpriests*, edited by Elsie Hainz McGrath, Bridget Mary Meehan, and Ida Raming, 115–121. College Station, TX: Virtualbookworm.com Publishing, 2008.

Rodriguez, Jeanette, and Ted Fortier. *Cultural Memory: Resistance, Faith, and Identity.* Austin, TX: University of Texas Press, 2007.

Ross, Maggie. *Pillars of Flame: Power, Priesthood and Spiritual Maturity.* San Francisco, CA: Harper & Row, 1988.

Saldana, Johnny. *The Coding Manual for Qualitative Researchers.* Thousand Oaks, CA: Sage, 2016

Schaaf, Kathe, Kay Lindahl, Kathleen S. Hurty, and Reverend Gua Cheen, eds. *Women, Spirituality and Transformative Leadership: Where Grace Meets Power.* Woodstock, VT: Skylight Paths Publishing, 2012.

Shackelford, Stephanie, and Bill Denzel. *You on Purpose.* Barna Group, September 29, 2021. https://www.barna.com/research/pc-calling/?utm_source=Newsletter&utm_medium

Schaefer, Pamela. "Though Church Bans Women Priests More And More Women Are Saying 'Why Wait?'" *National Catholic Reporter*, December 7, 2007, 15–18.

Schenk, Christine. *To Speak the Truth in Love: A Biography of Theresa Kane, RSM.* Maryknoll, NY: Orbis Book, 2019.

Schlumpf, Heidi. "A Church at the Crossroads." *Sojourners Magazine*, March, 2005.

———. "Call Waiting: The Stories of Five Women Who Want to Be Priests." *U.S. Catholic*. February 2001, 12–17.

Schmidt, Frederick W. *A Still Small Voice: Women, Ordination, and the Church*. Syracuse, NY: Syracuse University Press, 1996.

Schneider, Sandra Marie. *The Revelatory Text: Interpreting the New Testament as Sacred Scripture*. San Francisco: Harper San Francisco, 1991.

Sensing, Timothy R. *Qualitative Research: A Multi-Methods Approach to Projects for Doctor of Ministry Theses*. Eugene, OR: Wipf & Stock, 2011.

Shea, John. "The Religious Mission of the Parish." In *The Parish in Community and Ministry*, edited by Evelyn Eaton Whitehead, 53–71. New York: Paulist Press, 1992.

Small, Nancy. "A Catholic Woman Discovers Her Priesthood." *America Magazine*, January 22, 2018, 36–39.

Smith, Gregory A. "Just One-Third of U.S. Catholics Agree with Their Church That Eucharist Is Body, Blood of Christ." *Pew Report*. Pew Research Center, August 5, 2019, 1–5.

Sobrino, Jon. *Spirituality of Liberation: Toward Political Holiness*. Maryknoll, NY: Orbis Books, 1988.

Society of Jesus. *Decree 14: Jesuits and the Situation of Women in Church and Civil Society*. General Congregation 34 (1995).

Spazzi, Raimundo, O.P. "The Advancement of Women According to the Church." In *The Order of Priesthood: Nine Commentaries on the Vatican Decree Inter Insigniores*. An OSV Source Book, edited by Francis J. Sullivan. Huntington, IN: Our Sunday Visitor, 1978.

Stendhal, Kristen. *The Bible and the Role of Women: A Case Study in Hermeneutics*. Translated by Emilie T. Sander. Philadelphia: Fortress Press, 1966.

Stott, John. *Basic Christian Leadership, Biblical Models of Church, Gospel, and Ministry*. Downers Grove, IL: InterVarsity, 2002.

Stuhlmueller, Carroll, C.P. "Priesthood, Unity and the Ordination of Women: The Call to Dialog with the Church." In *Women and Priesthood: Future Directions: A Call to Dialogue from the Faculty of the Catholic Theological Union at Chicago*, edited by Carroll Stuhmueller, C.P., 3–22. Collegeville, MN: The Liturgical Press, 1978.

———. "Culture, Leadership and Symbolism in the Old Testament." In *Women and Priesthood: Future Directions: A Call to Dialogue from the*

Faculty of the Catholic Theological Union at Chicago, edited by Carroll Stuhmueller, C.P., 25–45. Collegeville, MN: The Liturgical Press, 1978.

Sullivan, Francis J., ed. *The Order of Priesthood: Nine Commentaries on the Vatican Decree Inter Insigniores*. An OSV Source Book. Huntington, IN: Our Sunday Visitor, 1978.

Swidler, Leonard. "Introduction: Roma Locuta, Causa Finita?" in *Women Priests: A Catholic Commentary on the Vatican Declaration*, edited by Leonard Swidler, and Arlene Swidler, 3–18. New York: Paulist Press, 1977.

Tarr-Whelan, Linda. *Women Lead the Way: Your Guide to Stepping Up to Leadership and Changing the World*. San Francisco: Barrett-Kohler Publishers, 2009.

Terpin, Anna, "The Nature and Effects of Excommunication in the 1983 Code of Canon Law/Natura i skutki ekskomuniki wedlug Kodeksu Prawa Kanonicznego z 1983 roku." *Kosciót I prawo* 3, no.1 (2014): 191–207.

Torjesen, Karen Jo. *When Women Were Priests: Women's Leadership in the Early Church & the Scandal of their Subordination in the Rise of Christianity*. San Francisco: Harper, 1995.

Trible, Phyllis. *God and the Rhetoric of Sexuality*. Philadelphia: Fortress Press, 1978.

Turnbull, Tiffanie. "Late Cardinal Pell called Pope a 'catastrophe' in Anonymous Memo." *BBC News*. Jan 13, 2023, https://www.bbc.com/news/world-australia-64258319

United States Conference of Catholic Bishops. *Catechism of the Catholic Church*. Washington, DC, 1994.

———. *Co-Workers in the Vineyard of the Lord*. Washington, DC, 2005.

———. *The Mystery of the Eucharist in the Life of the Church*. Washington, DC, 2022.

Vagle, Mark D. *Crafting Phenomenological Research*. New York: Routledge, 2014.

Van Gelder, Craig. *The Essence of The Church: A Community Created by The Spirit*. Grand Rapids, MI: Baker Books, 2000.

Van Manen, Max. *Phenomenology of Practice: Meaning-Giving Methods in Phenomenological Research and Writing*. New York, NY: Routledge, 2014.

Via, Jane. "Response 1 to Rosemary Radford Ruether: 'Should Women Want Women Priests or Women-Church?'" *Feminist Theology* 20, no. 1 (2011): 73–84. https://doi.org/10.1177/0966735011411815

Via, Jane, and Nancy Corran. *The Comprehensive Catholic Lectionary*, 2013. Accessed, April 6, 2023. https://www.inclusivelectionary.org/theresource

Von Balthasar, Hans Urs. "The Uninterrupted Tradition of the Church." In *The Order of Priesthood: Nine Commentaries on the Vatican Decree Inter Insigniores*. An OSV Source Book, edited by Francis J. Sullivan, 75–83. Huntington, IN: Our Sunday Visitor, 1978.

Ward, Gabriella Velardi. "Draw Me, We Shall Run." In *Women Find a Way: The Movement and Stories of Roman Catholic Womenpriests*, edited by Elsie Hainz McGrath, Bridget Mary Meehan, and Ida Raming, 68–75. College Station, TX: Virtualbookworm.com Publishing, 2008.

Watson, Natalie K. *Introducing Feminist Ecclesiology*. Eugene, OR: Wipf & Stock, 1996.

Weems, Renita J. *Just a Sister Away: A Womanist Vision of Women's Relationships in the Bible*. Philadelphia, PA: Innisfree Press, 1988.

Whalen, Diane. "Point of No Return." Olympia, WA: TEDx Talk, July, 2015. https://www.ted.com/tedx/events/14091

Wheatley, Margaret J. *Leadership and the New Science: Learning About Organization from an Orderly Universe*. San Francisco: Berrett-Koehler Publishers, 1992.

Wijngaards, John. *Did Christ Rule Out Women Priests?* Great Wakering, UK: McCrimmons, 1977.

———. *The Ordination of Women in the Catholic Church. Unmasking a Cuckoo's Egg Tradition*. New York: Continuum, 2001.

———. *Women Deacons in the Early Church: Historical Texts and Contemporary Debates*. New York: Herder & Herder Crossroad, 2006.

———. *What They Don't Teach You in Catholic College: Women in the Priesthood and the Mind of Christ*. Lafayette, LA: Acadian House Publishing, 2020.

———. *Ten Commandments for Church Reform: Memoirs of a Catholic Priest*. Lafayette, LA: Acadian House Publishing, 2021.

Wills, Garry. *Why Priests? A Failed Tradition*. New York: Viking, 2013.

Wilson, George. *Clericalism: The Death of Priesthood*. Collegeville, MN: Liturgical Press, 2008.

Wilson, Marie C. *Closing the Leadership Gap: Add Women, Change Everything.* New York: Penguin, 2007.

Winter, Miriam Therese. *Eucharist With a Small 'e'.* Maryknoll, NY: Orbis, 2007.

———. *Out of the Depths. The Story of Ludmila Javarova Ordained Roman Catholic Priest.* New York: Crossroad Publishing, 2001.

Zagano, Phyllis, ed. *Women Deacons? Essays with Answers.* Collegeville, MN: Liturgical Press, 2016.

———. *Women: Icons of Christ.* New York: Paulist Press, 2020.

Zikmund, Barbara Brown, Adair T. Lummis, and Patricia Mei Yin Chang. *Clergy Women: An Uphill Calling.* Louisville, KY: Westminster John Knox Press, 1998.

Zubiria, Georgina. "Mi corazón me dice que te busque (Sal 26,8)" [My heart tells me to look for you]. In *Diabonia Servicio De La Fe y Promoción De La Justicia*, translated by Jeanette Rodriguez, 61–65. Managua, Nicaragua: Centro Ignaciano de Centroamerica, 2001.